BATMAN
DETECTIVE COMICS

VOL. 1:
MYTHOLOGY

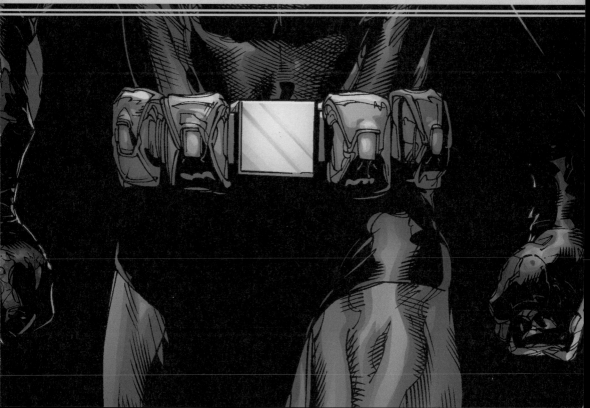

BATMAN
DETECTIVE COMICS

VOL. 1:
MYTHOLOGY

PETER J. TOMASI
WRITER

DOUG MAHNKE
PENCILLER

DAVID BARON
COLORIST

ROB LEIGH
LETTERER

JAIME MENDOZA
MARK IRWIN
CHRISTIAN ALAMY
KEITH CHAMPAGNE
INKERS

DOUG MAHNKE
JAIME MENDOZA
and **DAVID BARON**
COLLECTION COVER ARTISTS

BATMAN CREATED BY **BOB KANE** WITH **BILL FINGER**

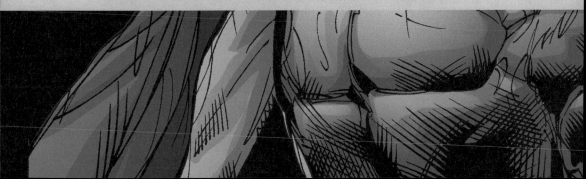

BATMAN: DETECTIVE COMICS VOL. 1: MYTHOLOGY

Published by DC Comics. Compilation and all new material Copyright
© 2019 DC Comics. All Rights Reserved. Originally published in single
magazine form in DETECTIVE COMICS 994-999. Copyright © 2018, 2019
DC Comics. All Rights Reserved. All characters, their distinctive likenesses
and related elements featured in this publication are trademarks of DC
Comics. The stories, characters and incidents featured in this publication
are entirely fictional. DC Comics does not read or accept unsolicited
submissions of ideas, stories or artwork. DC – a WarnerMedia Company.

DC Comics, 2900 West Alameda Ave., Burbank, CA 91505
Printed by LSC Communications, Kendallville, IN, USA. 9/9/19.
First Printing.
ISBN: 978-1-77950-162-2

Library of Congress Cataloging-in-Publication Data is available.

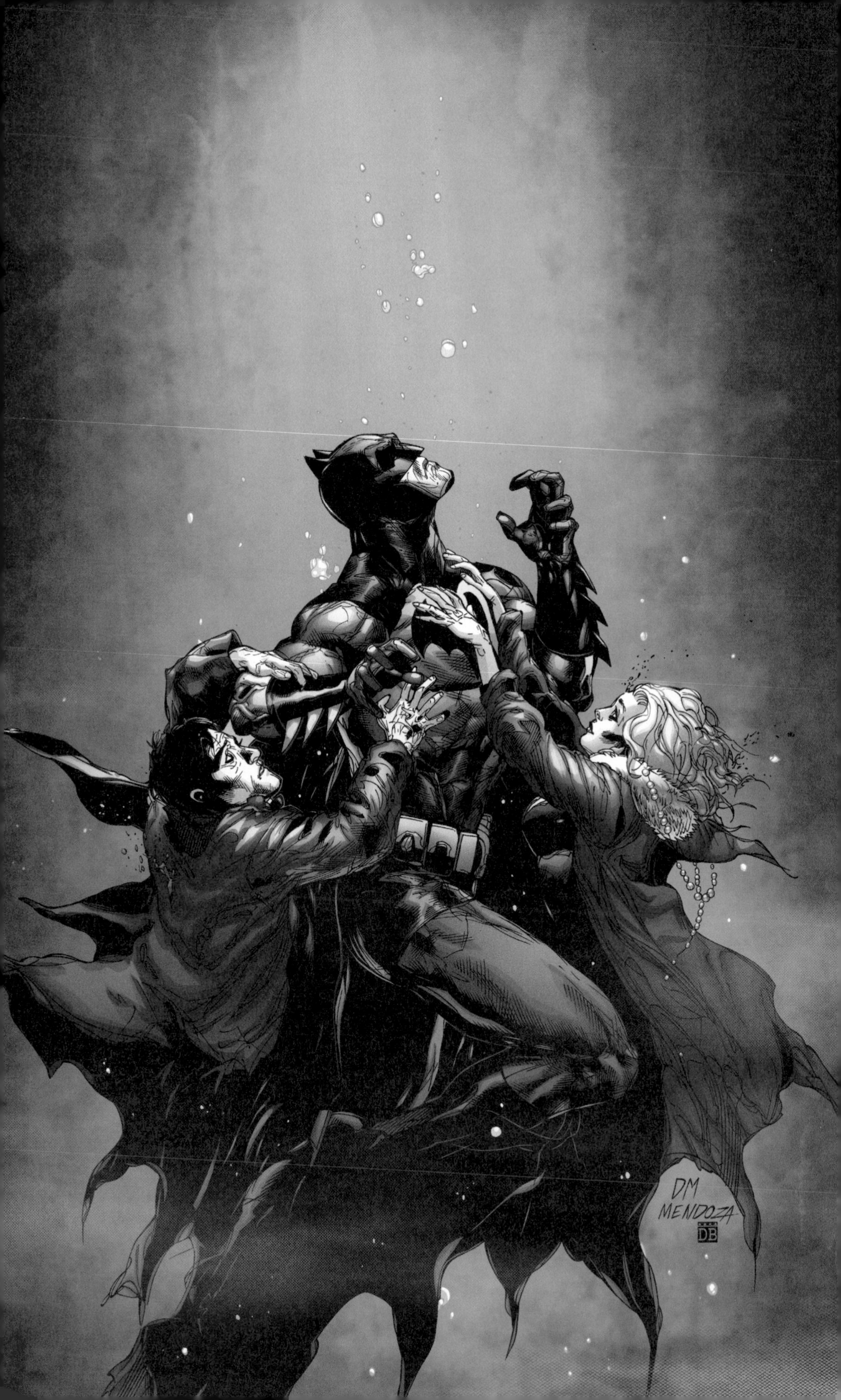
DM
MENDOZA
DB

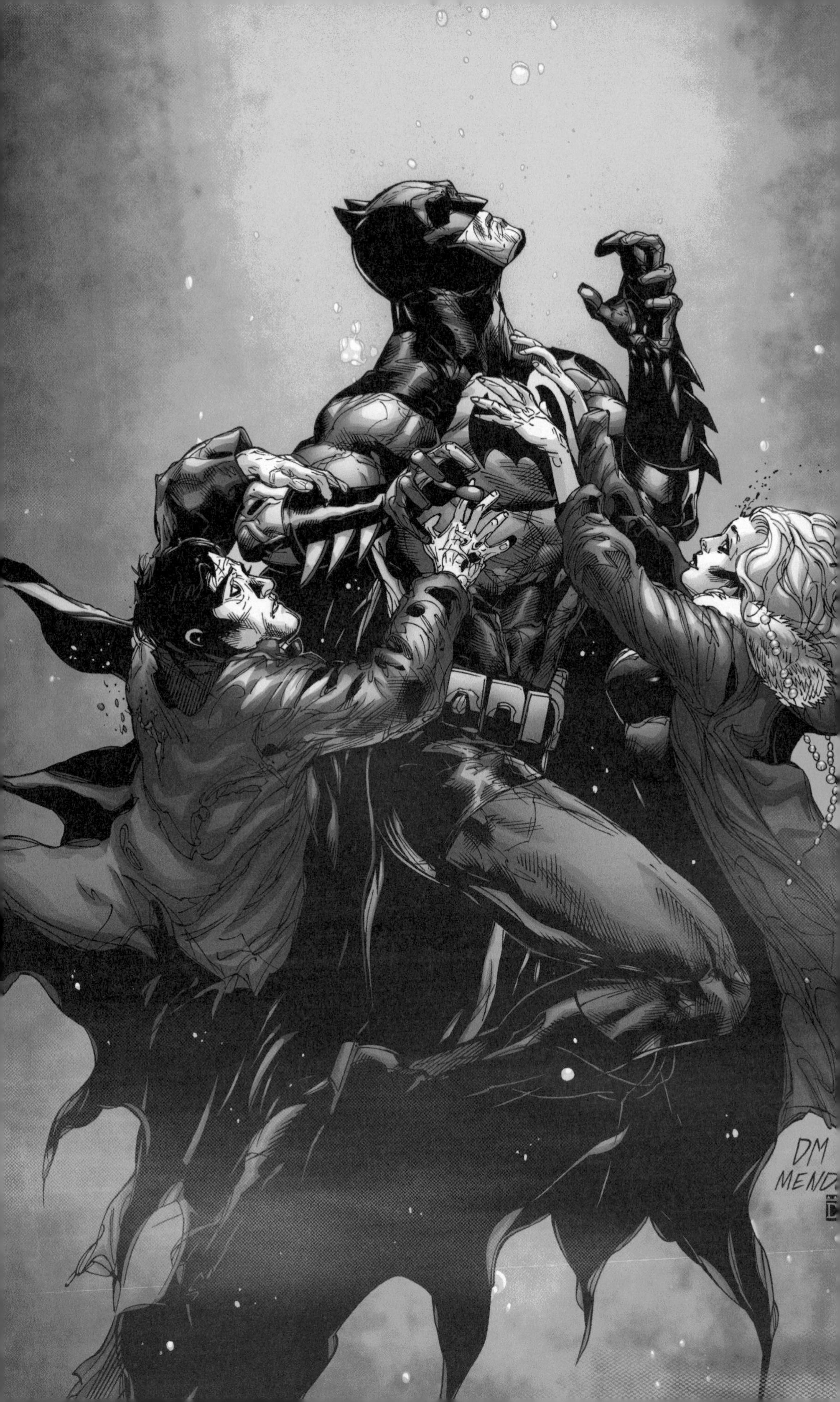

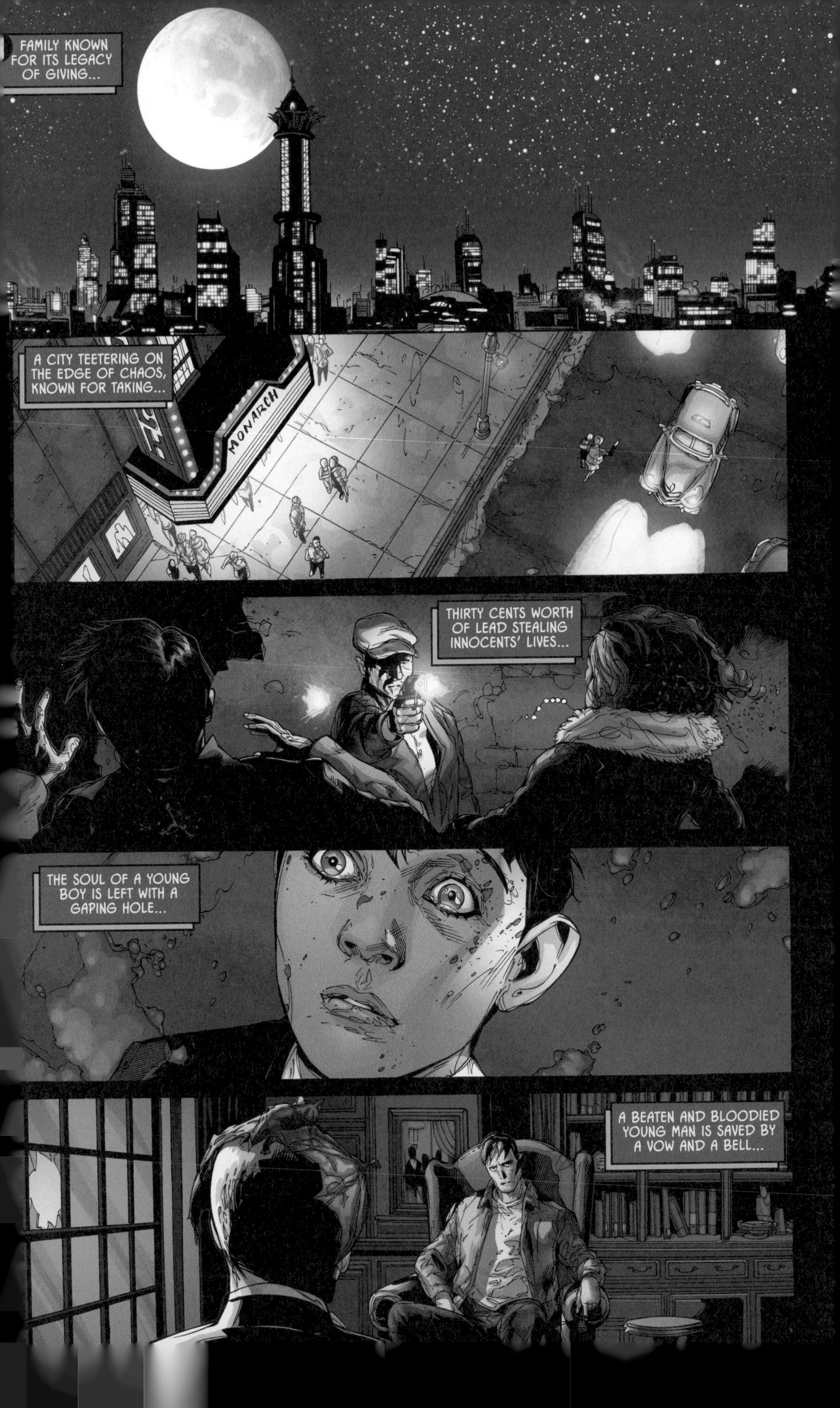

FAMILY KNOWN FOR ITS LEGACY OF GIVING...
A CITY TEETERING ON THE EDGE OF CHAOS, KNOWN FOR TAKING...
MONARCH
THIRTY CENTS WORTH OF LEAD STEALING INNOCENTS' LIVES...
THE SOUL OF A YOUNG BOY IS LEFT WITH A GAPING HOLE...
A BEATEN AND BLOODIED YOUNG MAN IS SAVED BY A VOW AND A BELL...

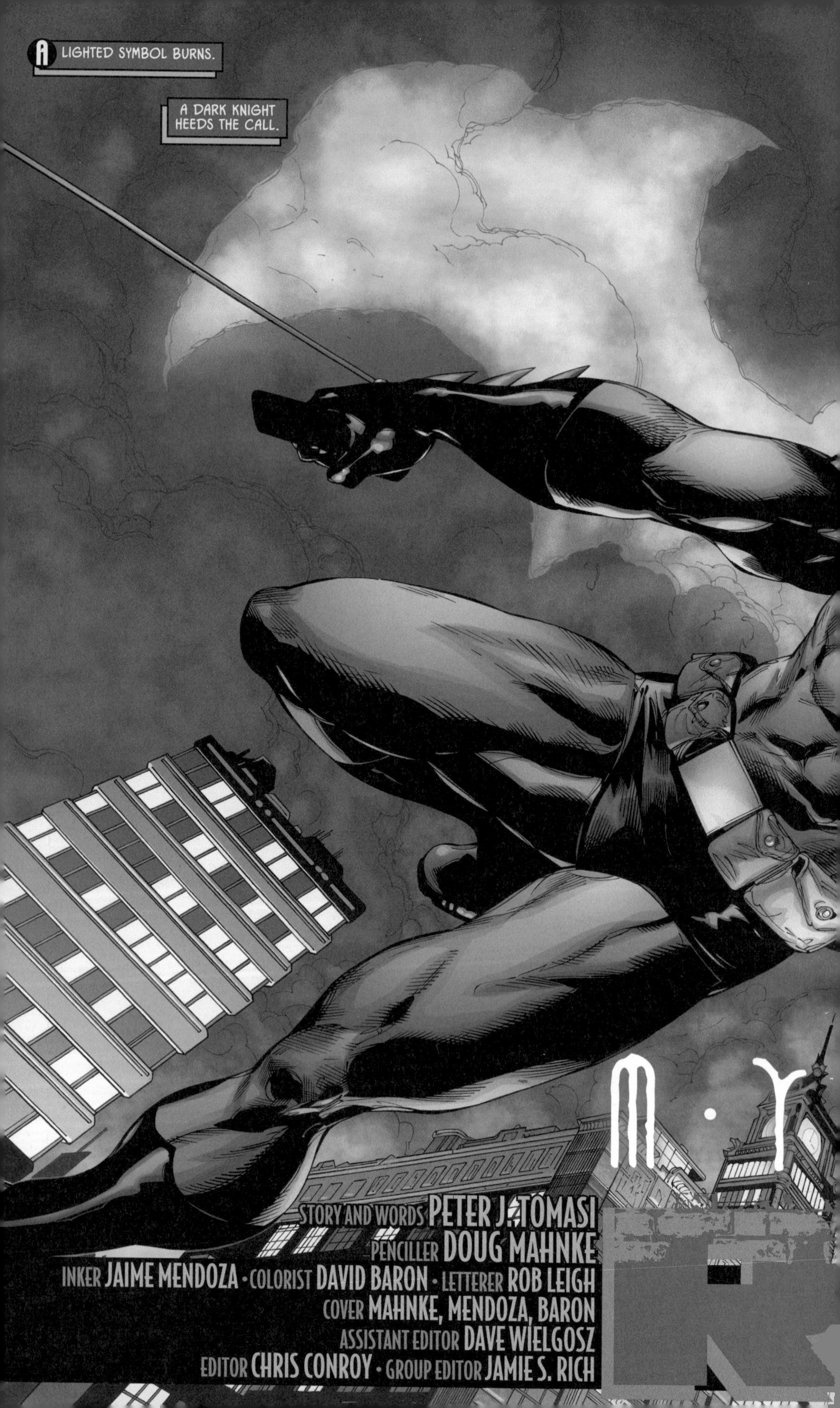
A LIGHTED SYMBOL BURNS.
A DARK KNIGHT HEEDS THE CALL.
STORY AND WORDS PETER J. TOMASI
PENCILLER DOUG MAHNKE
INKER JAIME MENDOZA · COLORIST DAVID BARON · LETTERER ROB LEIGH
COVER MAHNKE, MENDOZA, BARON
ASSISTANT EDITOR DAVE WIELGOSZ
EDITOR CHRIS CONROY · GROUP EDITOR JAMIE S. RICH

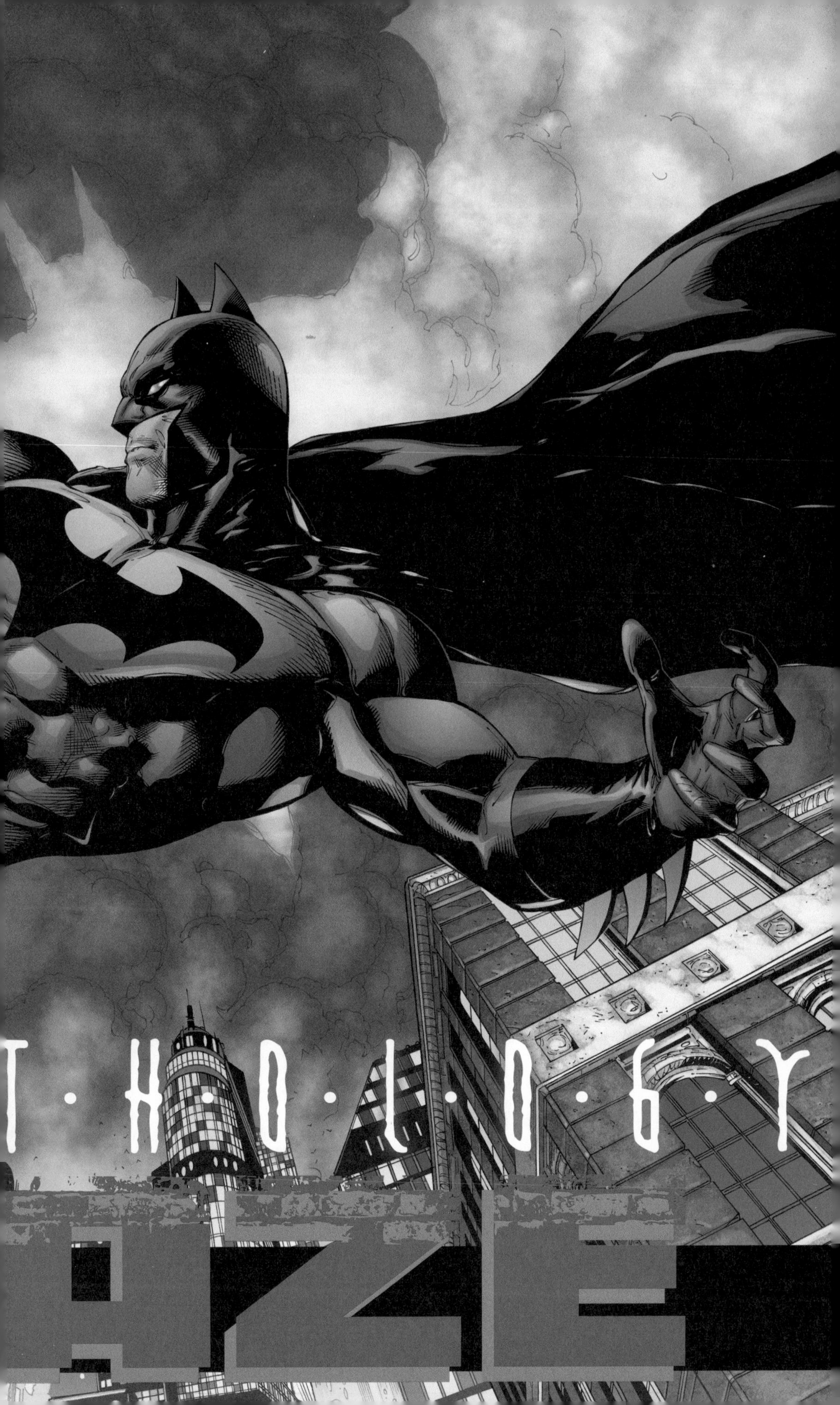
T · H · O · L · O · G · Y

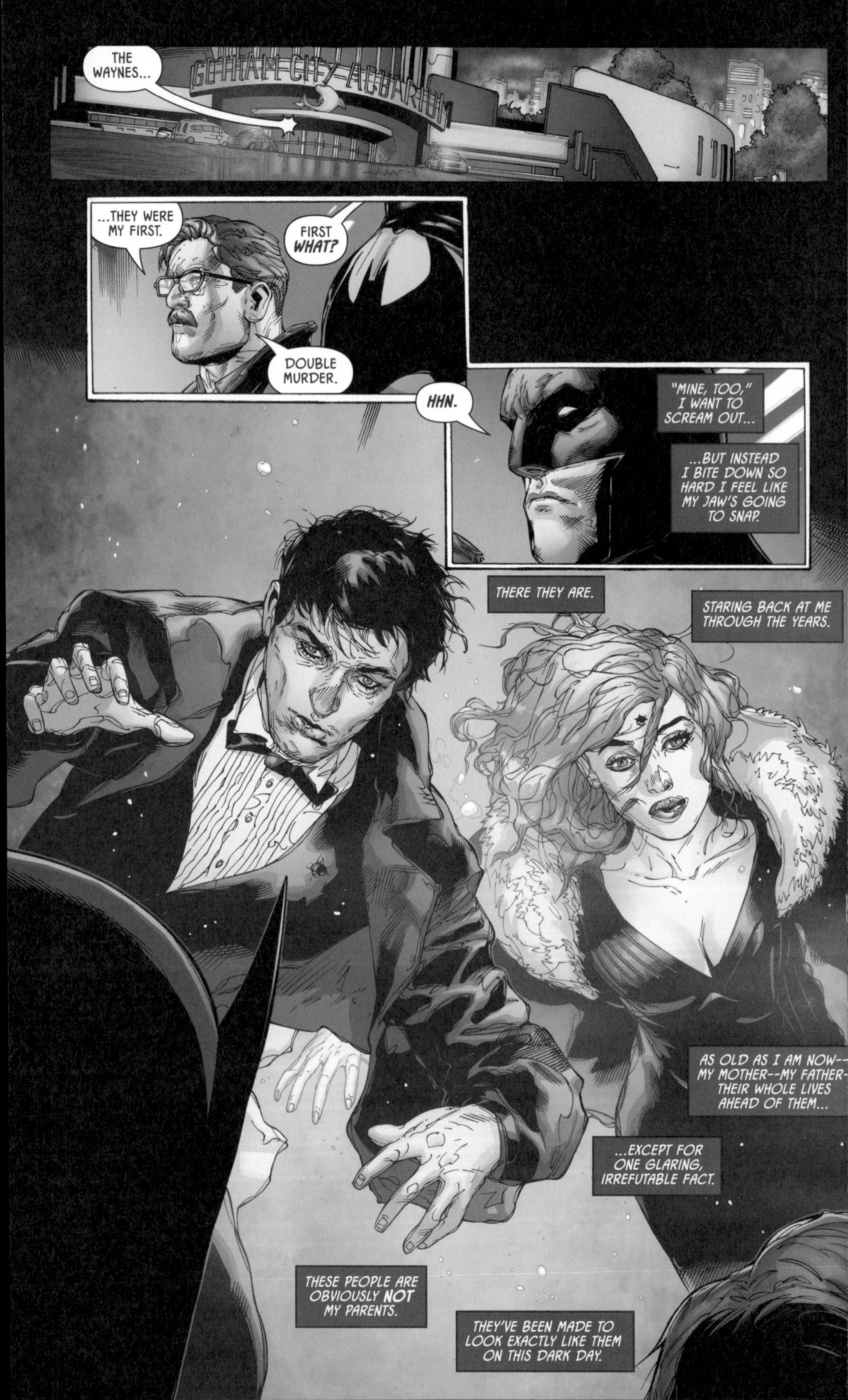
GOTHAM CITY AQUARIUM
THE WAYNES...
...THEY WERE MY FIRST.
FIRST WHAT?
DOUBLE MURDER.
HHN.
"MINE, TOO," I WANT TO SCREAM OUT...
...BUT INSTEAD I BITE DOWN SO HARD I FEEL LIKE MY JAW'S GOING TO SNAP.
THERE THEY ARE.
STARING BACK AT ME THROUGH THE YEARS.
AS OLD AS I AM NOW--MY MOTHER--MY FATHER-THEIR WHOLE LIVES AHEAD OF THEM...
...EXCEPT FOR ONE GLARING, IRREFUTABLE FACT.
THESE PEOPLE ARE OBVIOUSLY NOT MY PARENTS.
THEY'VE BEEN MADE TO LOOK EXACTLY LIKE THEM ON THIS DARK DAY.

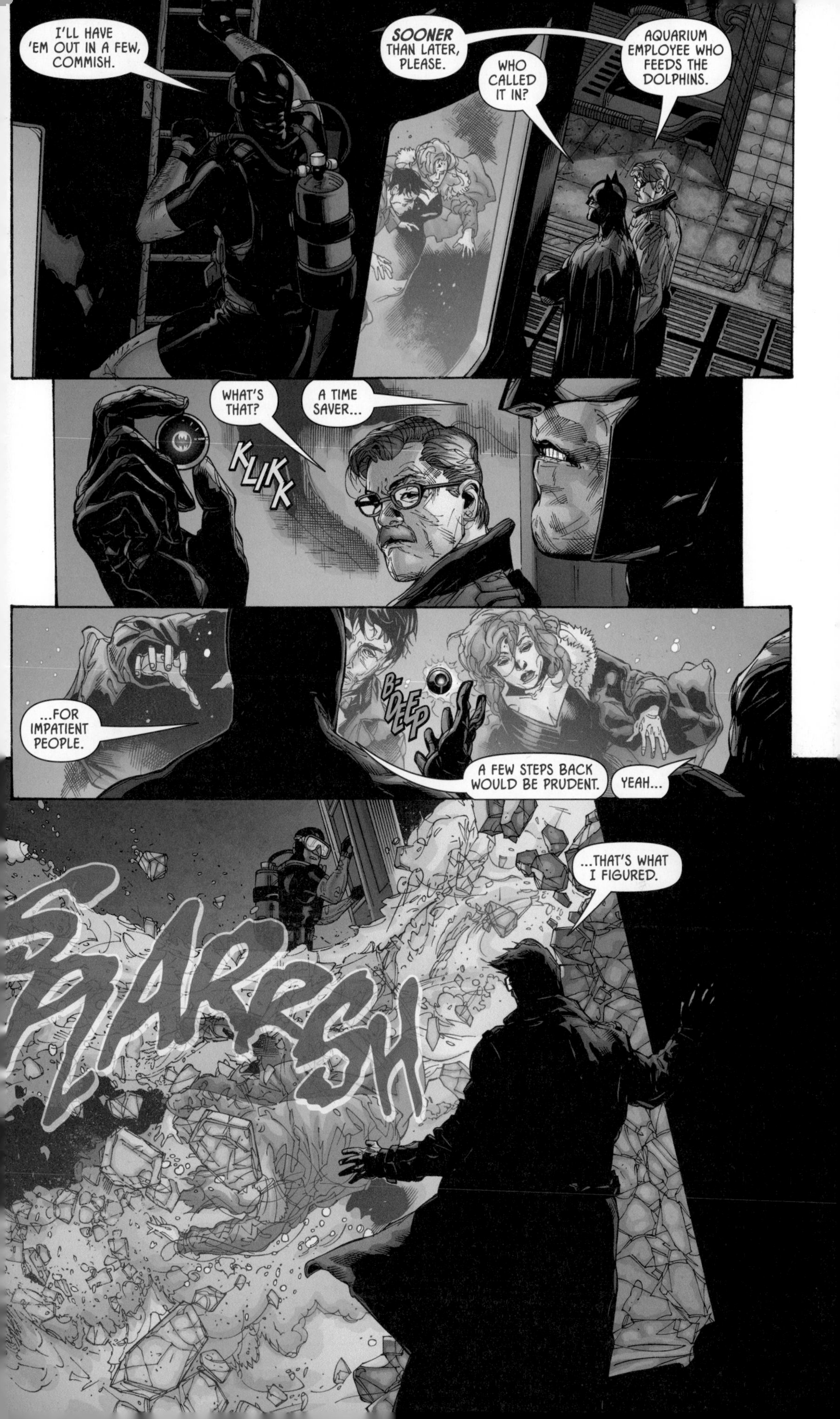
I'LL HAVE 'EM OUT IN A FEW, COMMISH.
SOONER THAN LATER, PLEASE.
WHO CALLED IT IN?
AQUARIUM EMPLOYEE WHO FEEDS THE DOLPHINS.
WHAT'S THAT?
A TIME SAVER...
KLIKK
...FOR IMPATIENT PEOPLE.
B-DEEP
A FEW STEPS BACK WOULD BE PRUDENT.
YEAH...
...THAT'S WHAT I FIGURED.
BLARRSH

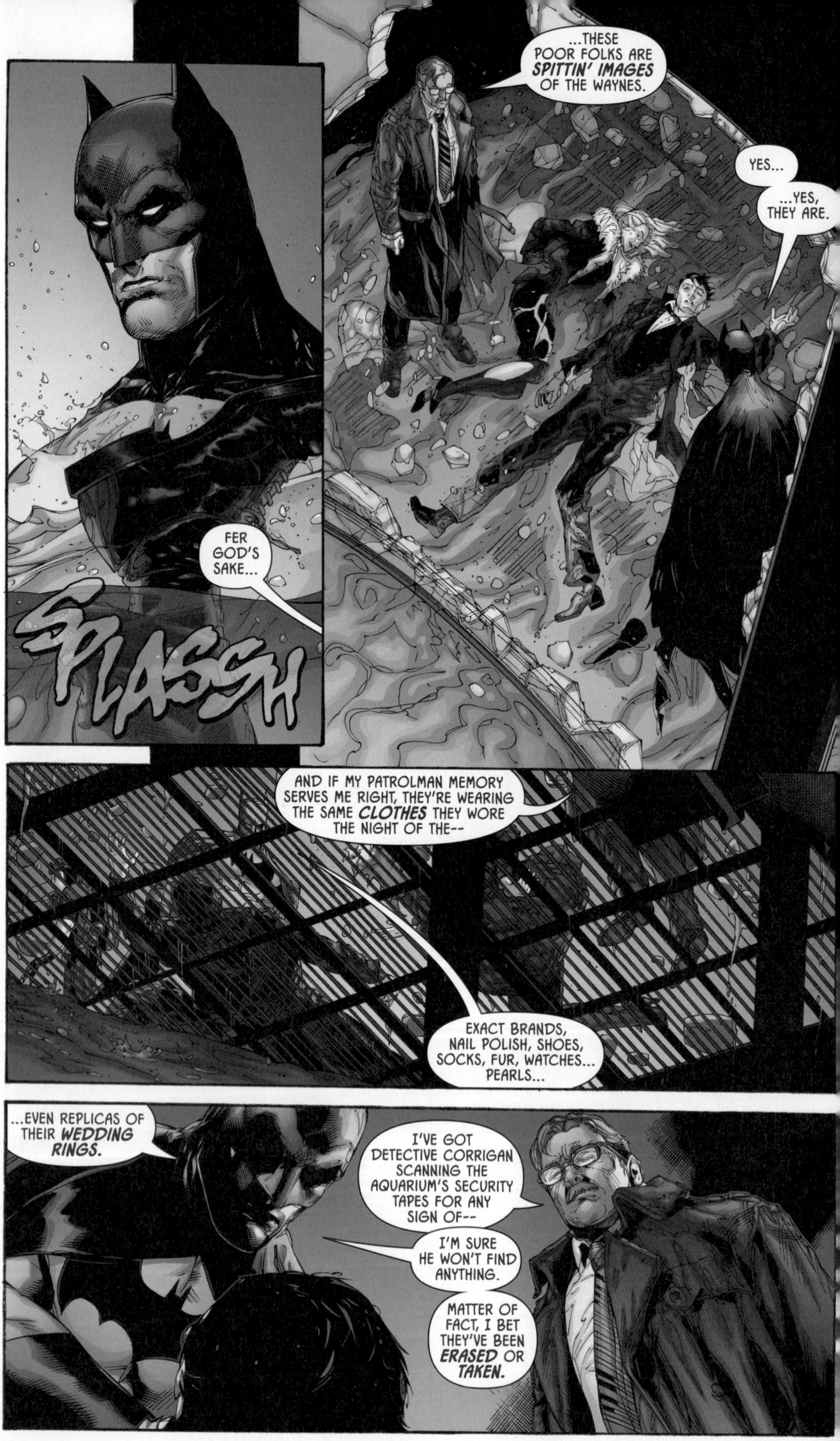
...THESE POOR FOLKS ARE SPITTIN' IMAGES OF THE WAYNES.
YES...
...YES, THEY ARE.
FER GOD'S SAKE...
SPLASSH
AND IF MY PATROLMAN MEMORY SERVES ME RIGHT, THEY'RE WEARING THE SAME CLOTHES THEY WORE THE NIGHT OF THE--
EXACT BRANDS, NAIL POLISH, SHOES, SOCKS, FUR, WATCHES... PEARLS...
...EVEN REPLICAS OF THEIR WEDDING RINGS.
I'VE GOT DETECTIVE CORRIGAN SCANNING THE AQUARIUM'S SECURITY TAPES FOR ANY SIGN OF--
I'M SURE HE WON'T FIND ANYTHING.
MATTER OF FACT, I BET THEY'VE BEEN ERASED OR TAKEN.

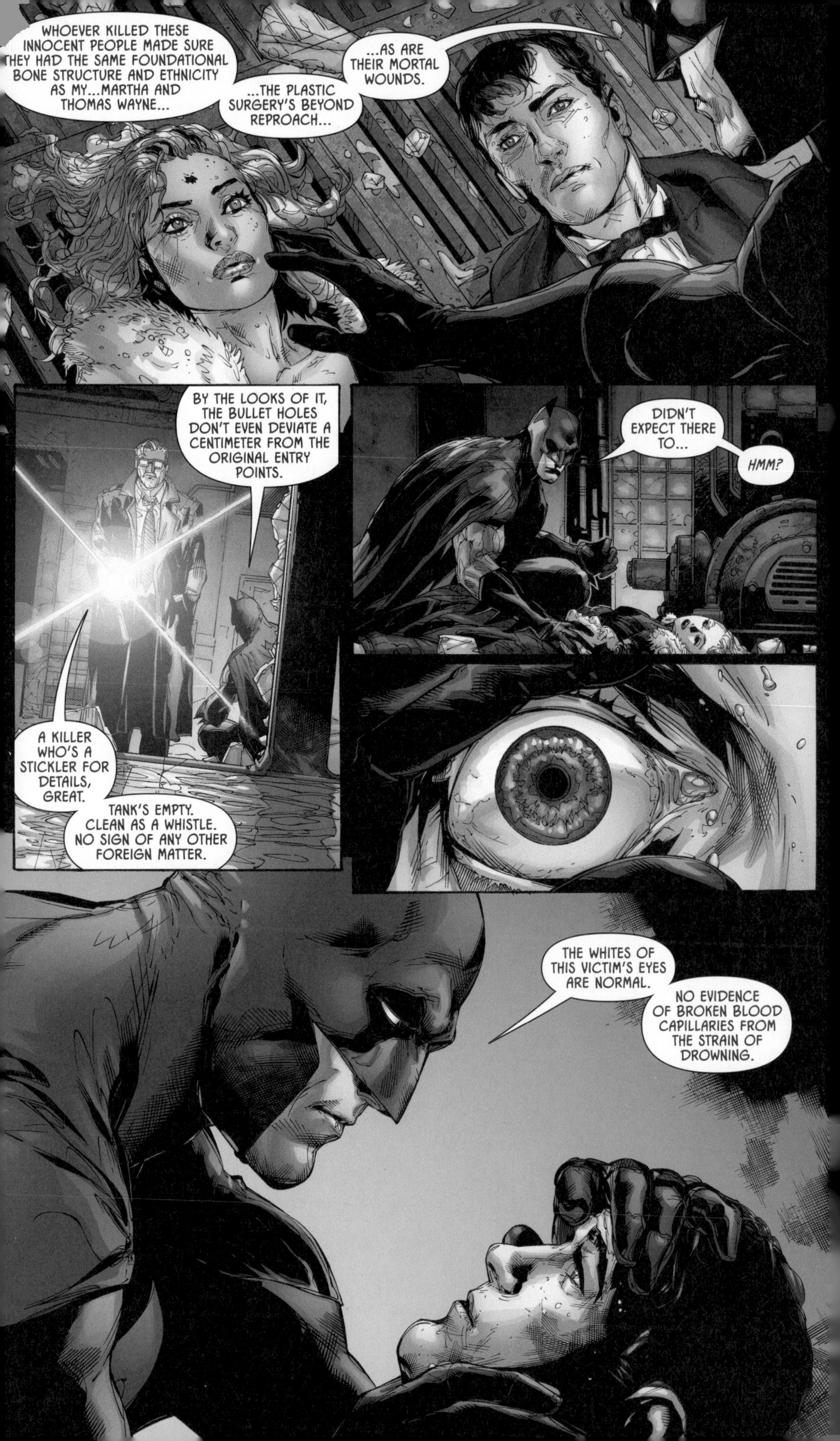
WHOEVER KILLED THESE INNOCENT PEOPLE MADE SURE THEY HAD THE SAME FOUNDATIONAL BONE STRUCTURE AND ETHNICITY AS MY...MARTHA AND THOMAS WAYNE...
...THE PLASTIC SURGERY'S BEYOND REPROACH...
...AS ARE THEIR MORTAL WOUNDS.
BY THE LOOKS OF IT, THE BULLET HOLES DON'T EVEN DEVIATE A CENTIMETER FROM THE ORIGINAL ENTRY POINTS.
A KILLER WHO'S A STICKLER FOR DETAILS, GREAT.
TANK'S EMPTY. CLEAN AS A WHISTLE. NO SIGN OF ANY OTHER FOREIGN MATTER.
DIDN'T EXPECT THERE TO...
HMM?
THE WHITES OF THIS VICTIM'S EYES ARE NORMAL.
NO EVIDENCE OF BROKEN BLOOD CAPILLARIES FROM THE STRAIN OF DROWNING.

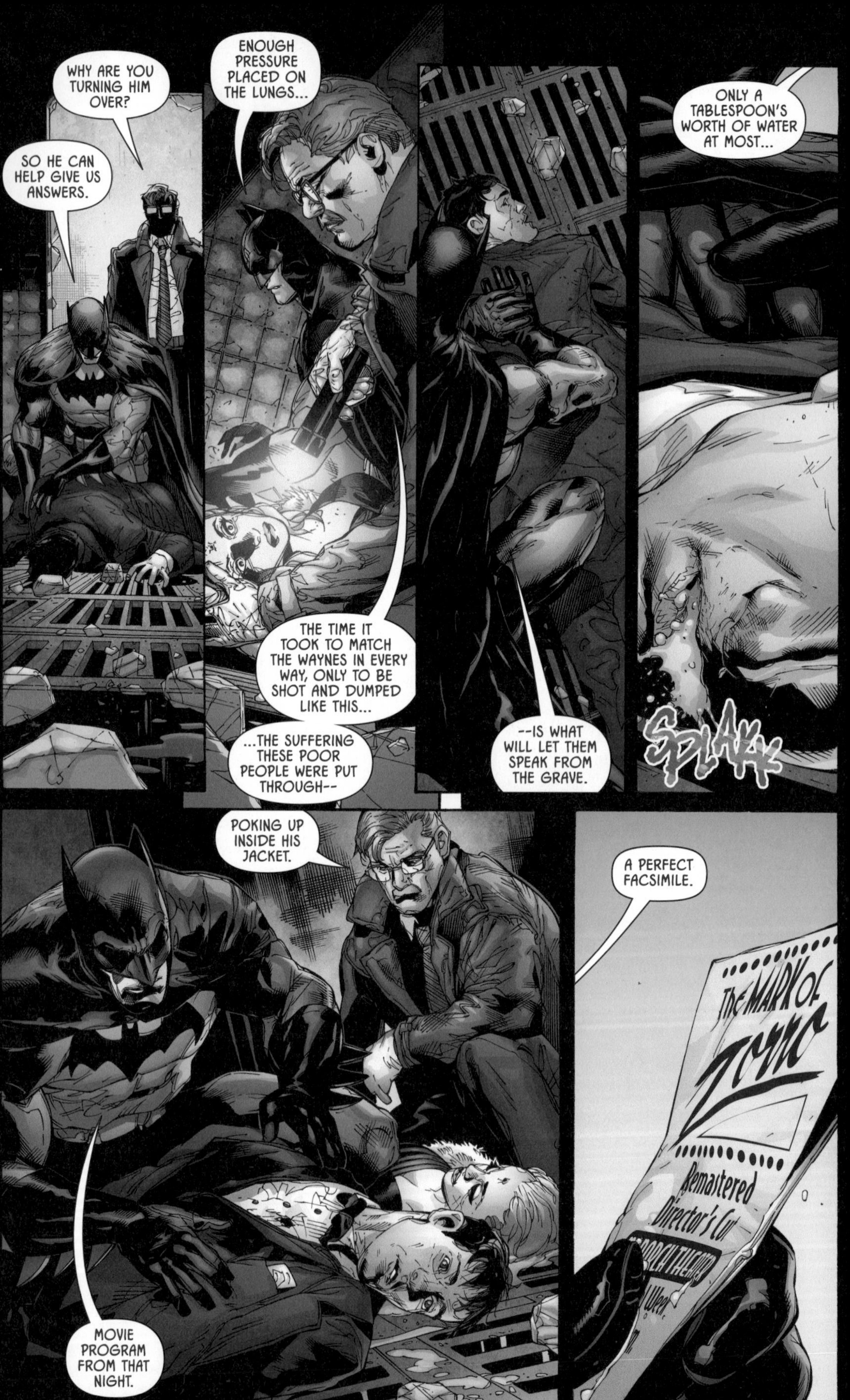
WHY ARE YOU TURNING HIM OVER?
SO HE CAN HELP GIVE US ANSWERS.
ENOUGH PRESSURE PLACED ON THE LUNGS...
THE TIME IT TOOK TO MATCH THE WAYNES IN EVERY WAY, ONLY TO BE SHOT AND DUMPED LIKE THIS...
...THE SUFFERING THESE POOR PEOPLE WERE PUT THROUGH--
--IS WHAT WILL LET THEM SPEAK FROM THE GRAVE.
ONLY A TABLESPOON'S WORTH OF WATER AT MOST...
SPLAKK
POKING UP INSIDE HIS JACKET.
MOVIE PROGRAM FROM THAT NIGHT.
A PERFECT FACSIMILE.
THE MARK OF ZORRO
Remastered Director's Cut

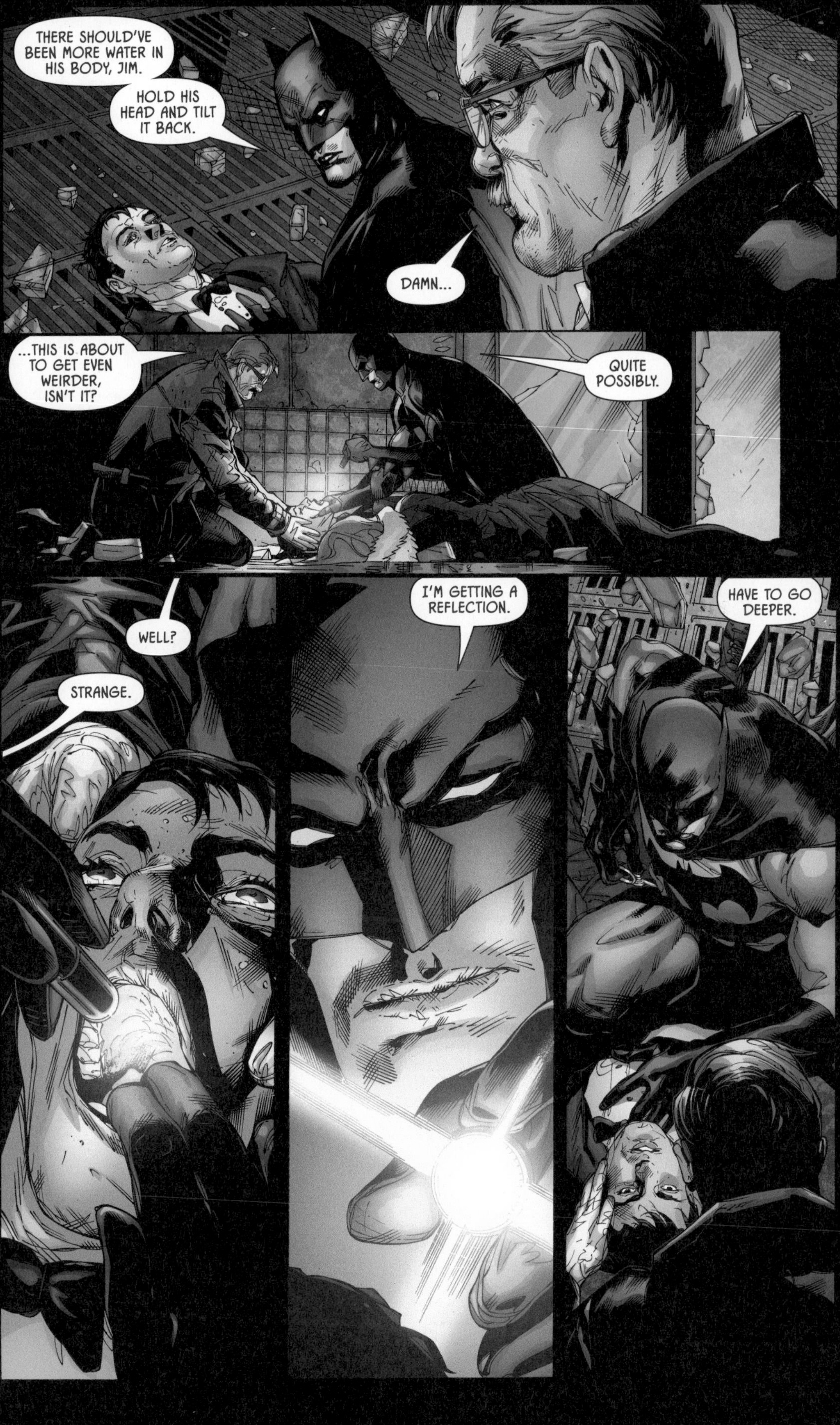
THERE SHOULD'VE BEEN MORE WATER IN HIS BODY, JIM.
HOLD HIS HEAD AND TILT IT BACK.
DAMN...
...THIS IS ABOUT TO GET EVEN WEIRDER, ISN'T IT?
QUITE POSSIBLY.
WELL?
STRANGE.
I'M GETTING A REFLECTION.
HAVE TO GO DEEPER.

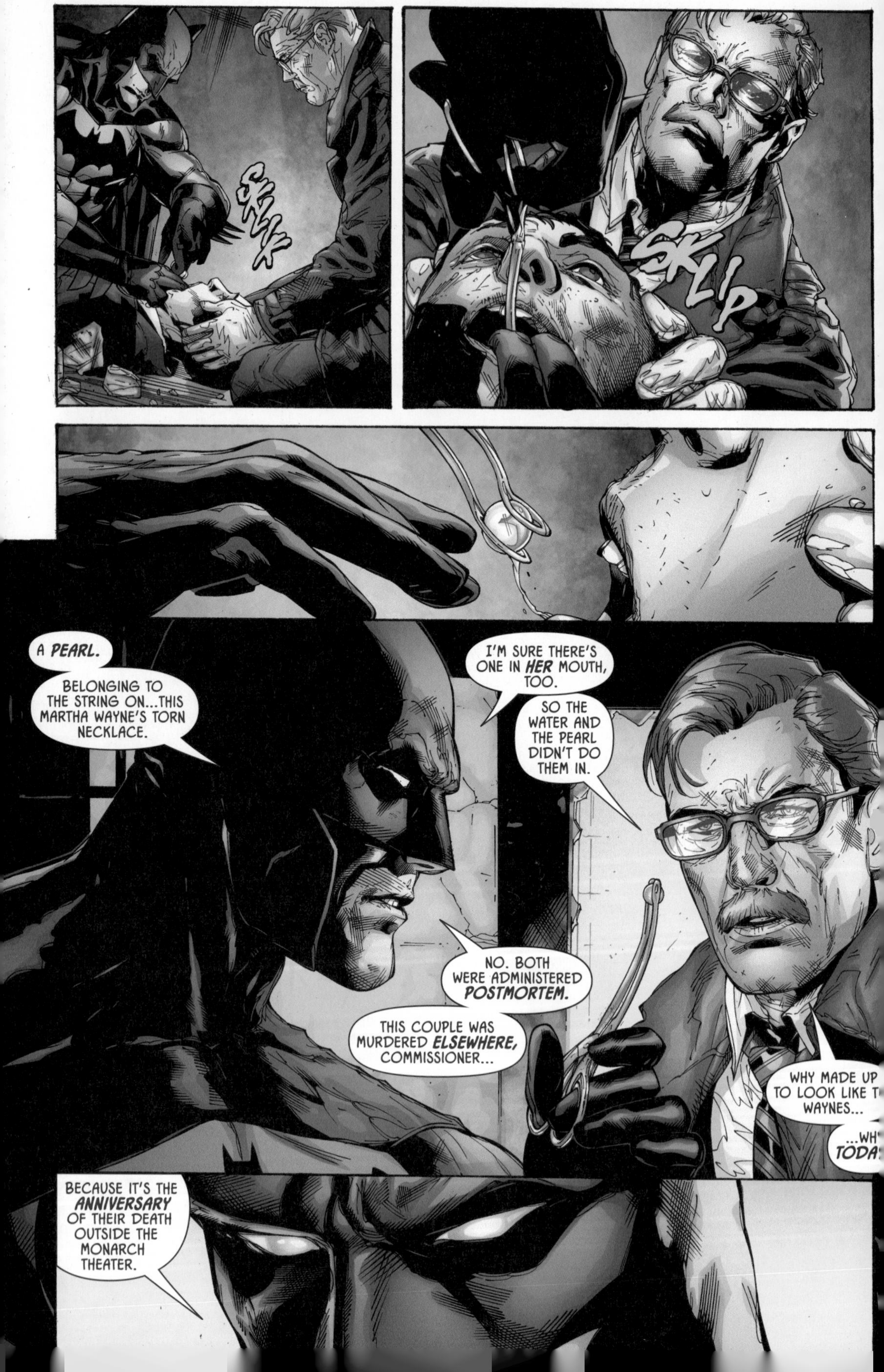
SKLIK
SKLIP
A PEARL.
BELONGING TO THE STRING ON...THIS MARTHA WAYNE'S TORN NECKLACE.
I'M SURE THERE'S ONE IN HER MOUTH, TOO.
SO THE WATER AND THE PEARL DIDN'T DO THEM IN.
NO. BOTH WERE ADMINISTERED POSTMORTEM.
THIS COUPLE WAS MURDERED ELSEWHERE, COMMISSIONER...
WHY MADE UP TO LOOK LIKE T WAYNES...
...WH TODA
BECAUSE IT'S THE ANNIVERSARY OF THEIR DEATH OUTSIDE THE MONARCH THEATER.

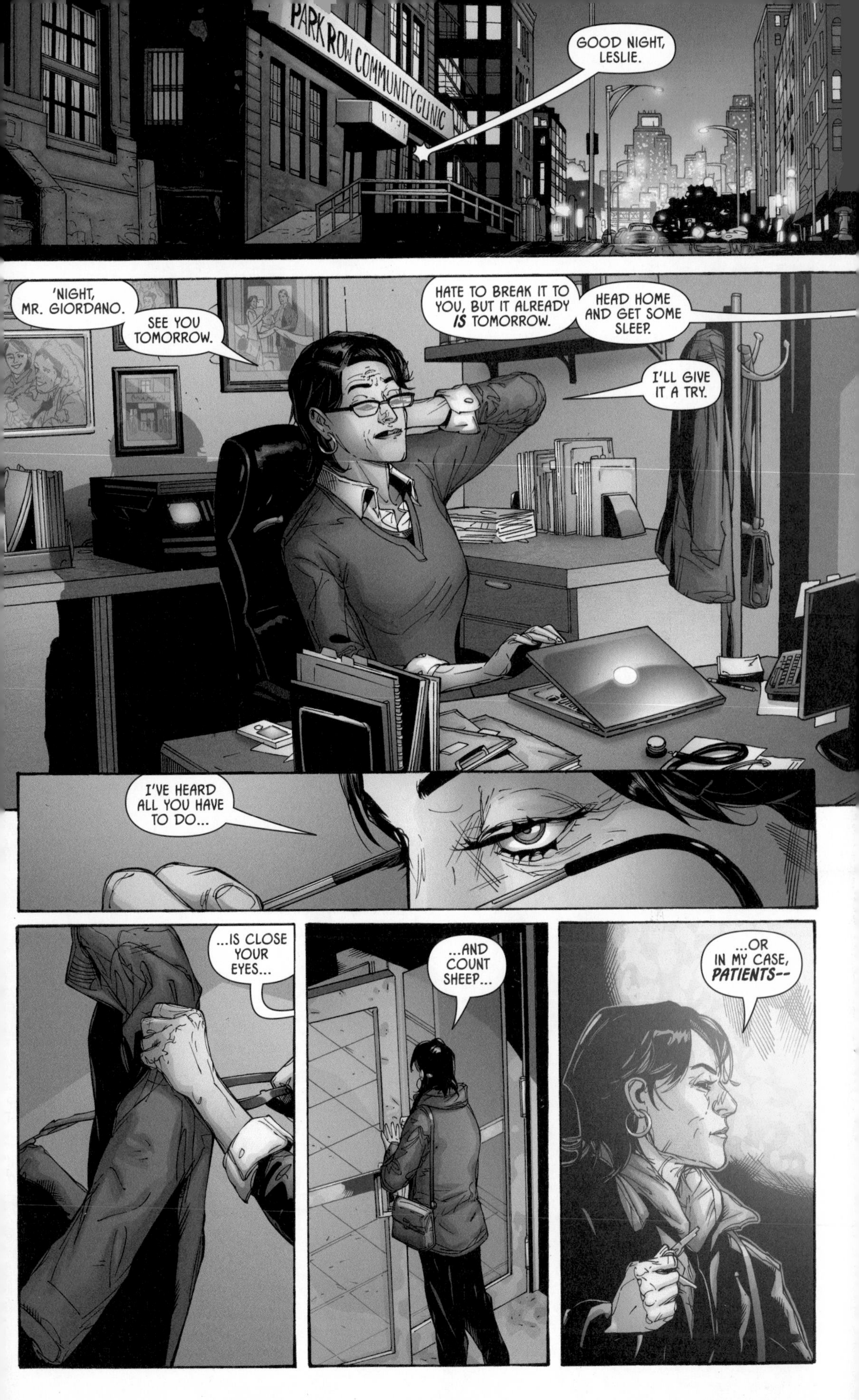
PARK ROW COMMUNITY CLINIC
GOOD NIGHT, LESLIE.
'NIGHT, MR. GIORDANO.
SEE YOU TOMORROW.
HATE TO BREAK IT TO YOU, BUT IT ALREADY IS TOMORROW.
HEAD HOME AND GET SOME SLEEP.
I'LL GIVE IT A TRY.
I'VE HEARD ALL YOU HAVE TO DO...
...IS CLOSE YOUR EYES...
...AND COUNT SHEEP...
...OR IN MY CASE, PATIENTS--

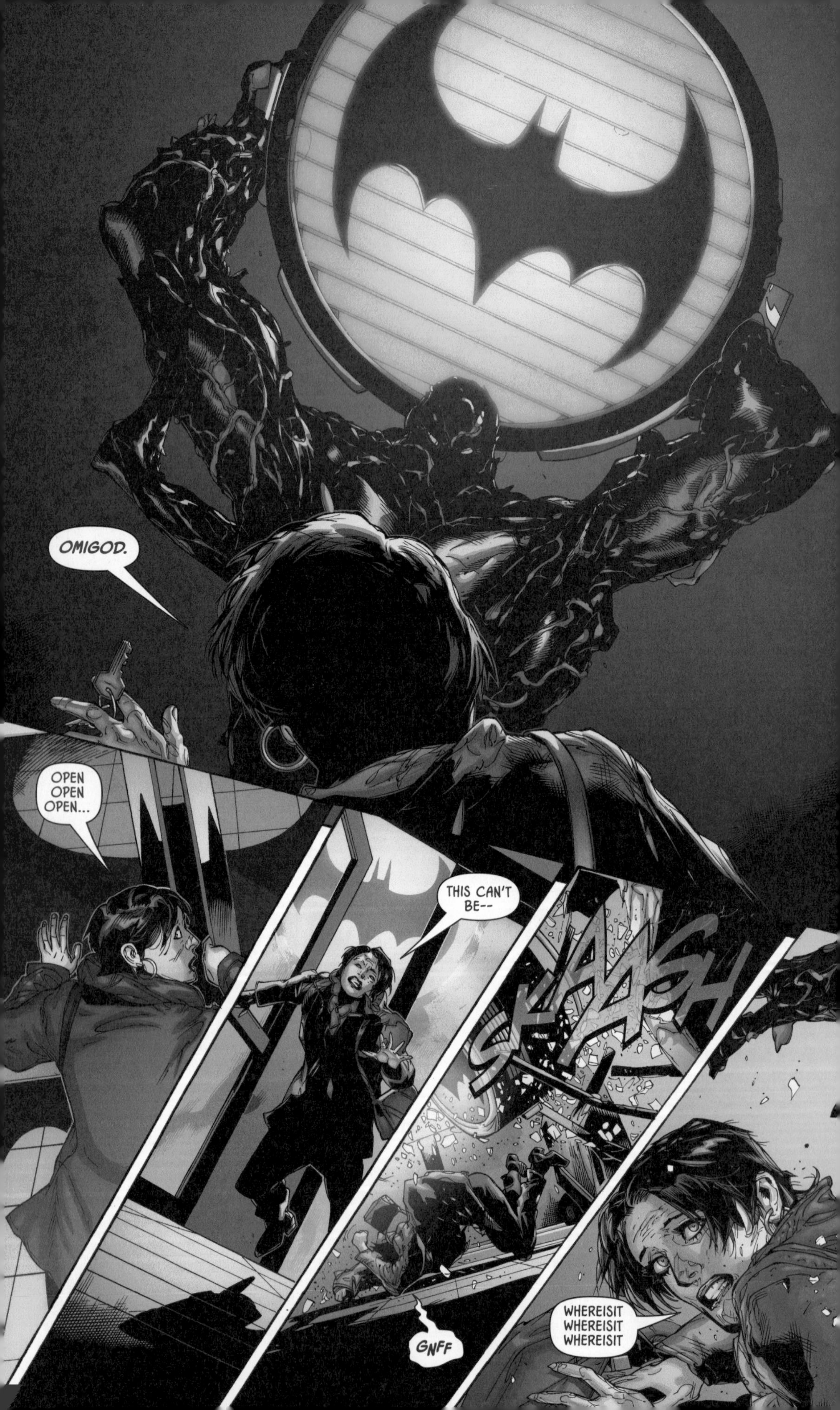
OMIGOD.
OPEN OPEN OPEN...
THIS CAN'T BE--
SKASH
GNFF
WHEREISIT WHEREISIT WHEREISIT

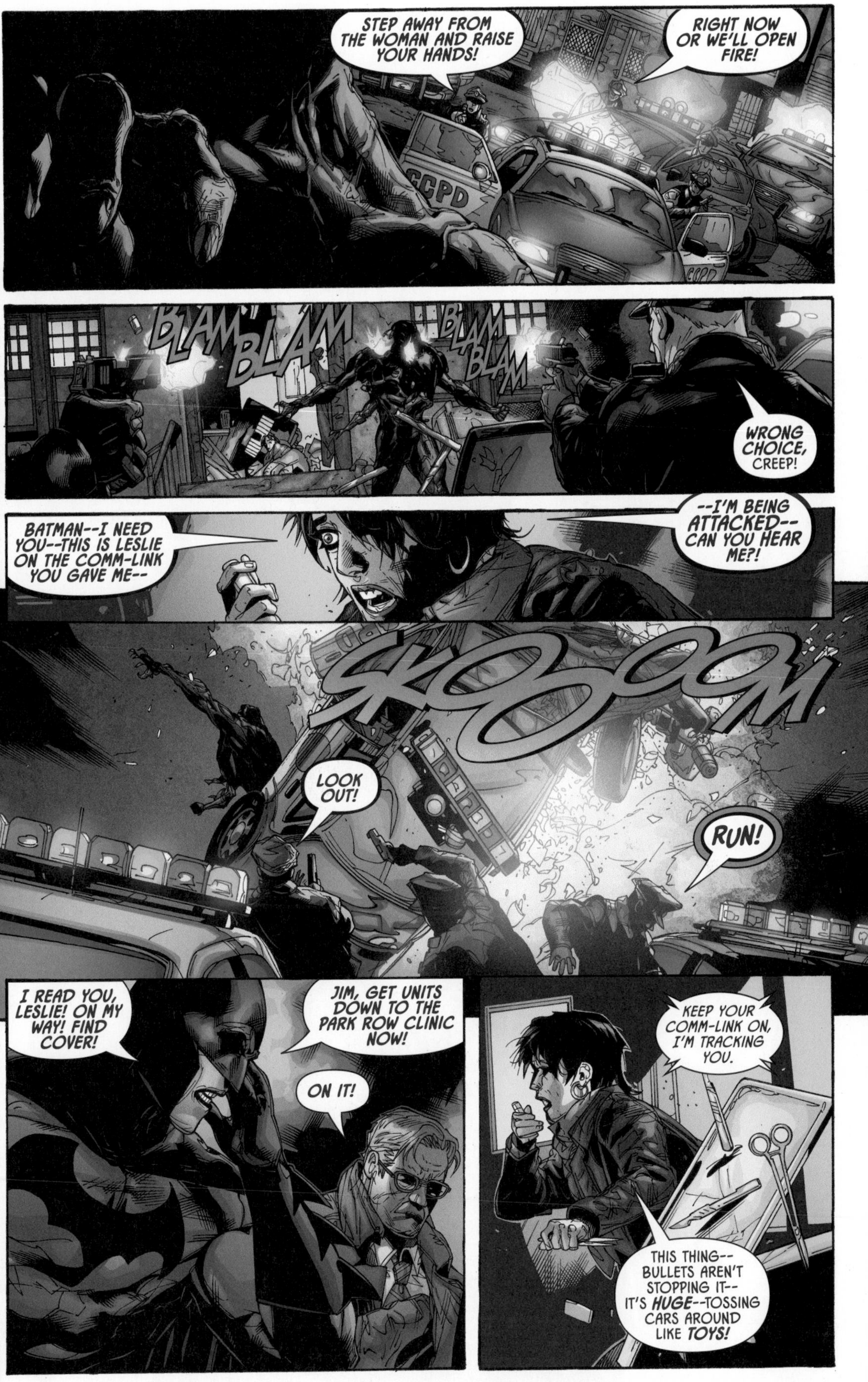
STEP AWAY FROM THE WOMAN AND RAISE YOUR HANDS!
RIGHT NOW OR WE'LL OPEN FIRE!
BLAM BLAM
BLAM BLAM
WRONG CHOICE, CREEP!
BATMAN--I NEED YOU--THIS IS LESLIE ON THE COMM-LINK YOU GAVE ME--
--I'M BEING ATTACKED--CAN YOU HEAR ME?!
SKOOOOM
LOOK OUT!
RUN!
I READ YOU, LESLIE! ON MY WAY! FIND COVER!
JIM, GET UNITS DOWN TO THE PARK ROW CLINIC NOW!
ON IT!
KEEP YOUR COMM-LINK ON, I'M TRACKING YOU.
THIS THING--BULLETS AREN'T STOPPING IT--IT'S HUGE--TOSSING CARS AROUND LIKE TOYS!

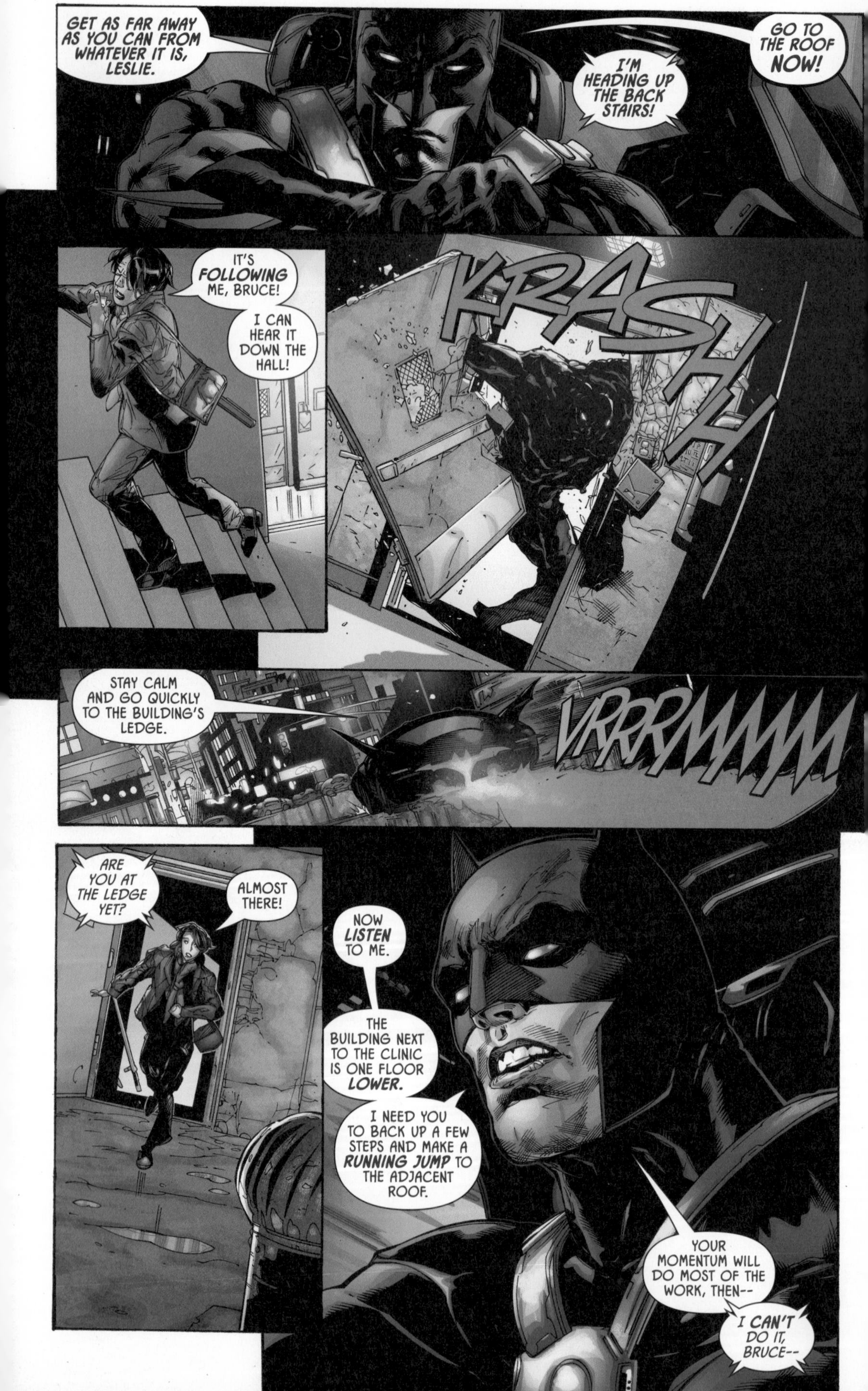

GET AS FAR AWAY AS YOU CAN FROM WHATEVER IT IS, LESLIE.
I'M HEADING UP THE BACK STAIRS!
GO TO THE ROOF NOW!
IT'S FOLLOWING ME, BRUCE!
I CAN HEAR IT DOWN THE HALL!
KRASHH
STAY CALM AND GO QUICKLY TO THE BUILDING'S LEDGE.
VRRRMMMM
ARE YOU AT THE LEDGE YET?
ALMOST THERE!
NOW LISTEN TO ME.
THE BUILDING NEXT TO THE CLINIC IS ONE FLOOR LOWER.
I NEED YOU TO BACK UP A FEW STEPS AND MAKE A RUNNING JUMP TO THE ADJACENT ROOF.
YOUR MOMENTUM WILL DO MOST OF THE WORK, THEN--
I CAN'T DO IT, BRUCE--

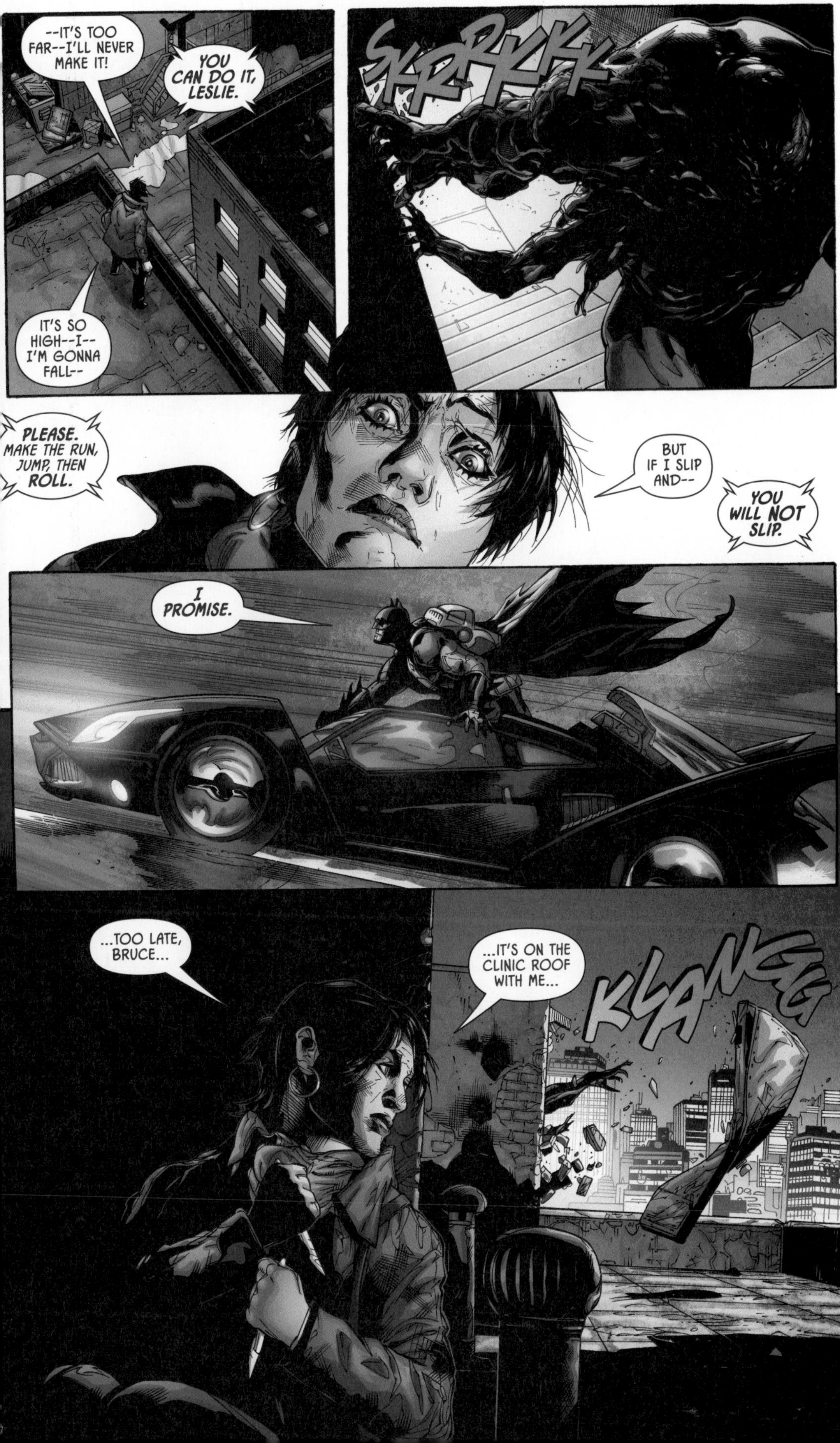
--IT'S TOO FAR--I'LL NEVER MAKE IT!
YOU CAN DO IT, LESLIE.
IT'S SO HIGH--I--I'M GONNA FALL--
SKRKKK
PLEASE. MAKE THE RUN, JUMP, THEN ROLL.
BUT IF I SLIP AND--
YOU WILL NOT SLIP.
I PROMISE.
...TOO LATE, BRUCE...
...IT'S ON THE CLINIC ROOF WITH ME...
KLANGG

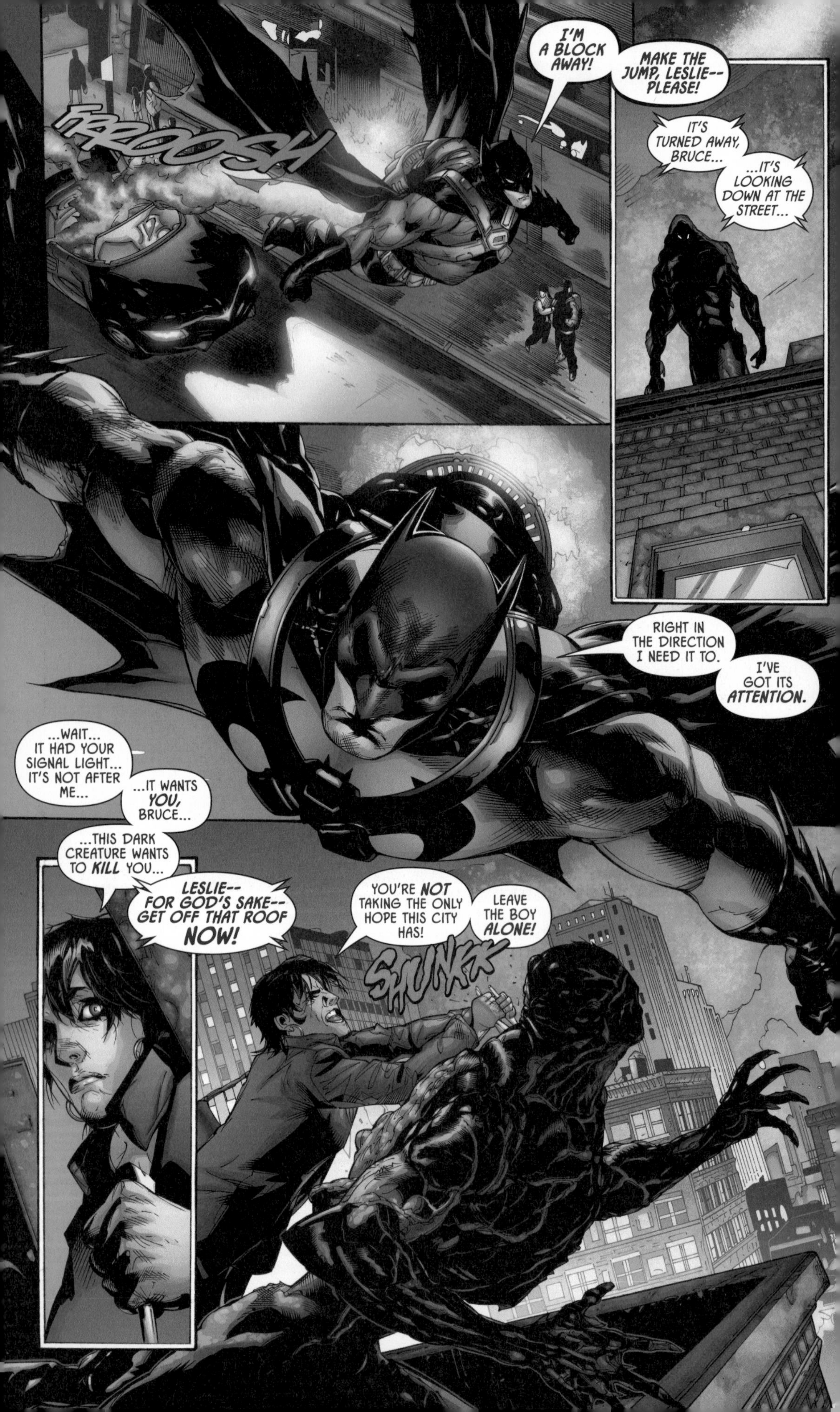

FRROOSH
I'M A BLOCK AWAY!
MAKE THE JUMP, LESLIE-- PLEASE!
IT'S TURNED AWAY, BRUCE...
...IT'S LOOKING DOWN AT THE STREET...
RIGHT IN THE DIRECTION I NEED IT TO.
I'VE GOT ITS ATTENTION.
...WAIT... IT HAD YOUR SIGNAL LIGHT... IT'S NOT AFTER ME...
...IT WANTS YOU, BRUCE...
...THIS DARK CREATURE WANTS TO KILL YOU...
LESLIE-- FOR GOD'S SAKE-- GET OFF THAT ROOF NOW!
YOU'RE NOT TAKING THE ONLY HOPE THIS CITY HAS!
LEAVE THE BOY ALONE!
SHUNKK

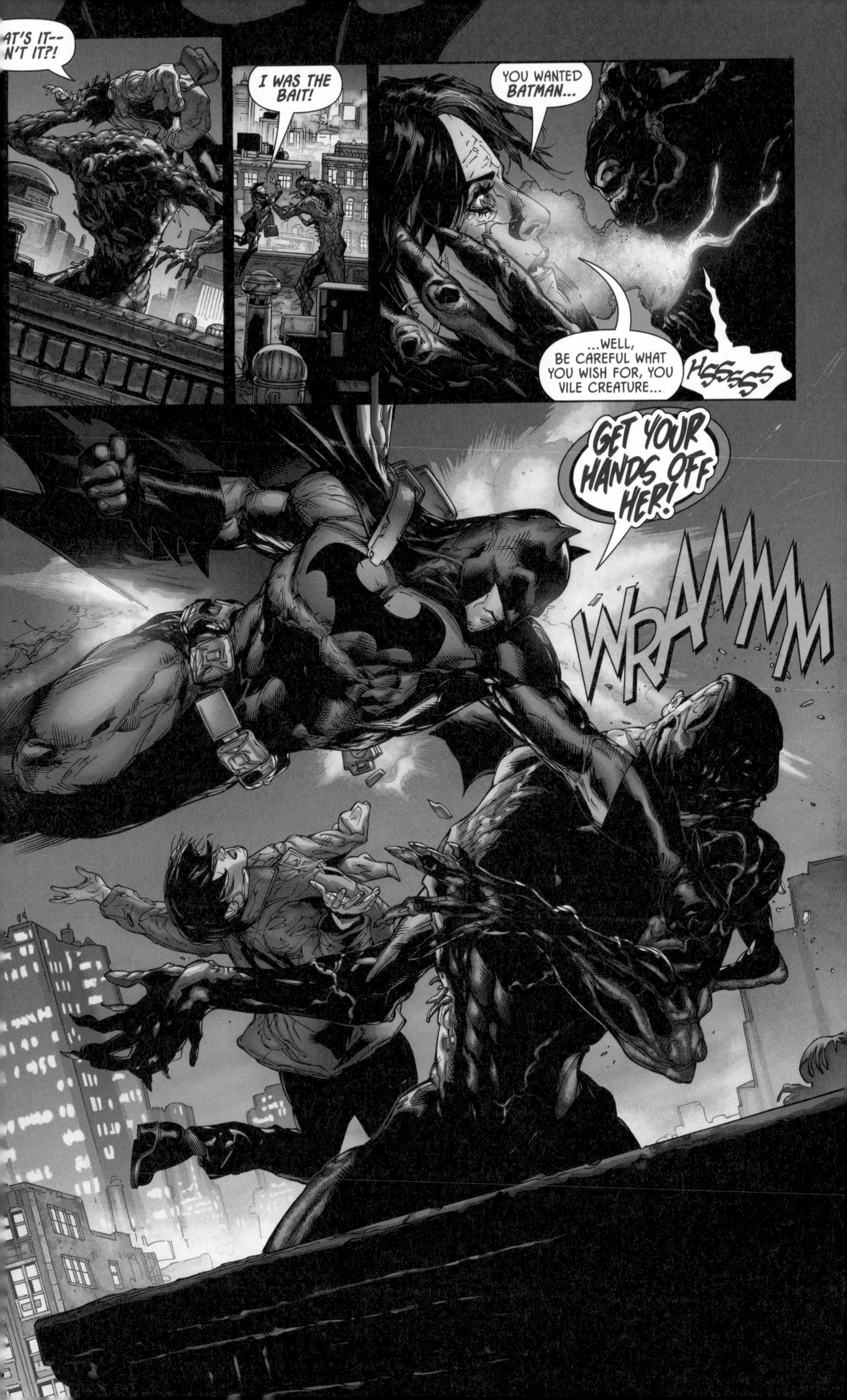
AT'S IT--
N'T IT?!
I WAS THE BAIT!
YOU WANTED BATMAN...
...WELL, BE CAREFUL WHAT YOU WISH FOR, YOU VILE CREATURE...
HSSSSS
GET YOUR HANDS OFF HER!
WRAMMM

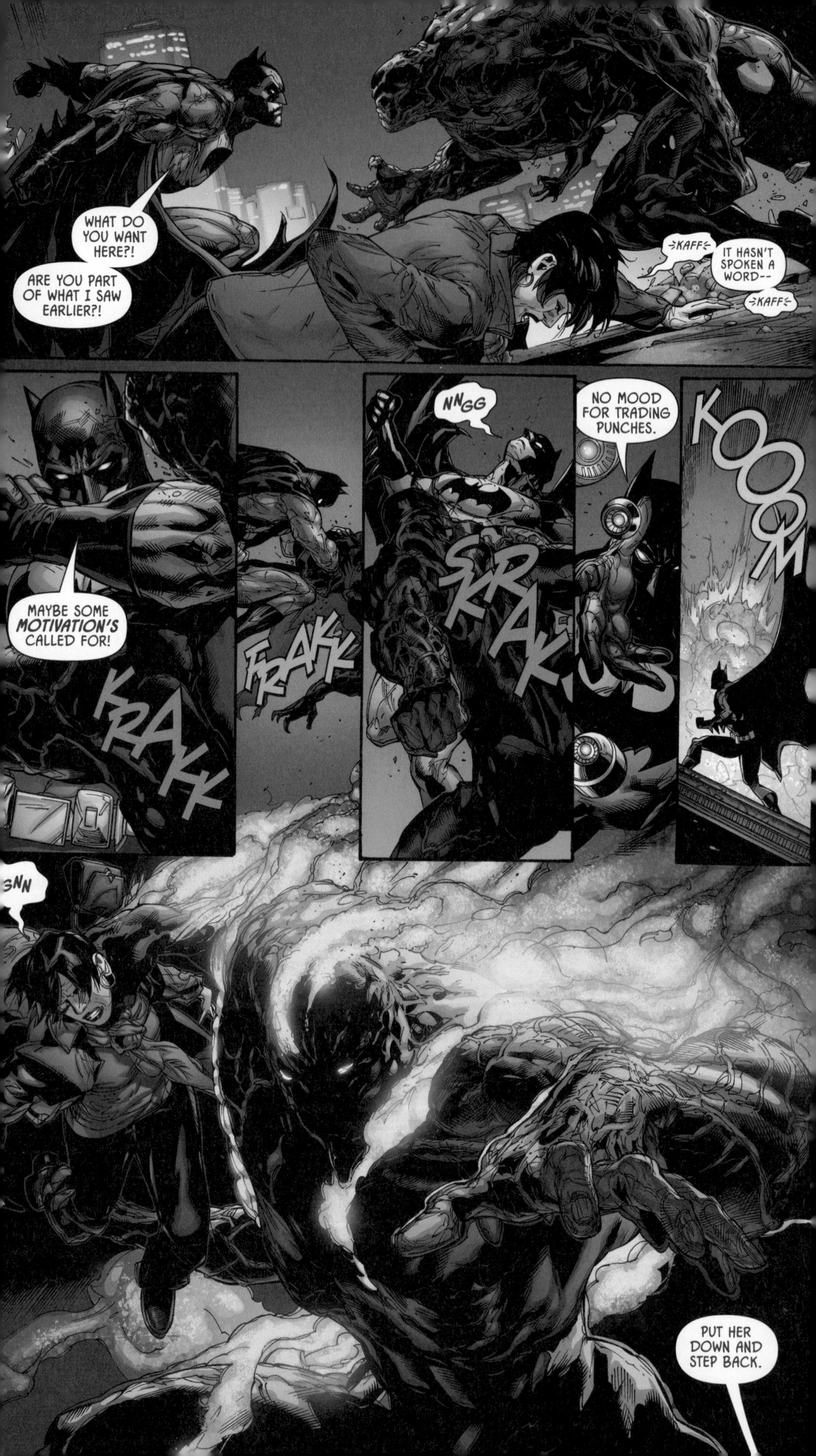
WHAT DO YOU WANT HERE?!
ARE YOU PART OF WHAT I SAW EARLIER?!
KAFF
IT HASN'T SPOKEN A WORD--
KAFF
MAYBE SOME MOTIVATION'S CALLED FOR!
KRAKK
FRAKK
NNGG
SKRAKK
NO MOOD FOR TRADING PUNCHES.
KOOOM
GNN
PUT HER DOWN AND STEP BACK.

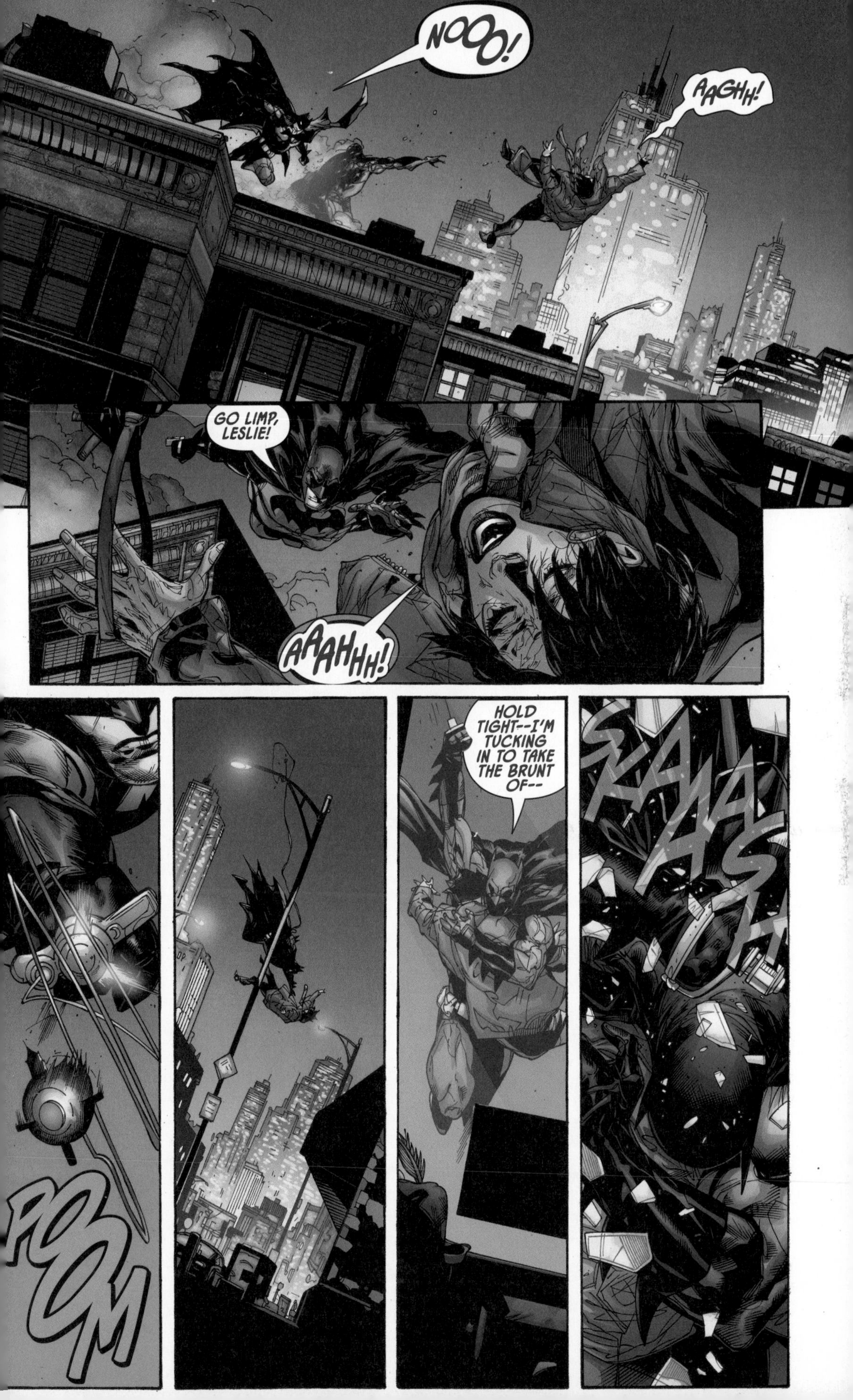
NOOO!
AAGHH!
GO LIMP, LESLIE!
AAAHHH!
POOM
HOLD TIGHT--I'M TUCKING IN TO TAKE THE BRUNT OF--
SKAAASH

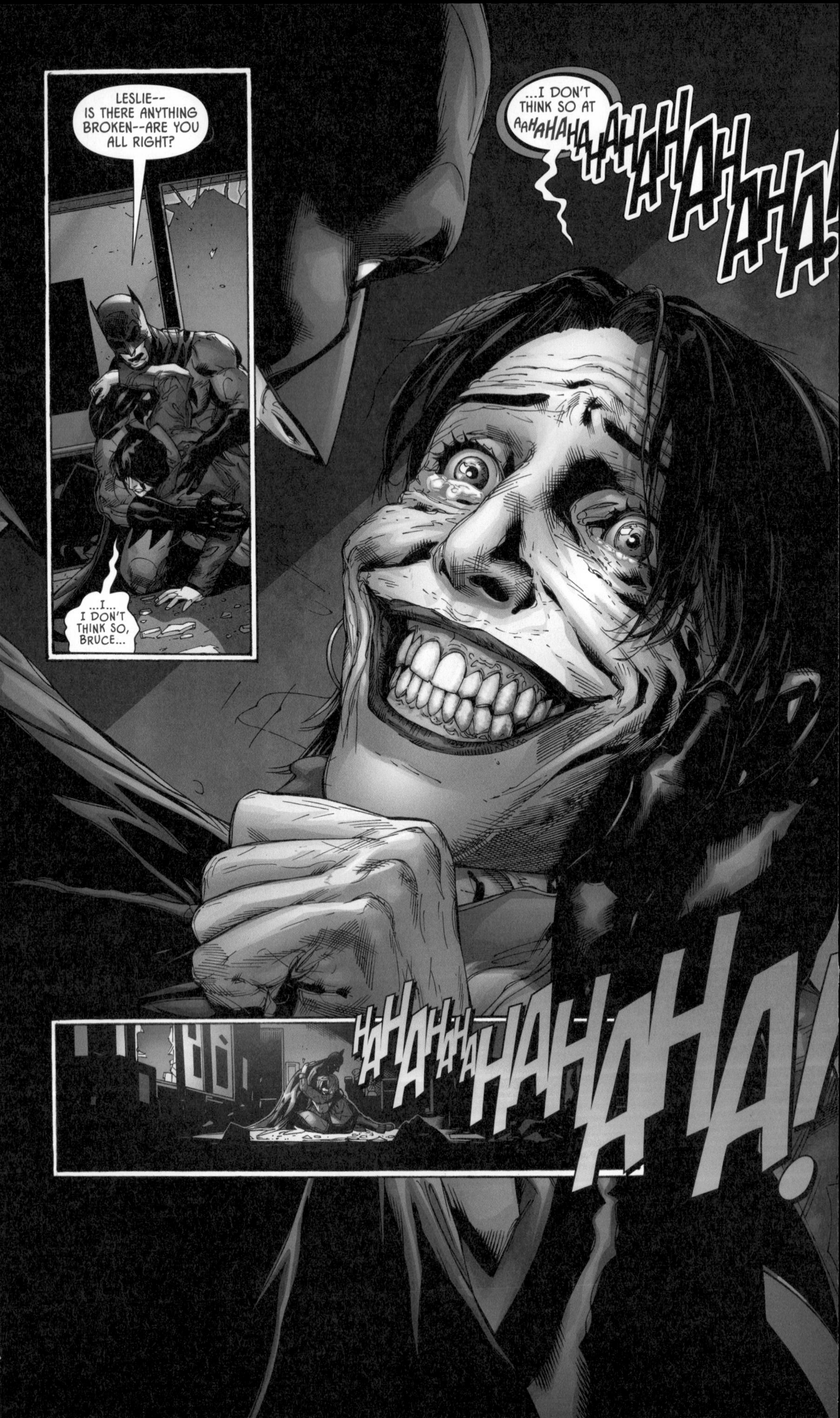
LESLIE-- IS THERE ANYTHING BROKEN--ARE YOU ALL RIGHT?
...I... I DON'T THINK SO, BRUCE...
...I DON'T THINK SO AT AAHAHAHAHAHAHAHAHAHA!
HAHAHAHAHAHAHAHAHA!

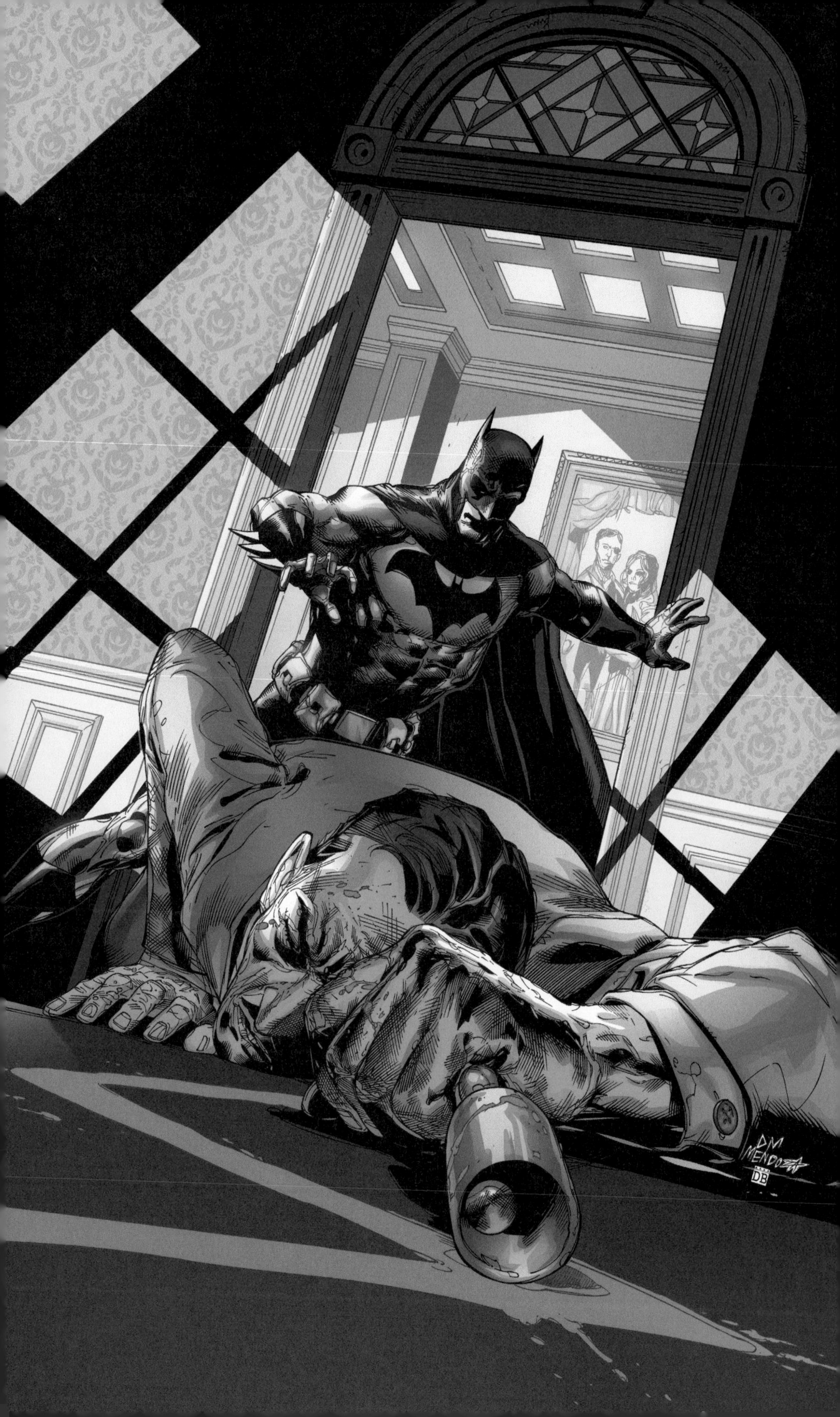
DM
MENDOZA
DB

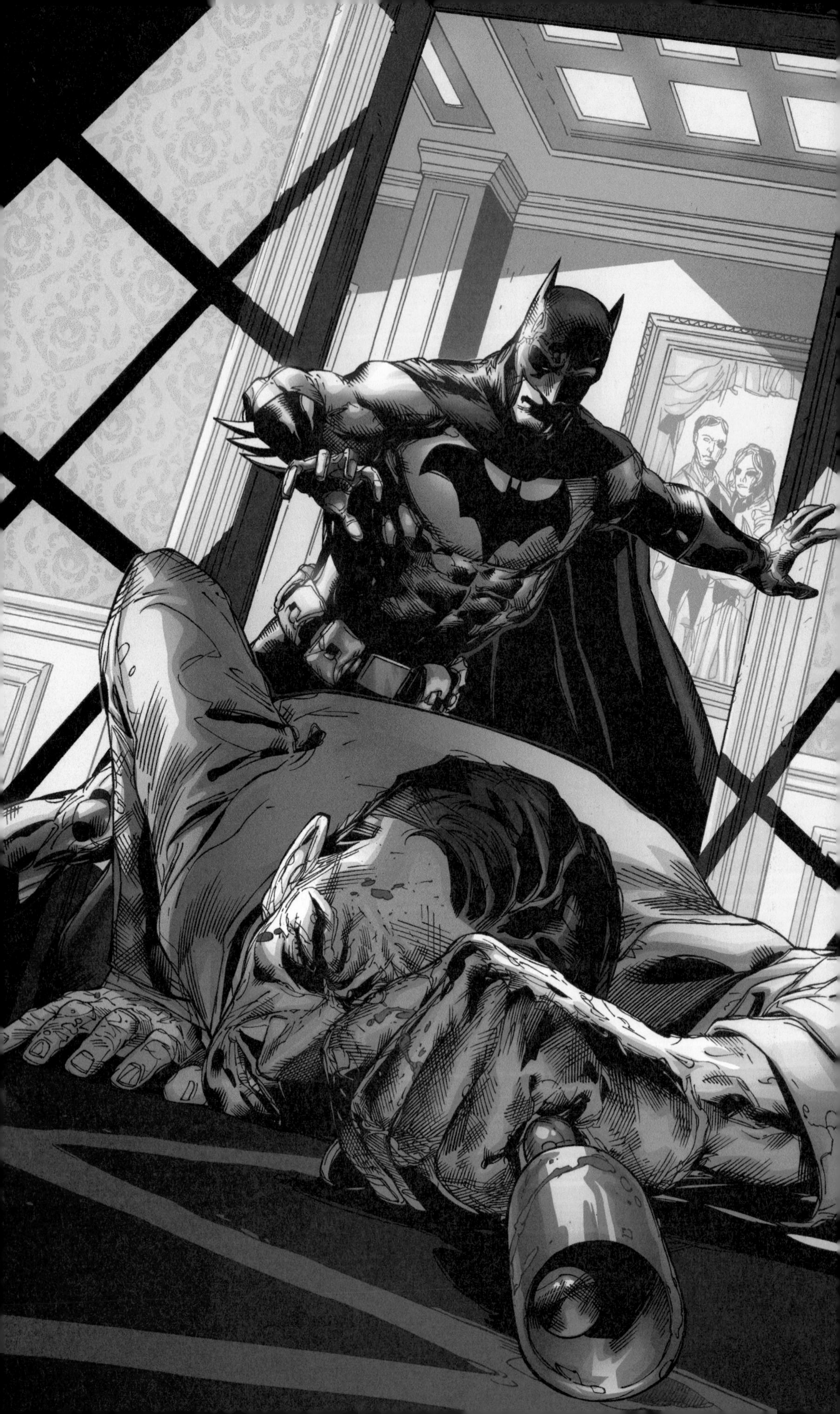

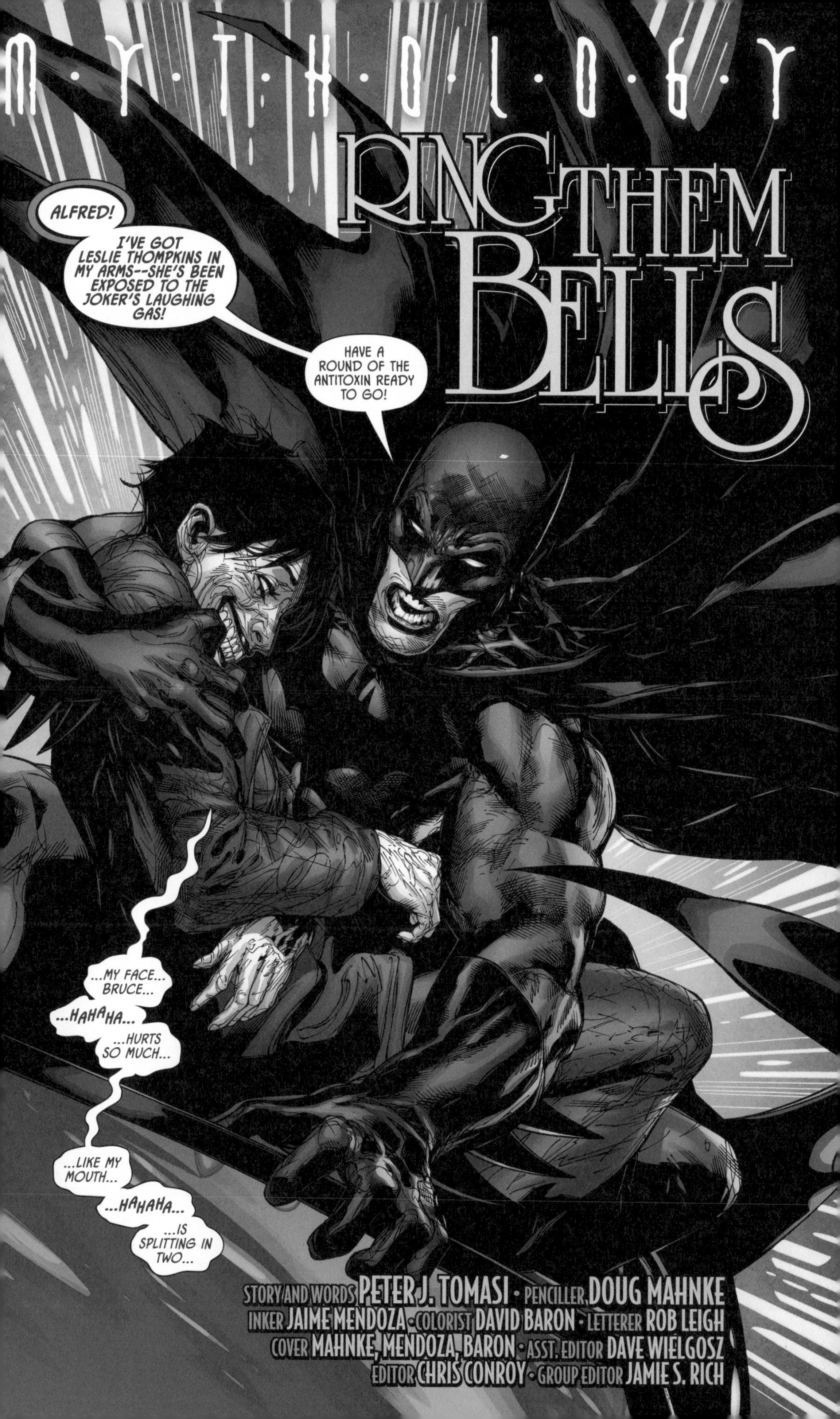
M·Y·T·H·O·L·O·G·Y
RING THEM BELLS
ALFRED!
I'VE GOT LESLIE THOMPKINS IN MY ARMS--SHE'S BEEN EXPOSED TO THE JOKER'S LAUGHING GAS!
HAVE A ROUND OF THE ANTITOXIN READY TO GO!
...MY FACE... BRUCE...
...HAHAHA...
...HURTS SO MUCH...
...LIKE MY MOUTH...
...HAHAHA...
...IS SPLITTING IN TWO...
STORY AND WORDS PETER J. TOMASI · PENCILLER DOUG MAHNKE
INKER JAIME MENDOZA · COLORIST DAVID BARON · LETTERER ROB LEIGH
COVER MAHNKE, MENDOZA, BARON · ASST. EDITOR DAVE WIELGOSZ
EDITOR CHRIS CONROY · GROUP EDITOR JAMIE S. RICH

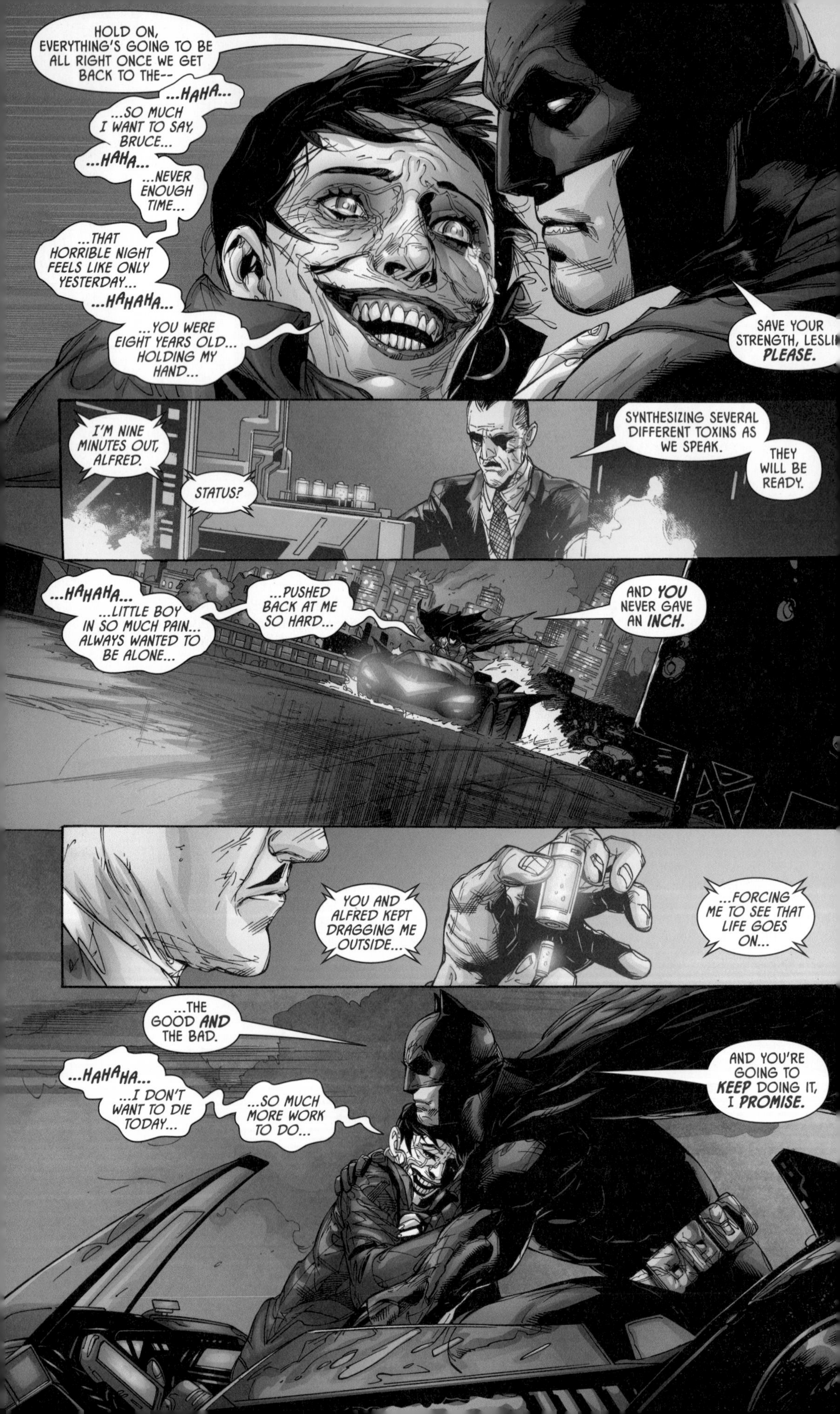
HOLD ON, EVERYTHING'S GOING TO BE ALL RIGHT ONCE WE GET BACK TO THE--
...HAHA...
...SO MUCH I WANT TO SAY, BRUCE...
...HAHA...
...NEVER ENOUGH TIME...
...THAT HORRIBLE NIGHT FEELS LIKE ONLY YESTERDAY...
...HAHAHA...
...YOU WERE EIGHT YEARS OLD... HOLDING MY HAND...
SAVE YOUR STRENGTH, LESLI
PLEASE.
I'M NINE MINUTES OUT, ALFRED.
STATUS?
SYNTHESIZING SEVERAL DIFFERENT TOXINS AS WE SPEAK.
THEY WILL BE READY.
...HAHAHA...
...LITTLE BOY IN SO MUCH PAIN... ALWAYS WANTED TO BE ALONE...
...PUSHED BACK AT ME SO HARD...
AND YOU NEVER GAVE AN INCH.
YOU AND ALFRED KEPT DRAGGING ME OUTSIDE...
...FORCING ME TO SEE THAT LIFE GOES ON...
...THE GOOD AND THE BAD.
...HAHAHA...
...I DON'T WANT TO DIE TODAY...
...SO MUCH MORE WORK TO DO...
AND YOU'RE GOING TO KEEP DOING IT, I PROMISE.

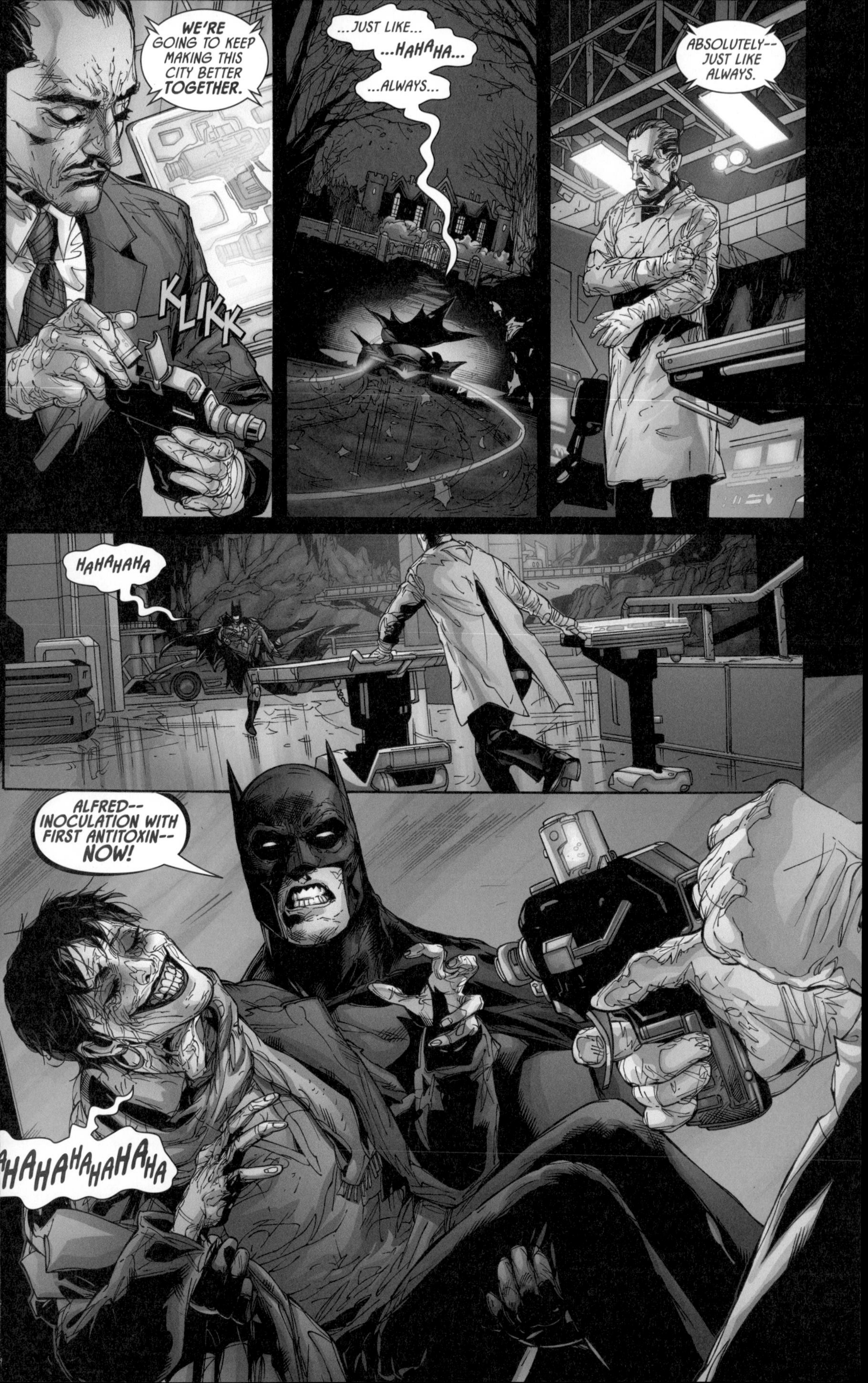
WE'RE GOING TO KEEP MAKING THIS CITY BETTER TOGETHER.
KLIKK
...JUST LIKE...
...HAHAHA...
...ALWAYS...
ABSOLUTELY-- JUST LIKE ALWAYS.
HAHAHAHA
ALFRED-- INOCULATION WITH FIRST ANTITOXIN-- NOW!
HAHAHAHAHAHAHA

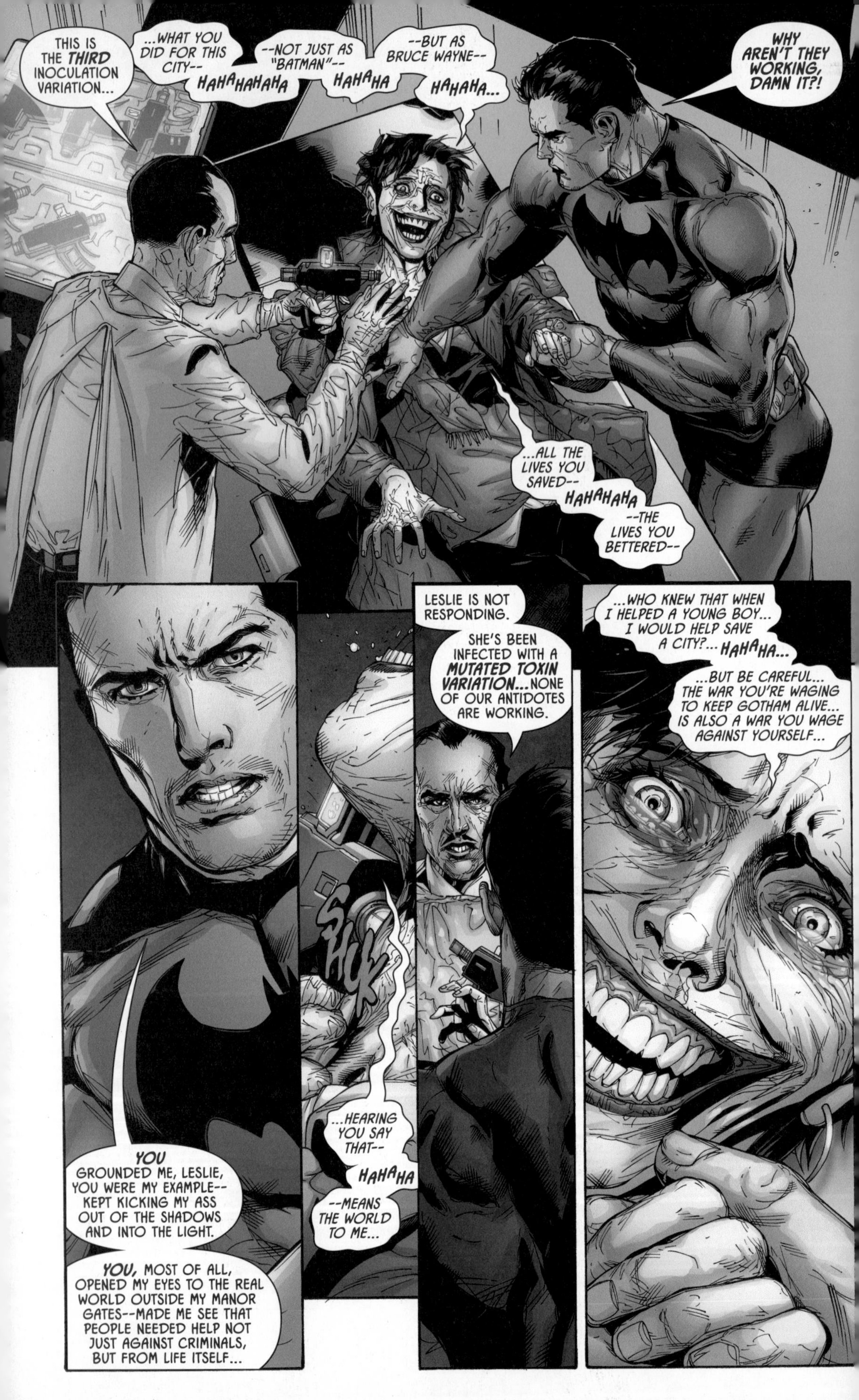

THIS IS THE THIRD INOCULATION VARIATION...
...WHAT YOU DID FOR THIS CITY-- HAHAHAHAHA
--NOT JUST AS "BATMAN"-- HAHAHA
--BUT AS BRUCE WAYNE-- HAHAHA...
WHY AREN'T THEY WORKING, DAMN IT?!
...ALL THE LIVES YOU SAVED-- HAHAHAHA
--THE LIVES YOU BETTERED--
YOU GROUNDED ME, LESLIE, YOU WERE MY EXAMPLE-- KEPT KICKING MY ASS OUT OF THE SHADOWS AND INTO THE LIGHT.
YOU, MOST OF ALL, OPENED MY EYES TO THE REAL WORLD OUTSIDE MY MANOR GATES--MADE ME SEE THAT PEOPLE NEEDED HELP NOT JUST AGAINST CRIMINALS, BUT FROM LIFE ITSELF...
SHUK
...HEARING YOU SAY THAT--
HAHAHA
--MEANS THE WORLD TO ME...
LESLIE IS NOT RESPONDING.
SHE'S BEEN INFECTED WITH A MUTATED TOXIN VARIATION... NONE OF OUR ANTIDOTES ARE WORKING.
...WHO KNEW THAT WHEN I HELPED A YOUNG BOY... I WOULD HELP SAVE A CITY?... HAHAHA...
...BUT BE CAREFUL... THE WAR YOU'RE WAGING TO KEEP GOTHAM ALIVE... IS ALSO A WAR YOU WAGE AGAINST YOURSELF...

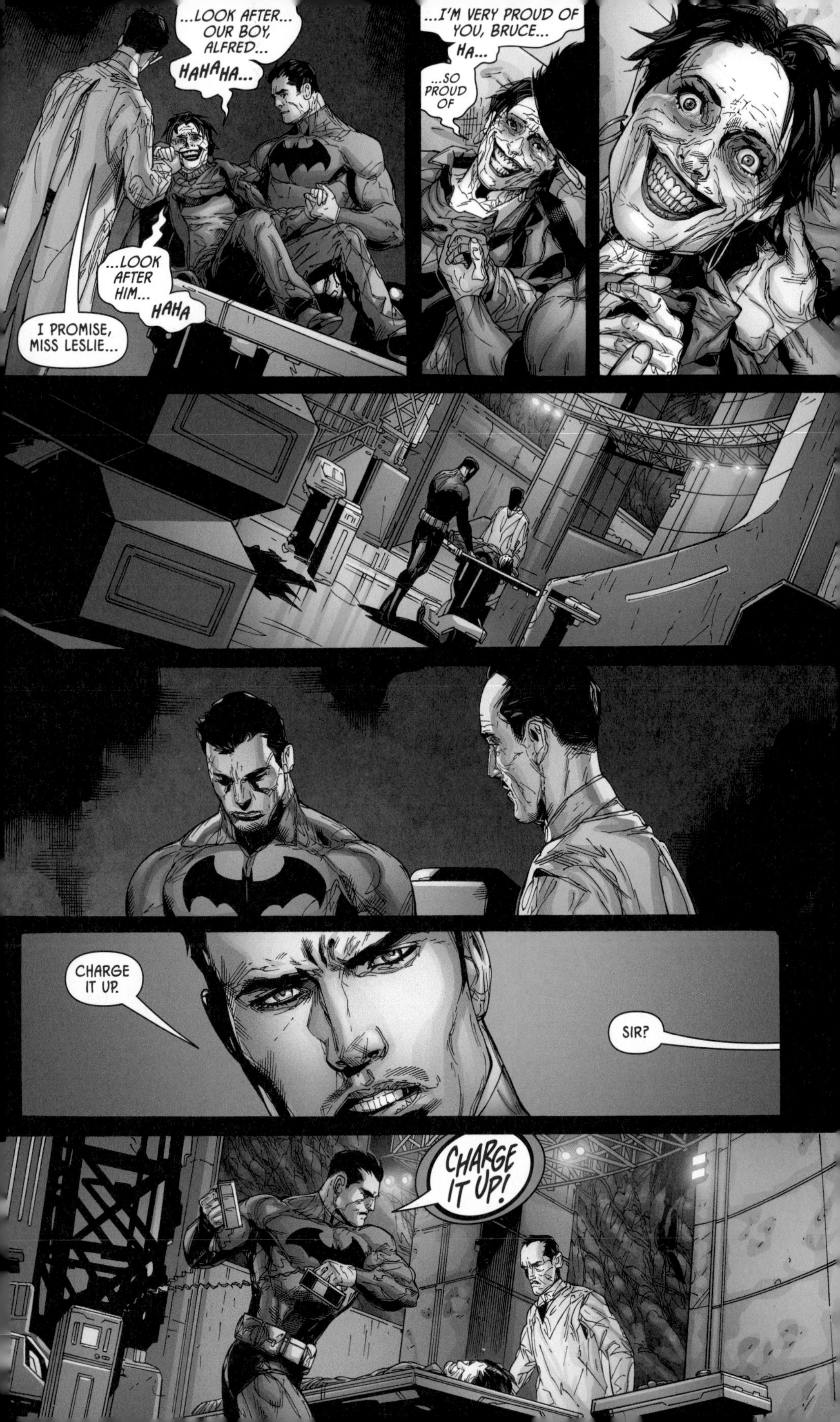
...LOOK AFTER... OUR BOY, ALFRED...
HAHAHA...
...LOOK AFTER HIM...
HAHA
I PROMISE, MISS LESLIE...
...I'M VERY PROUD OF YOU, BRUCE...
HA...
...SO PROUD OF
CHARGE IT UP.
SIR?
CHARGE IT UP!

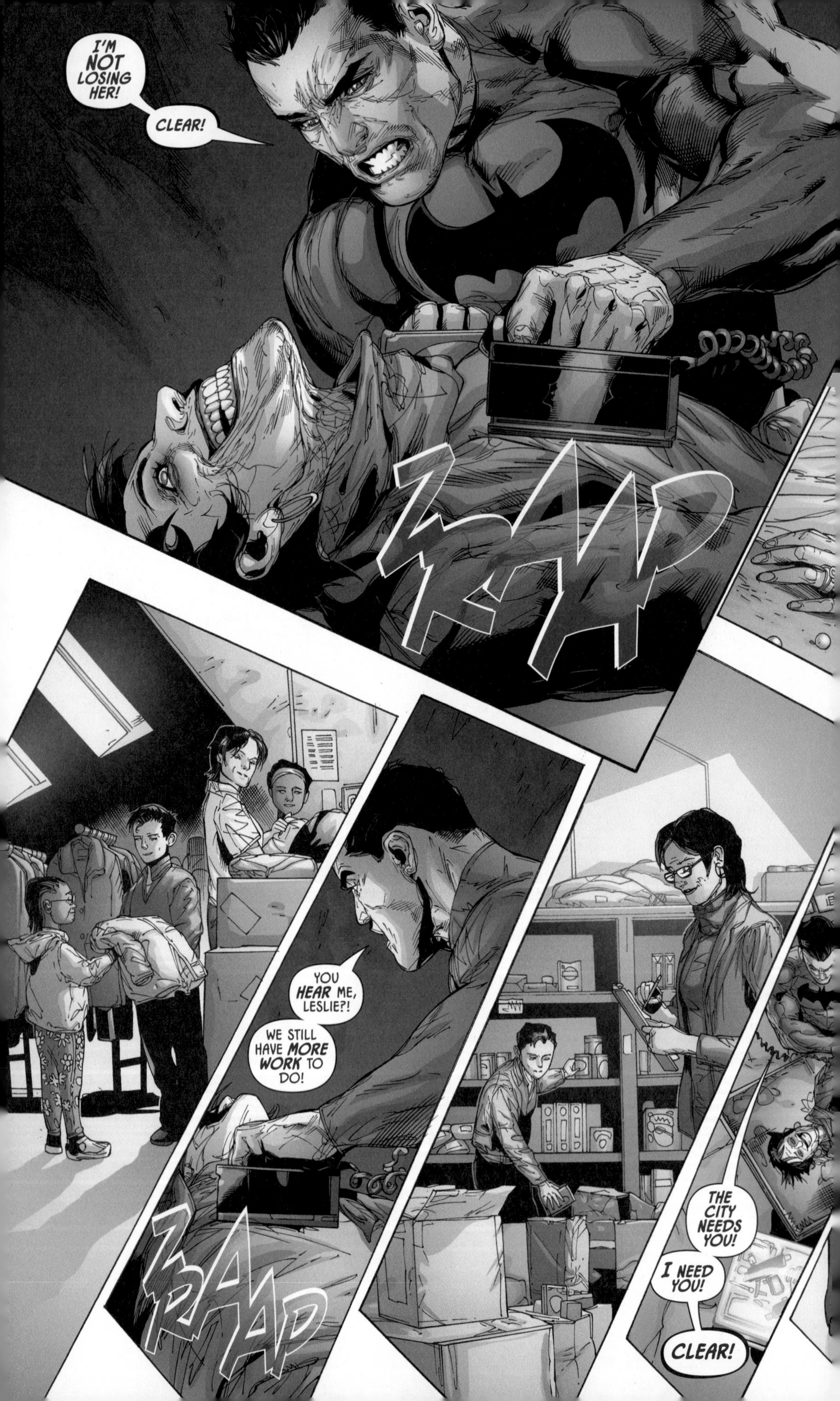

I'M NOT LOSING HER!
CLEAR!
ZAP
YOU HEAR ME, LESLIE?!
WE STILL HAVE MORE WORK TO DO!
ZAAP
THE CITY NEEDS YOU!
I NEED YOU!
CLEAR!

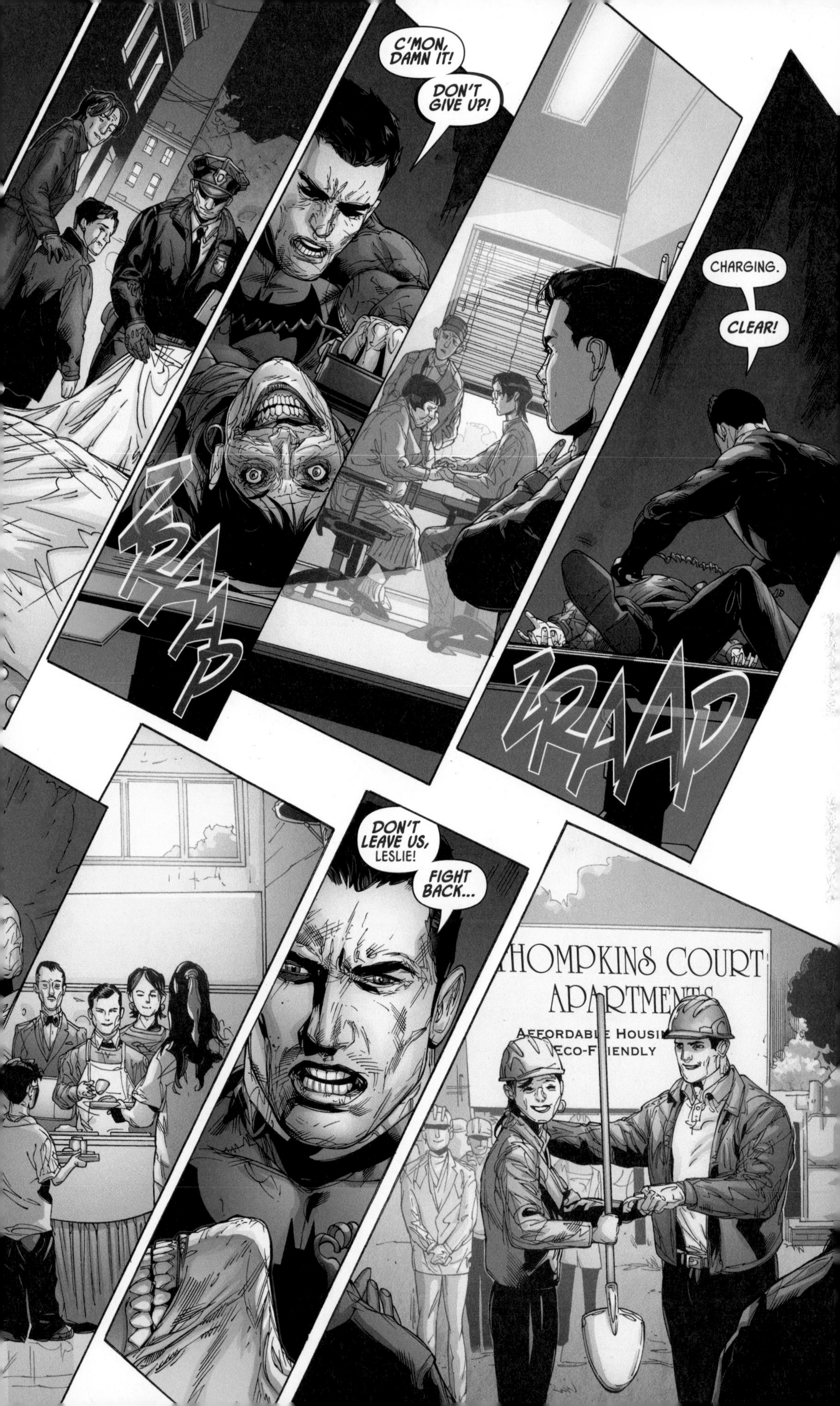
C'MON, DAMN IT!
DON'T GIVE UP!
ZRAAP
CHARGING.
CLEAR!
ZRAAP
DON'T LEAVE US, LESLIE!
FIGHT BACK...
THOMPKINS COURT APARTMENTS
AFFORDABLE HOUSING
ECO-FRIENDLY

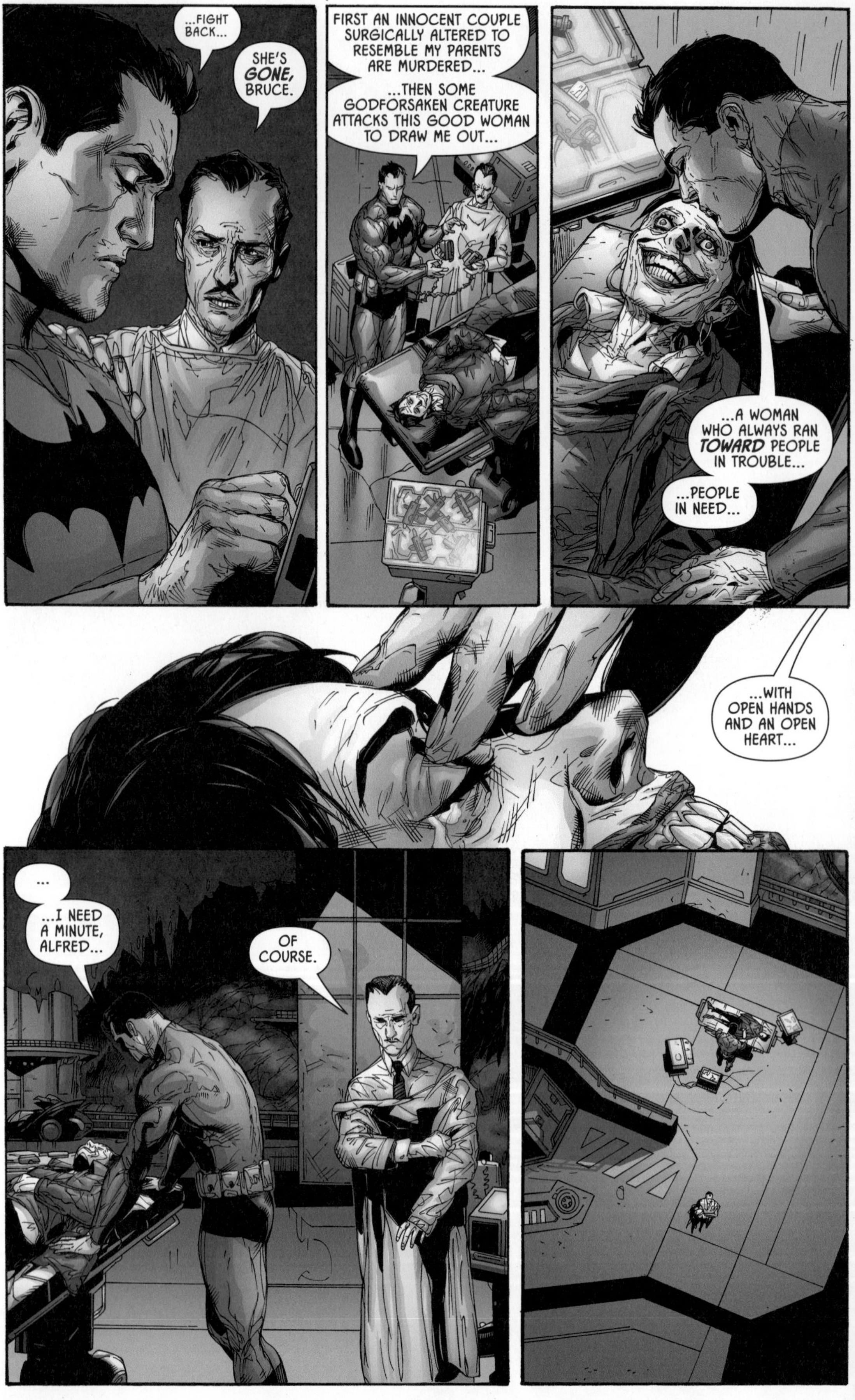

...FIGHT BACK...
SHE'S *GONE,* BRUCE.
FIRST AN INNOCENT COUPLE SURGICALLY ALTERED TO RESEMBLE MY PARENTS ARE MURDERED...
...THEN SOME GODFORSAKEN CREATURE ATTACKS THIS GOOD WOMAN TO DRAW ME OUT...
...A WOMAN WHO ALWAYS RAN *TOWARD* PEOPLE IN TROUBLE...
...PEOPLE IN NEED...
...WITH OPEN HANDS AND AN OPEN HEART...
...
...I NEED A MINUTE, ALFRED...
OF COURSE.

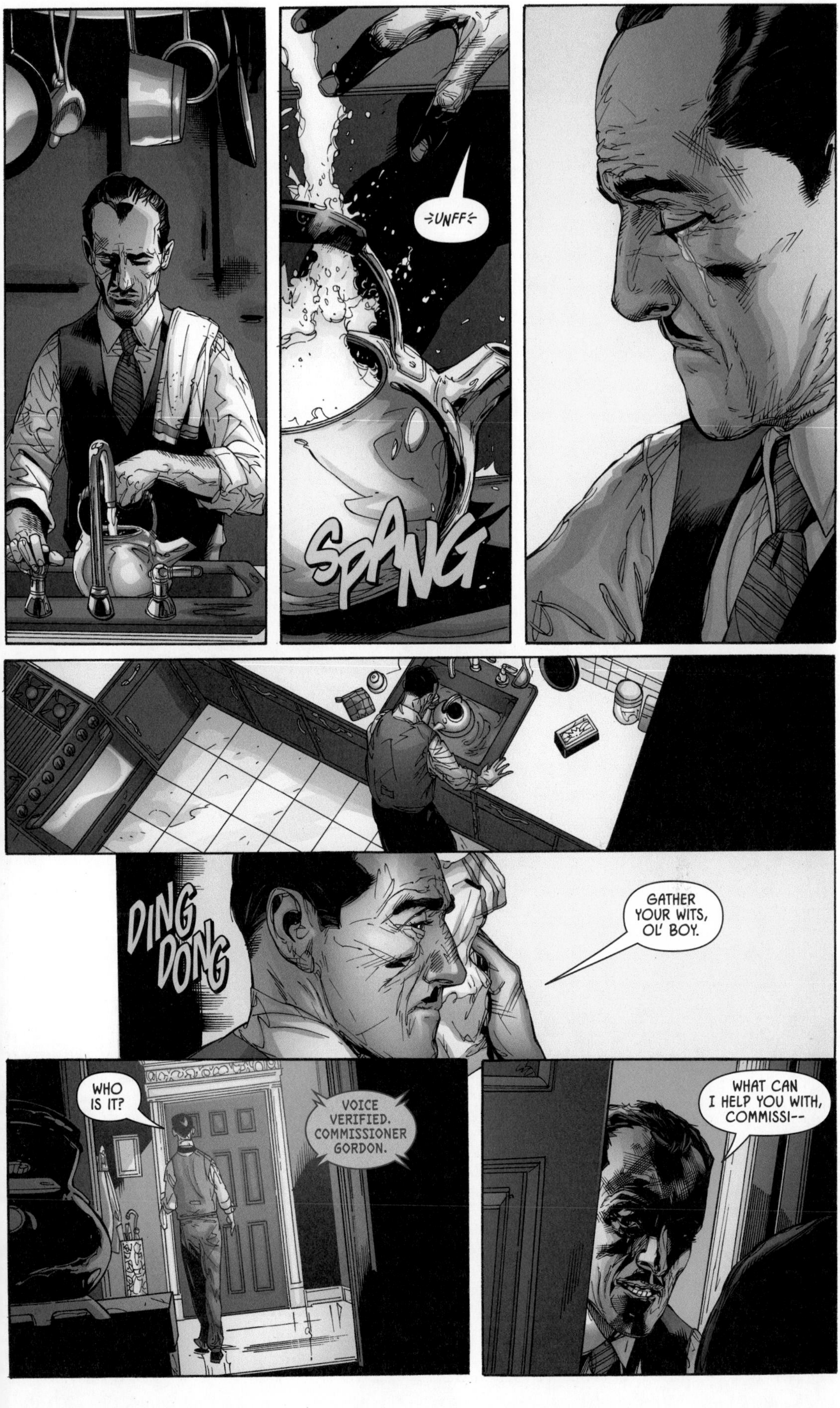

UNFF
SPANG
DING DONG
GATHER YOUR WITS, OL' BOY.
WHO IS IT?
VOICE VERIFIED. COMMISSIONER GORDON.
WHAT CAN I HELP YOU WITH, COMMISSI--

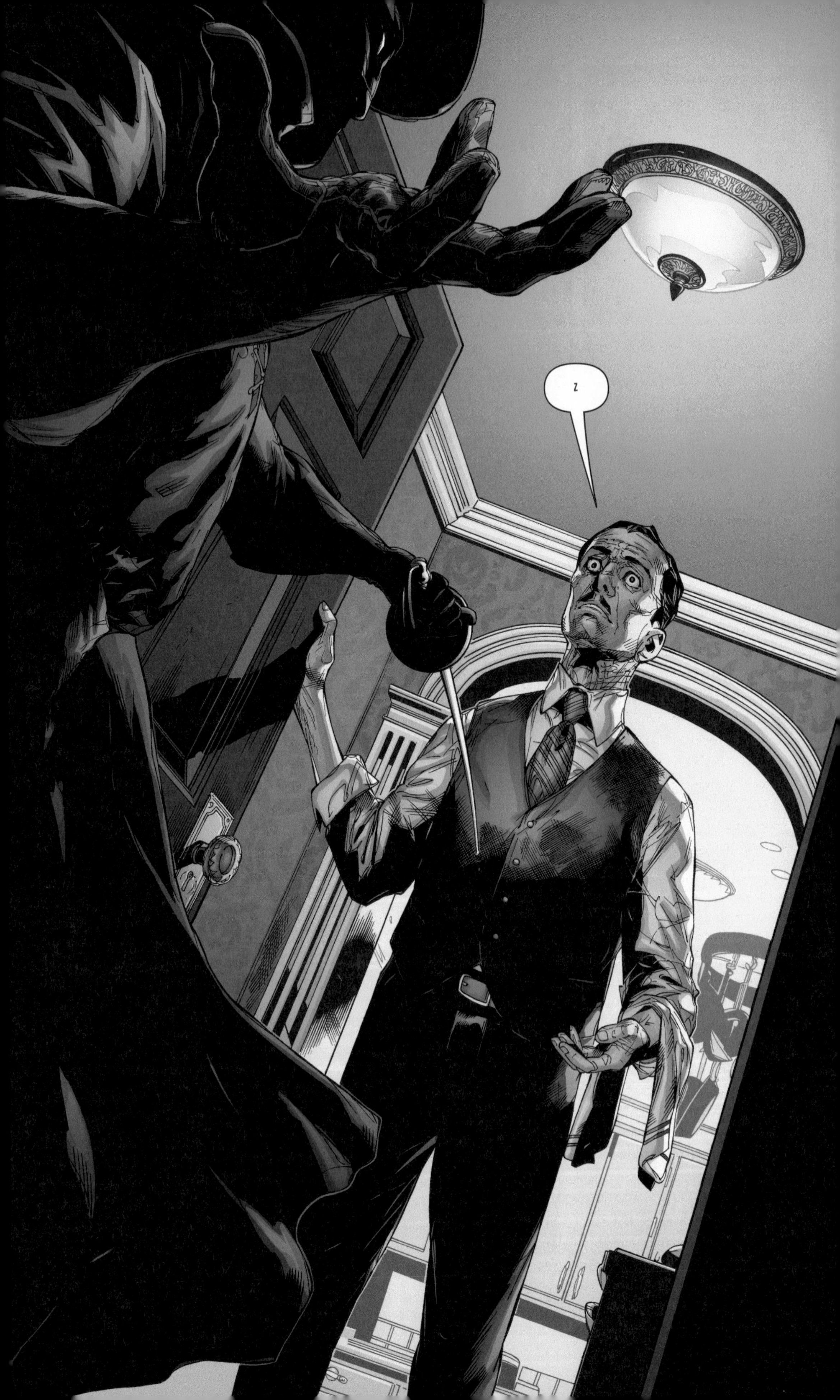
Z

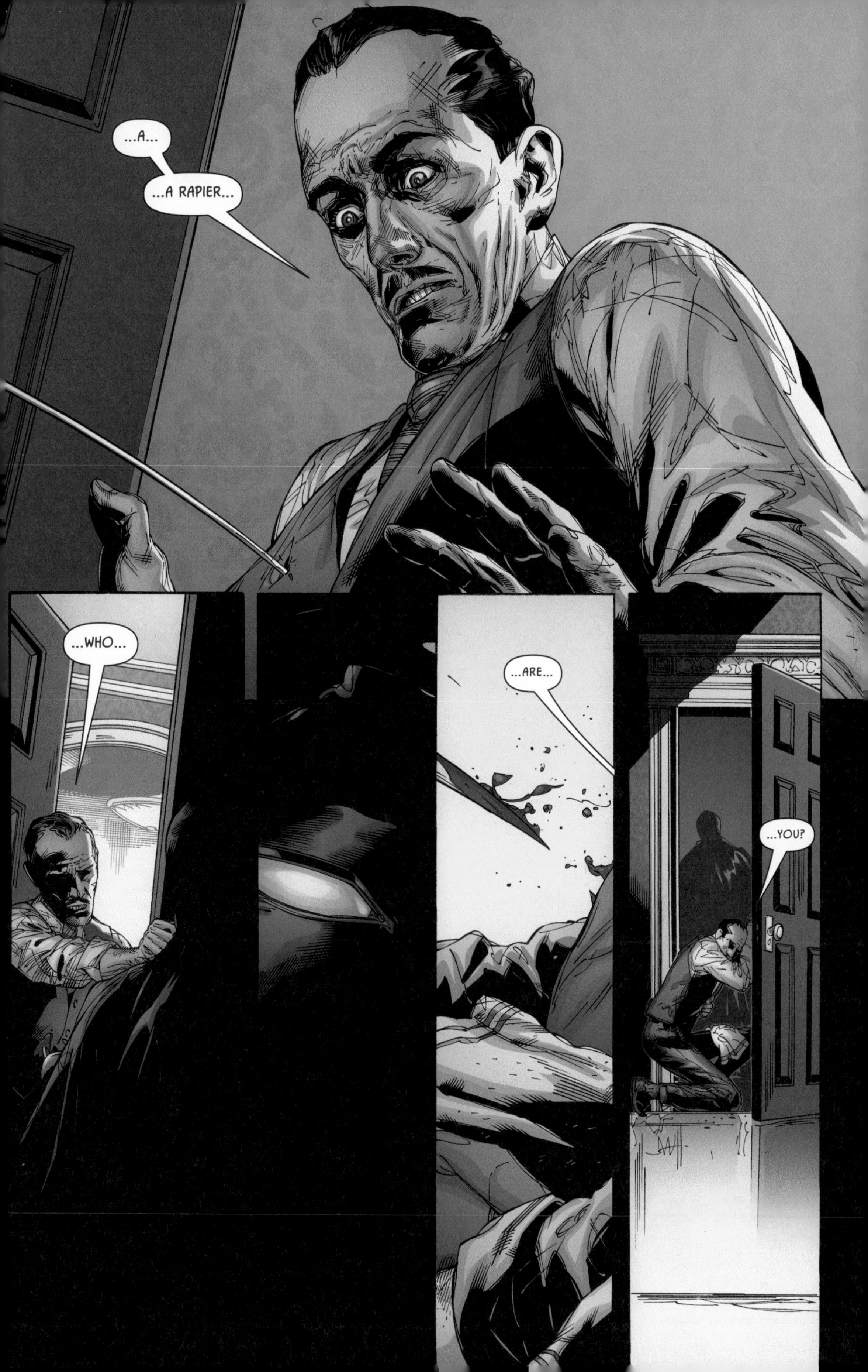
...A...
...A RAPIER...
...WHO...
...ARE...
...YOU?

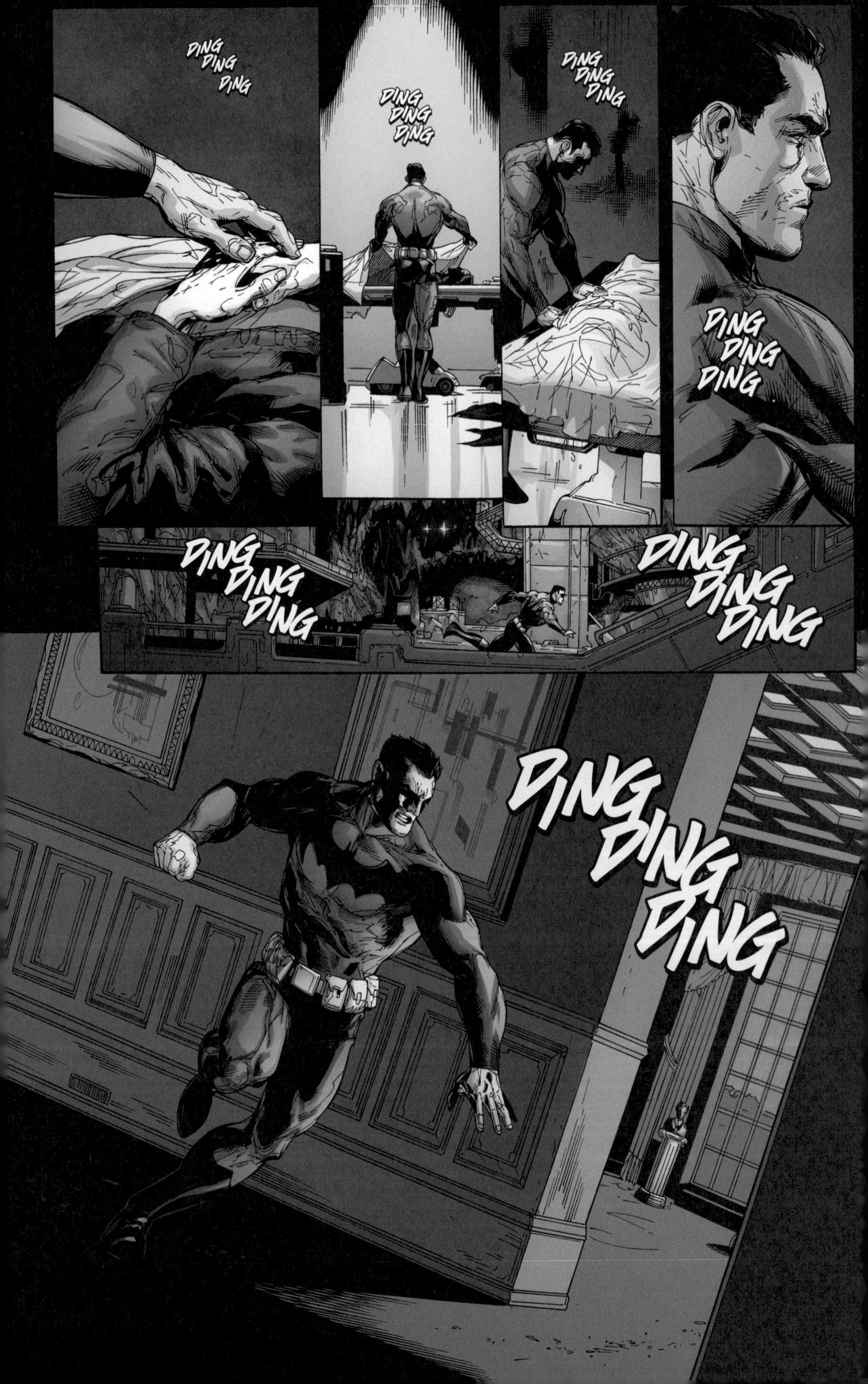
DING DING DING
DING DING DING
DING DING DING
DING DING DING
DING DING DING
DING DING DING
DING DING DING

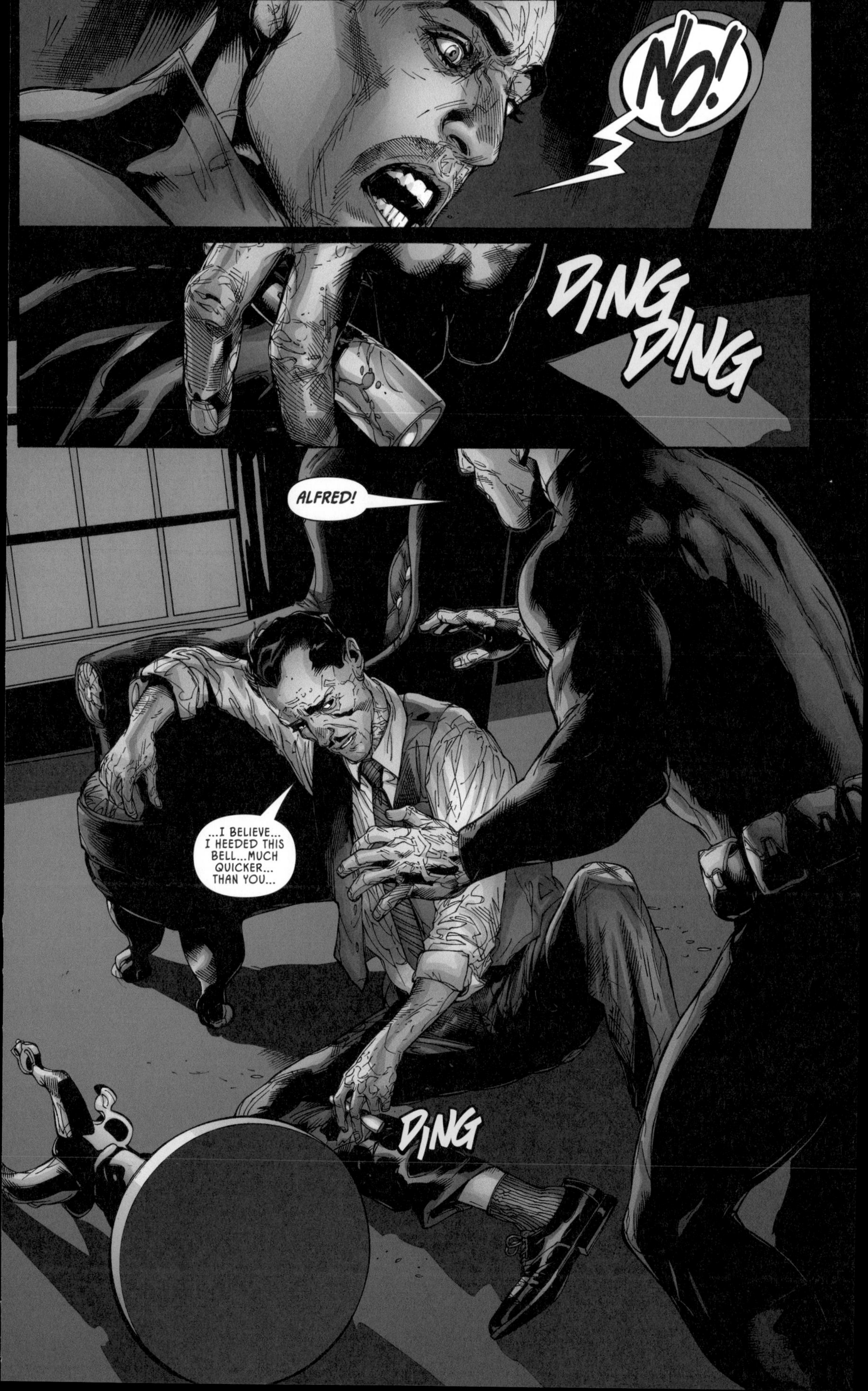
NO!
DING DING
ALFRED!
...I BELIEVE... I HEEDED THIS BELL...MUCH QUICKER... THAN YOU...
DING

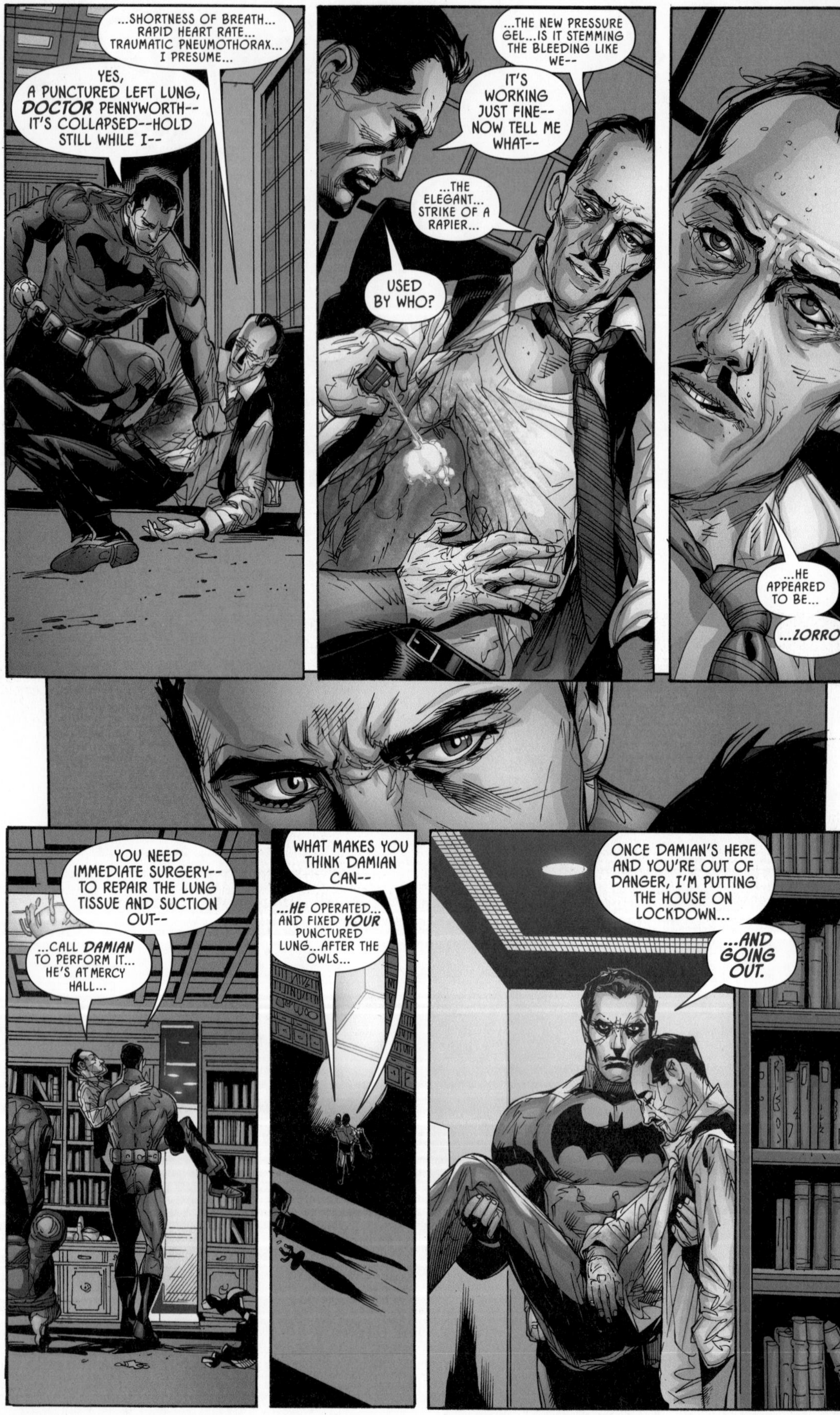

...SHORTNESS OF BREATH... RAPID HEART RATE... TRAUMATIC PNEUMOTHORAX... I PRESUME...
YES, A PUNCTURED LEFT LUNG, DOCTOR PENNYWORTH-- IT'S COLLAPSED--HOLD STILL WHILE I--
...THE NEW PRESSURE GEL...IS IT STEMMING THE BLEEDING LIKE WE--
IT'S WORKING JUST FINE-- NOW TELL ME WHAT--
...THE ELEGANT... STRIKE OF A RAPIER...
USED BY WHO?
...HE APPEARED TO BE...
...ZORRO.
YOU NEED IMMEDIATE SURGERY-- TO REPAIR THE LUNG TISSUE AND SUCTION OUT--
...CALL DAMIAN TO PERFORM IT... HE'S AT MERCY HALL...
WHAT MAKES YOU THINK DAMIAN CAN--
...HE OPERATED... AND FIXED YOUR PUNCTURED LUNG...AFTER THE OWLS...
ONCE DAMIAN'S HERE AND YOU'RE OUT OF DANGER, I'M PUTTING THE HOUSE ON LOCKDOWN...
...AND GOING OUT.

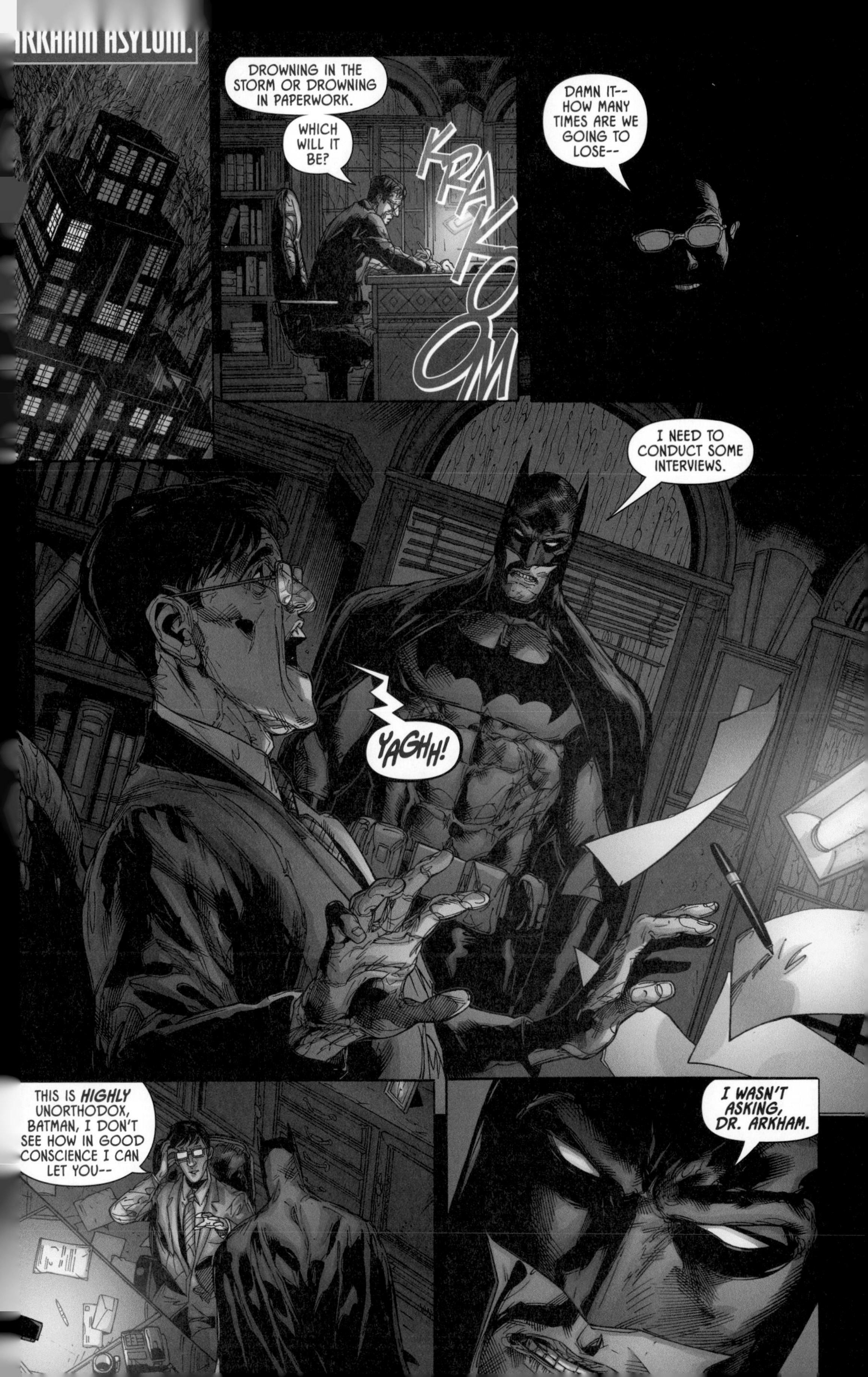
RKHAM ASYLUM.
DROWNING IN THE STORM OR DROWNING IN PAPERWORK.
WHICH WILL IT BE?
KRAKOOOM
DAMN IT-- HOW MANY TIMES ARE WE GOING TO LOSE--
I NEED TO CONDUCT SOME INTERVIEWS.
YAGHH!
THIS IS HIGHLY UNORTHODOX, BATMAN, I DON'T SEE HOW IN GOOD CONSCIENCE I CAN LET YOU--
I WASN'T ASKING, DR. ARKHAM.

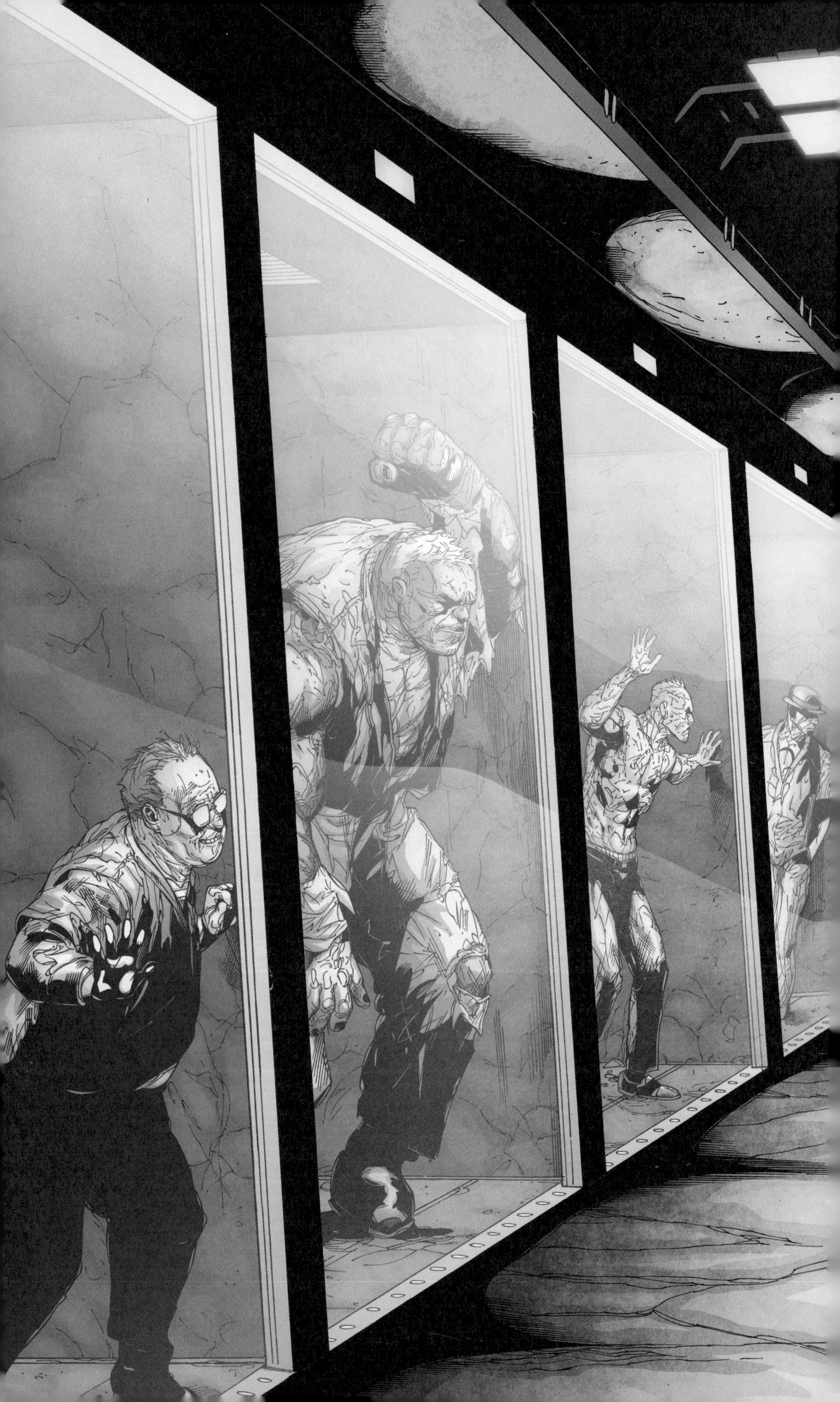

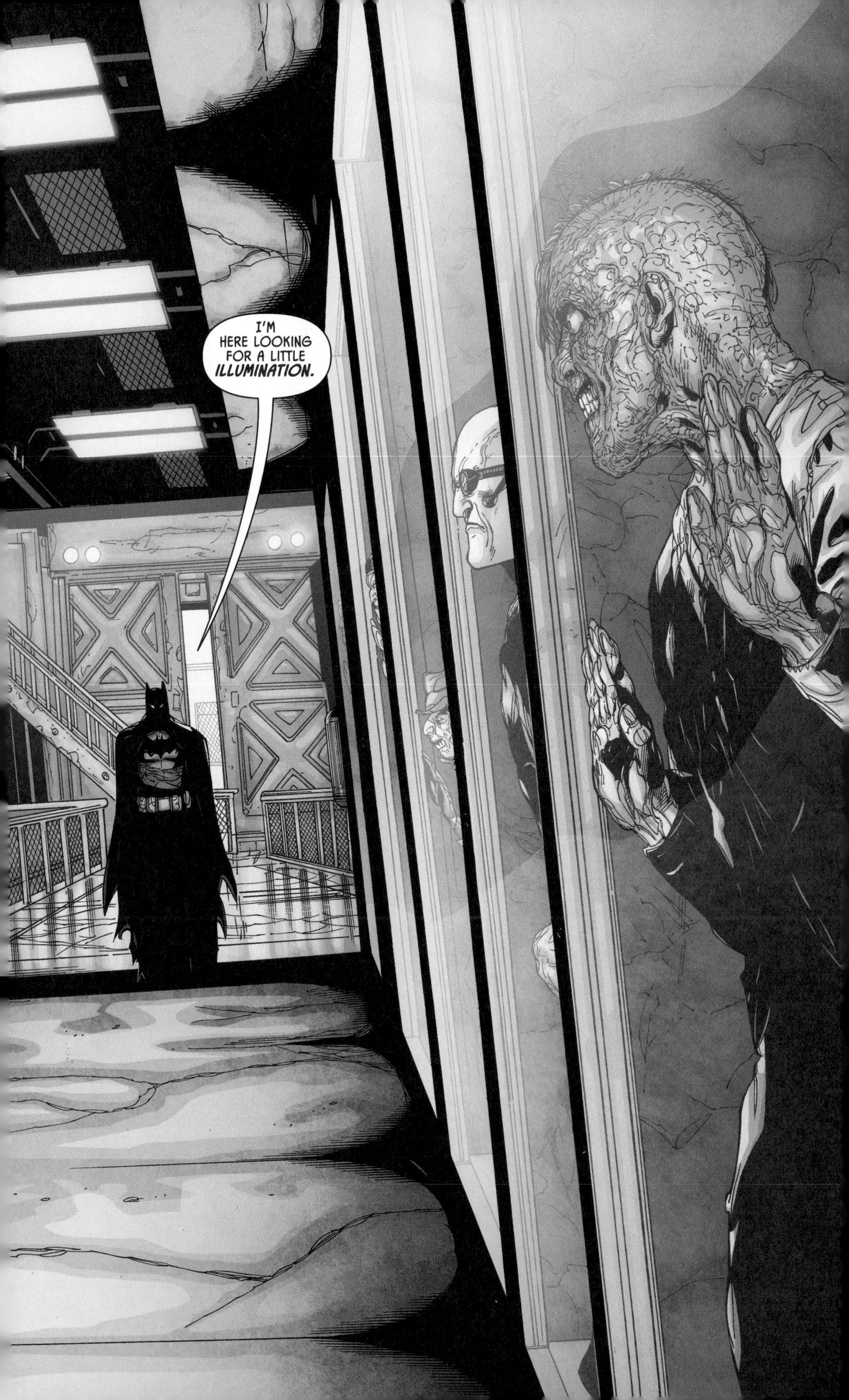
I'M HERE LOOKING FOR A LITTLE ILLUMINATION.

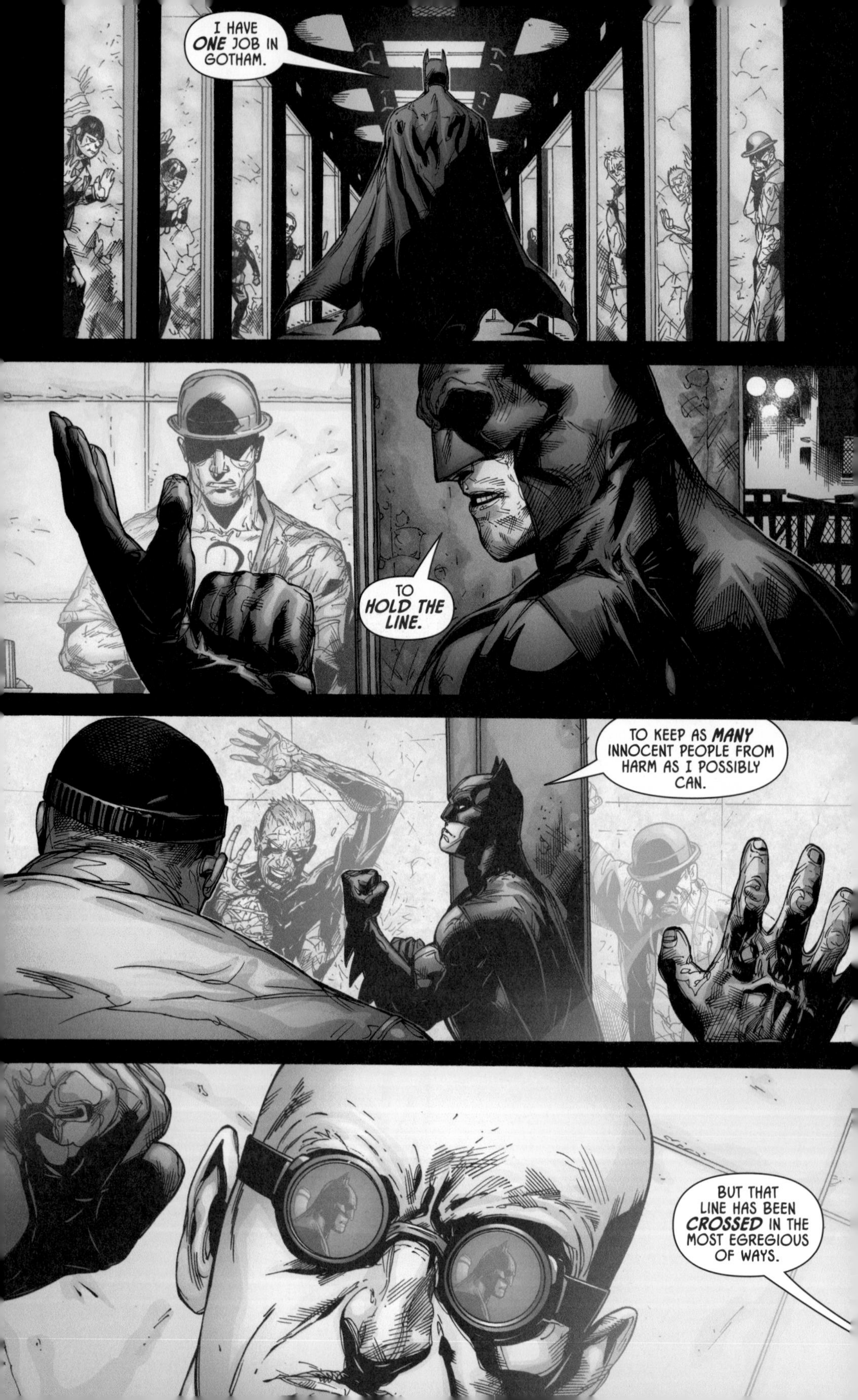
I HAVE ONE JOB IN GOTHAM.
TO HOLD THE LINE.
TO KEEP AS MANY INNOCENT PEOPLE FROM HARM AS I POSSIBLY CAN.
BUT THAT LINE HAS BEEN CROSSED IN THE MOST EGREGIOUS OF WAYS.

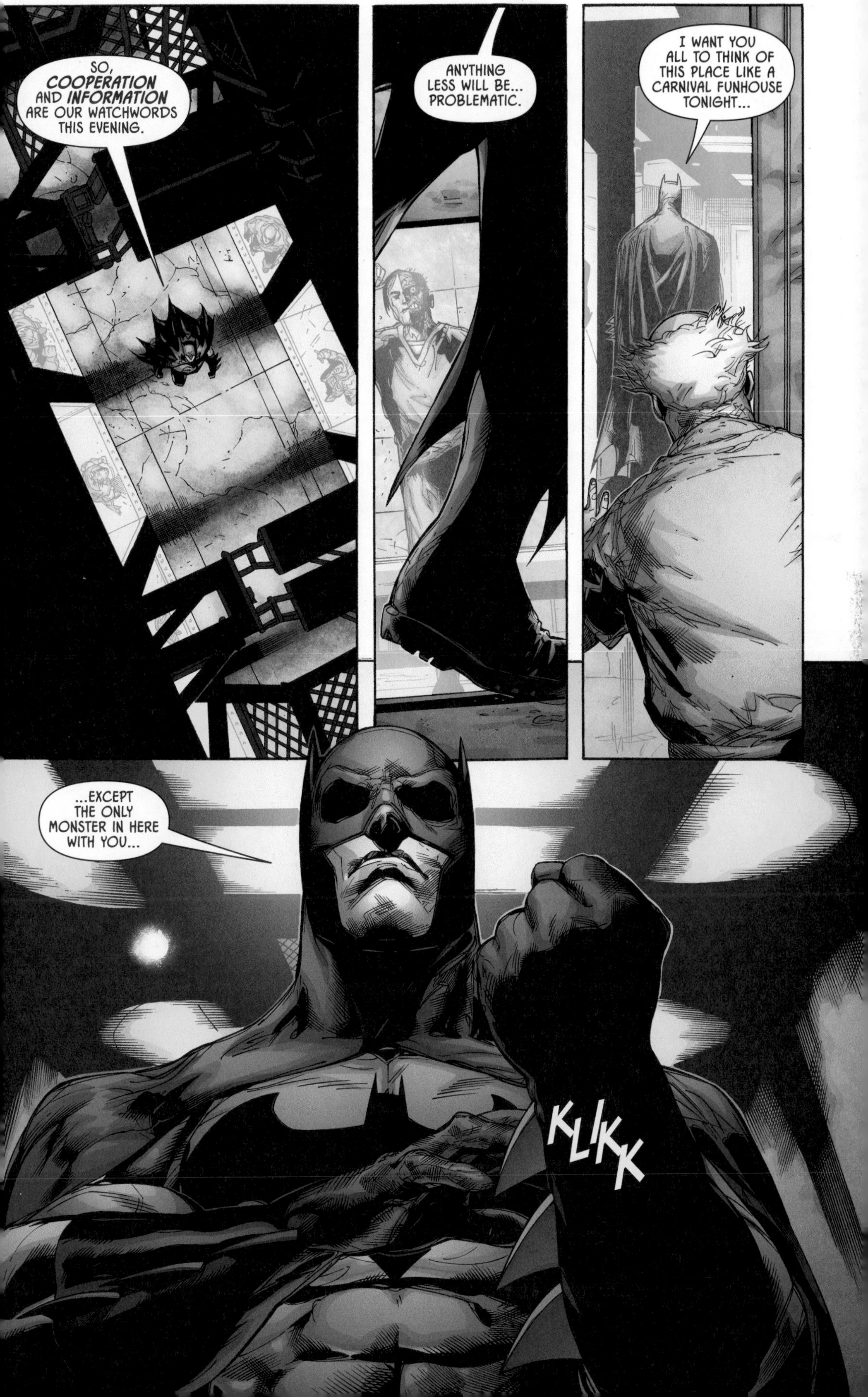
SO, COOPERATION AND INFORMATION ARE OUR WATCHWORDS THIS EVENING.
ANYTHING LESS WILL BE... PROBLEMATIC.
I WANT YOU ALL TO THINK OF THIS PLACE LIKE A CARNIVAL FUNHOUSE TONIGHT...
...EXCEPT THE ONLY MONSTER IN HERE WITH YOU...
KLIKK

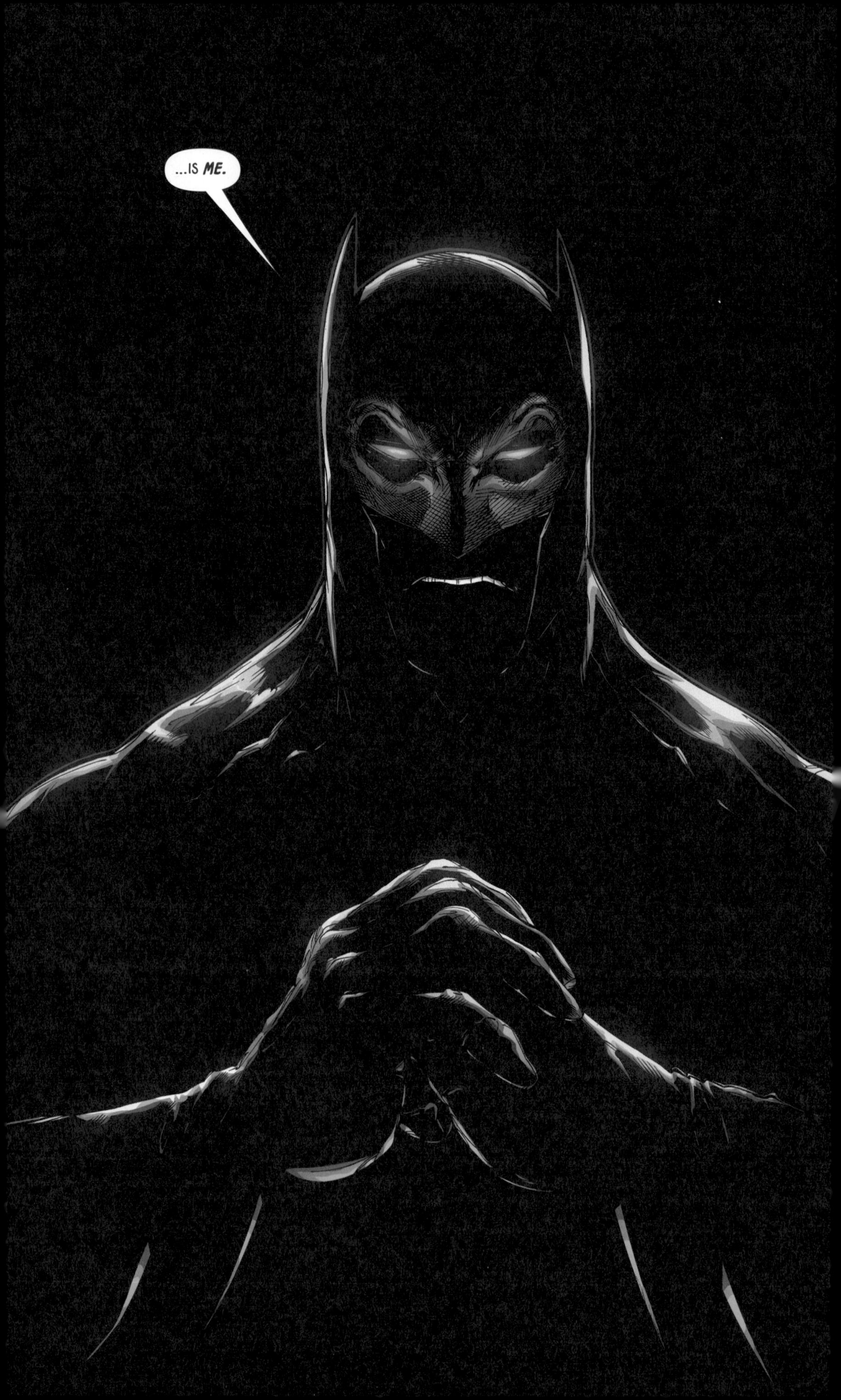
...IS ME.

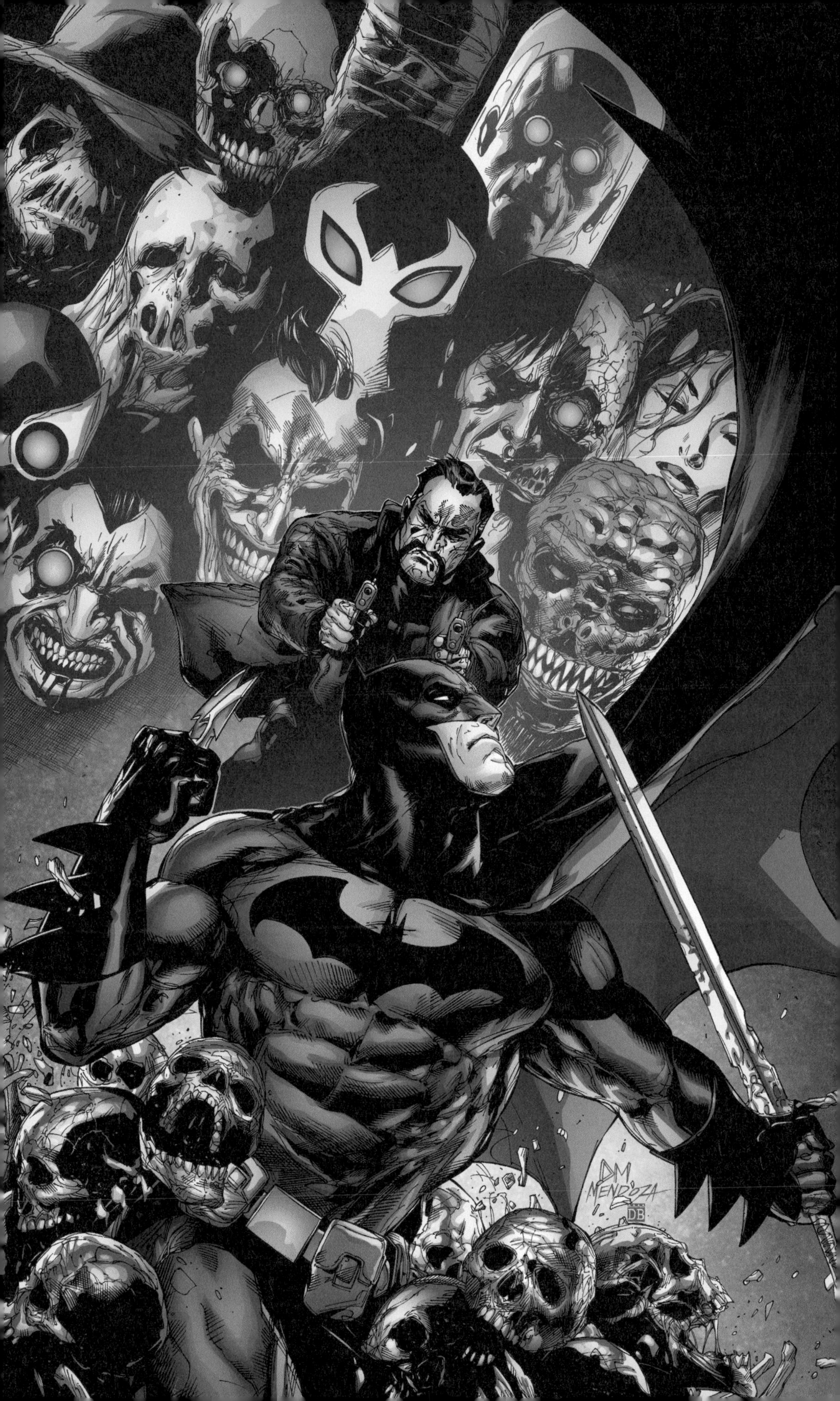
DM
MENDOZA
DB

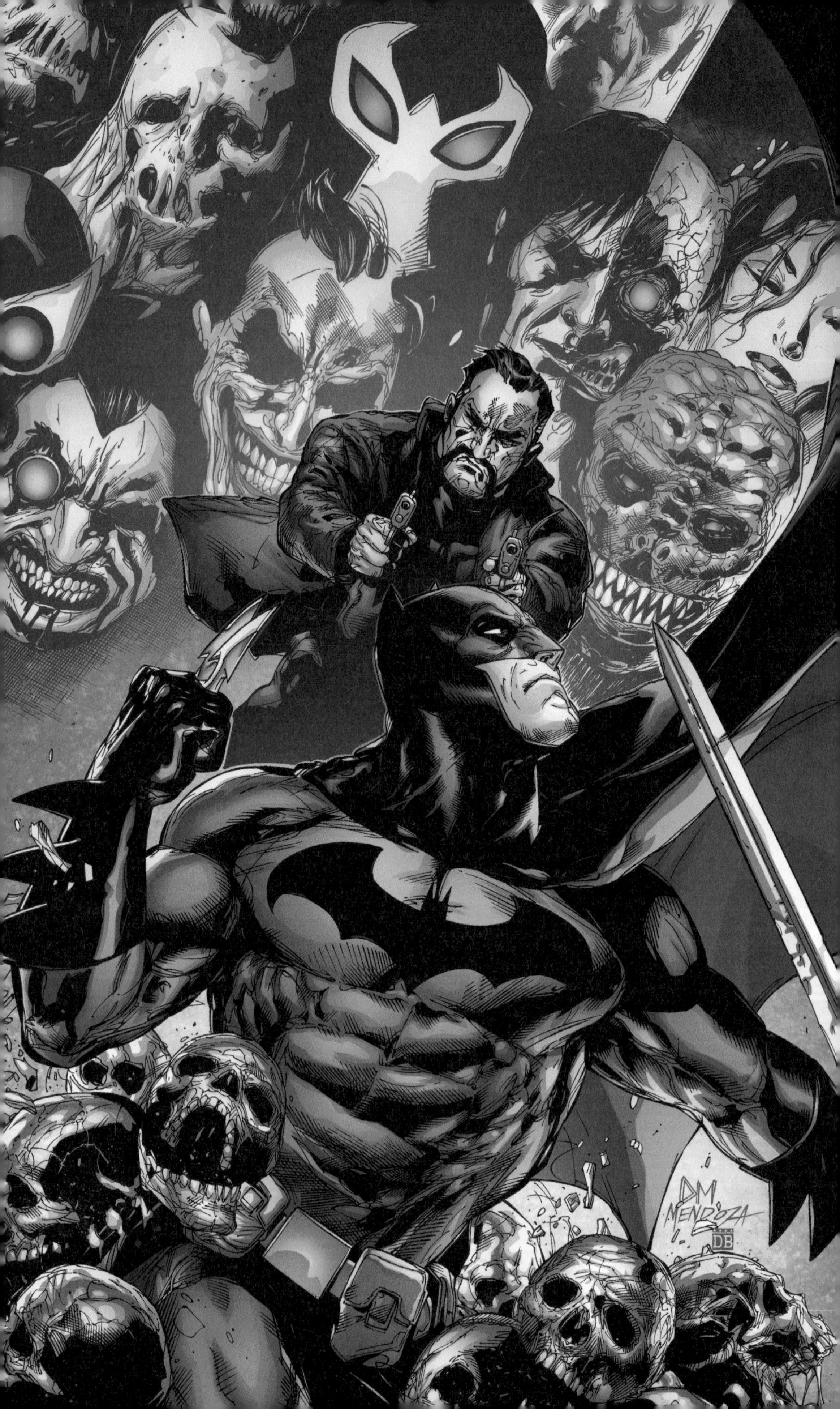
DM
MENDOZA
DB

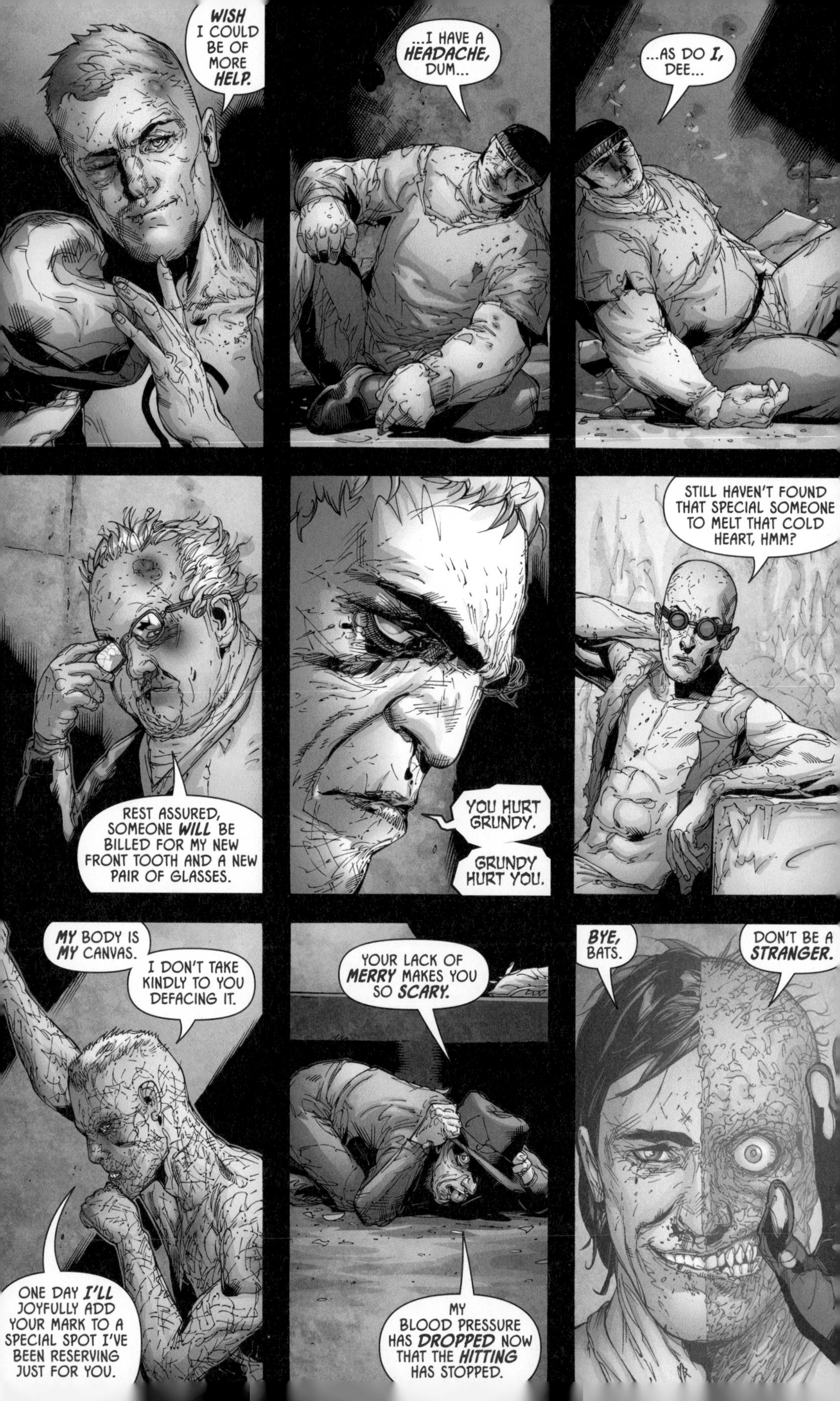

WISH I COULD BE OF MORE HELP.
...I HAVE A HEADACHE, DUM...
...AS DO I, DEE...
REST ASSURED, SOMEONE WILL BE BILLED FOR MY NEW FRONT TOOTH AND A NEW PAIR OF GLASSES.
YOU HURT GRUNDY.
GRUNDY HURT YOU.
STILL HAVEN'T FOUND THAT SPECIAL SOMEONE TO MELT THAT COLD HEART, HMM?
MY BODY IS MY CANVAS.
I DON'T TAKE KINDLY TO YOU DEFACING IT.
ONE DAY I'LL JOYFULLY ADD YOUR MARK TO A SPECIAL SPOT I'VE BEEN RESERVING JUST FOR YOU.
YOUR LACK OF MERRY MAKES YOU SO SCARY.
MY BLOOD PRESSURE HAS DROPPED NOW THAT THE HITTING HAS STOPPED.
BYE, BATS.
DON'T BE A STRANGER.

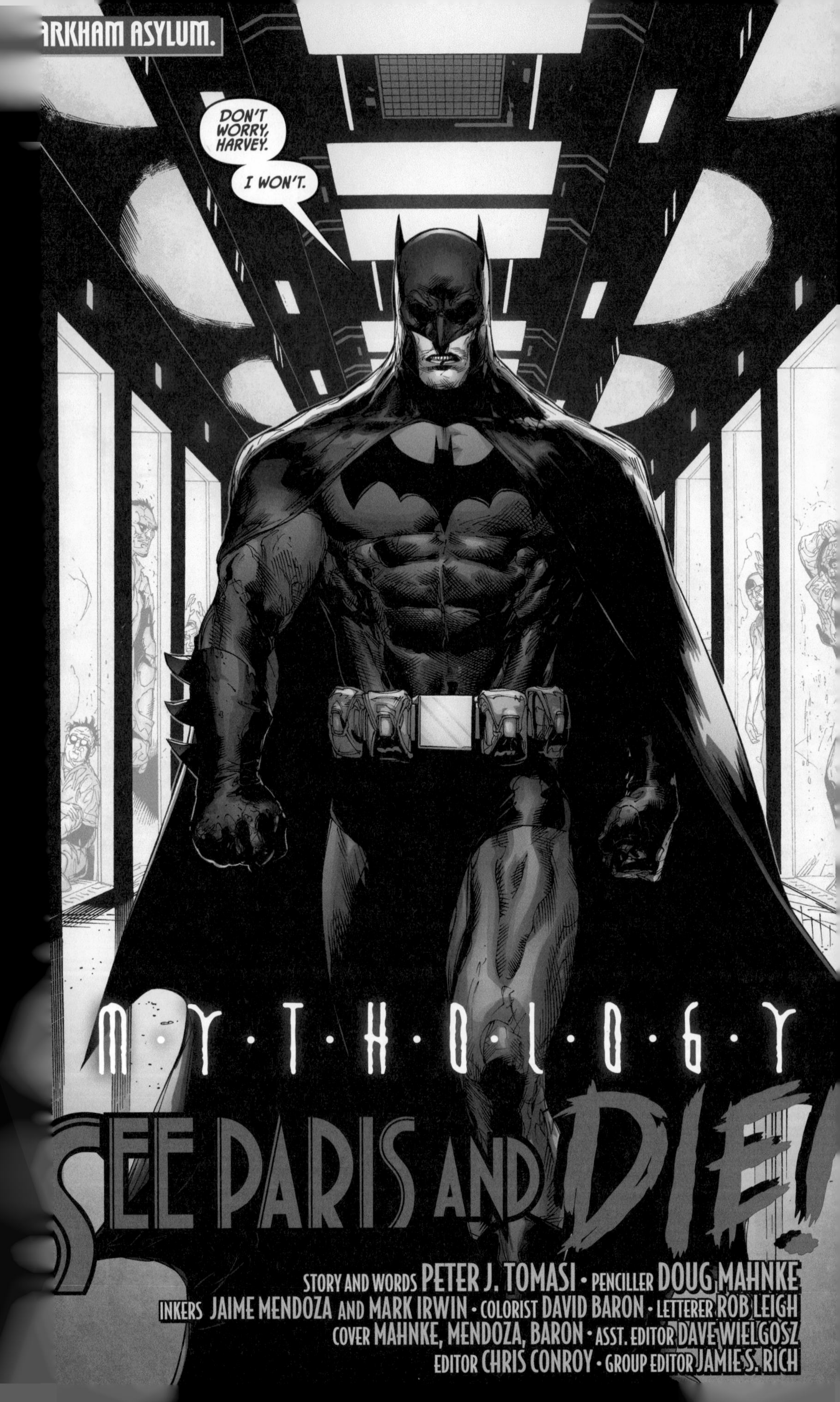
ARKHAM ASYLUM.
DON'T WORRY, HARVEY.
I WON'T.
M·Y·T·H·O·L·O·G·Y
SEE PARIS AND DIE!
STORY AND WORDS PETER J. TOMASI · PENCILLER DOUG MAHNKE
INKERS JAIME MENDOZA AND MARK IRWIN · COLORIST DAVID BARON · LETTERER ROB LEIGH
COVER MAHNKE, MENDOZA, BARON · ASST. EDITOR DAVE WIELGOSZ
EDITOR CHRIS CONROY · GROUP EDITOR JAMIE S. RICH

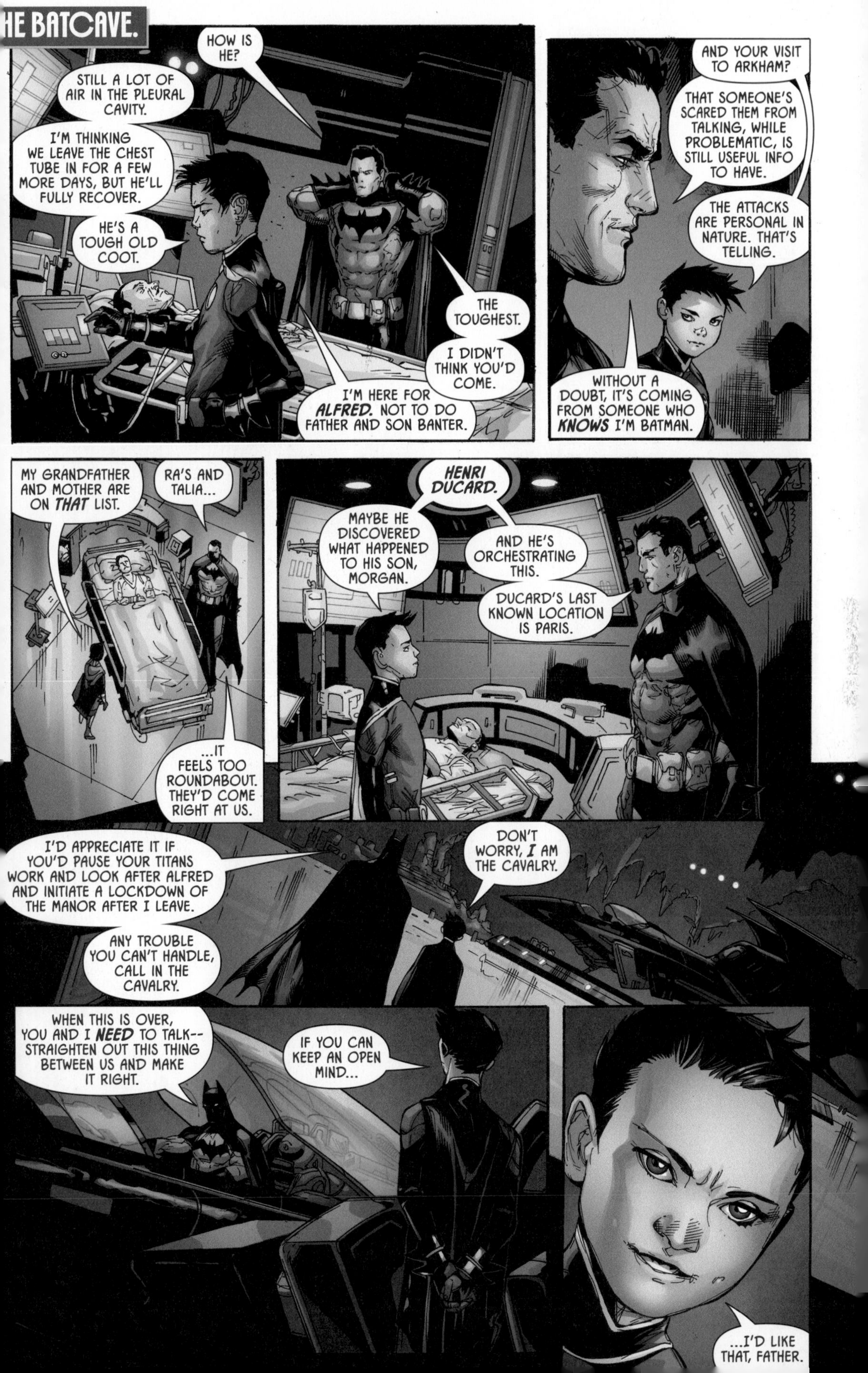
HE BATCAVE.
HOW IS HE?
STILL A LOT OF AIR IN THE PLEURAL CAVITY.
I'M THINKING WE LEAVE THE CHEST TUBE IN FOR A FEW MORE DAYS, BUT HE'LL FULLY RECOVER.
HE'S A TOUGH OLD COOT.
THE TOUGHEST.
I DIDN'T THINK YOU'D COME.
I'M HERE FOR ALFRED. NOT TO DO FATHER AND SON BANTER.
AND YOUR VISIT TO ARKHAM?
THAT SOMEONE'S SCARED THEM FROM TALKING, WHILE PROBLEMATIC, IS STILL USEFUL INFO TO HAVE.
THE ATTACKS ARE PERSONAL IN NATURE. THAT'S TELLING.
WITHOUT A DOUBT, IT'S COMING FROM SOMEONE WHO KNOWS I'M BATMAN.
MY GRANDFATHER AND MOTHER ARE ON THAT LIST.
RA'S AND TALIA...
...IT FEELS TOO ROUNDABOUT. THEY'D COME RIGHT AT US.
HENRI DUCARD.
MAYBE HE DISCOVERED WHAT HAPPENED TO HIS SON, MORGAN.
AND HE'S ORCHESTRATING THIS.
DUCARD'S LAST KNOWN LOCATION IS PARIS.
I'D APPRECIATE IT IF YOU'D PAUSE YOUR TITANS WORK AND LOOK AFTER ALFRED AND INITIATE A LOCKDOWN OF THE MANOR AFTER I LEAVE.
ANY TROUBLE YOU CAN'T HANDLE, CALL IN THE CAVALRY.
DON'T WORRY, I AM THE CAVALRY.
WHEN THIS IS OVER, YOU AND I NEED TO TALK-- STRAIGHTEN OUT THIS THING BETWEEN US AND MAKE IT RIGHT.
IF YOU CAN KEEP AN OPEN MIND...
...I'D LIKE THAT, FATHER.

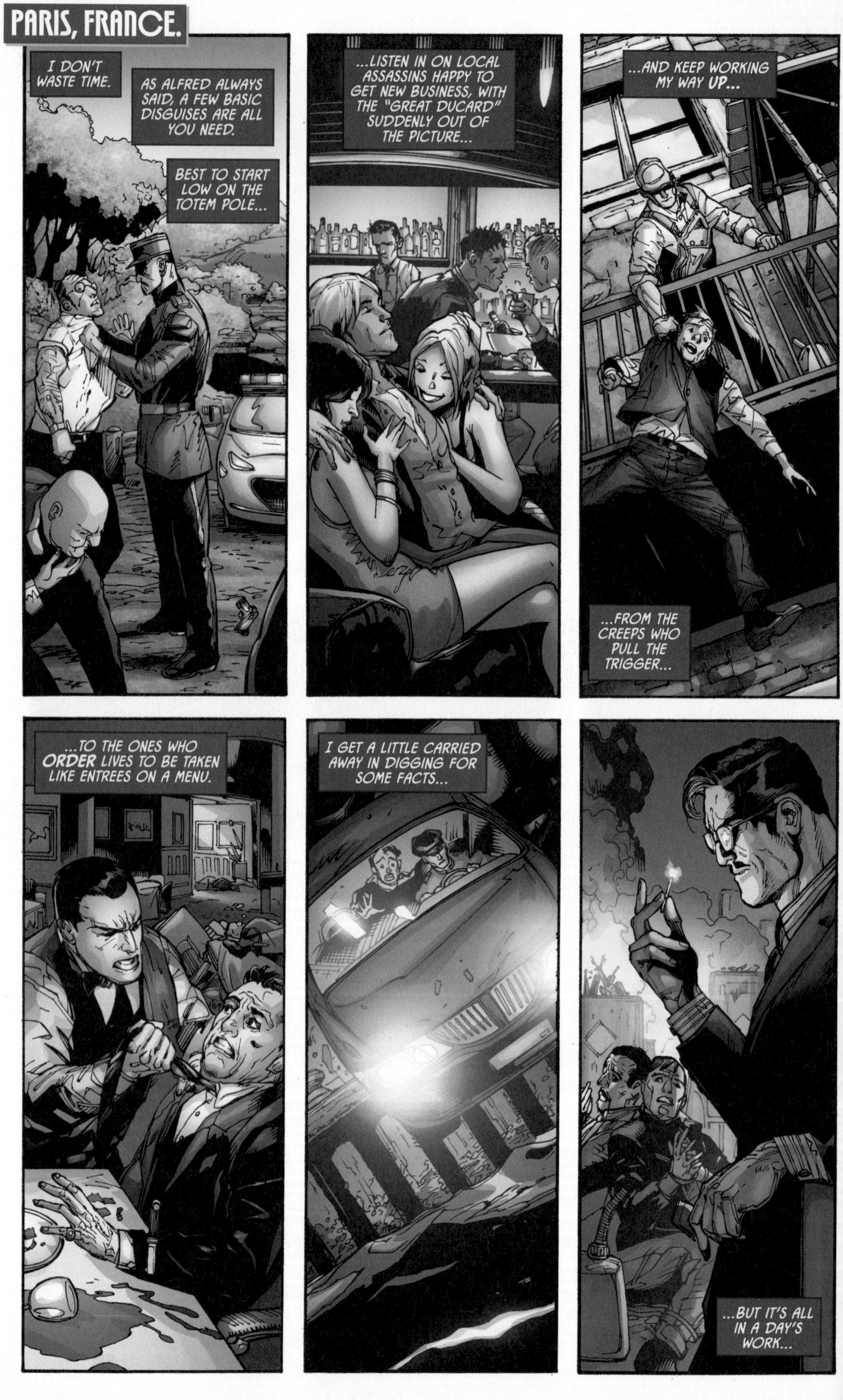

PARIS, FRANCE.
I DON'T WASTE TIME.
AS ALFRED ALWAYS SAID, A FEW BASIC DISGUISES ARE ALL YOU NEED.
BEST TO START LOW ON THE TOTEM POLE...
...LISTEN IN ON LOCAL ASSASSINS HAPPY TO GET NEW BUSINESS, WITH THE "GREAT DUCARD" SUDDENLY OUT OF THE PICTURE...
...AND KEEP WORKING MY WAY UP...
...FROM THE CREEPS WHO PULL THE TRIGGER...
...TO THE ONES WHO ORDER LIVES TO BE TAKEN LIKE ENTREES ON A MENU.
I GET A LITTLE CARRIED AWAY IN DIGGING FOR SOME FACTS...
...BUT IT'S ALL IN A DAY'S WORK...

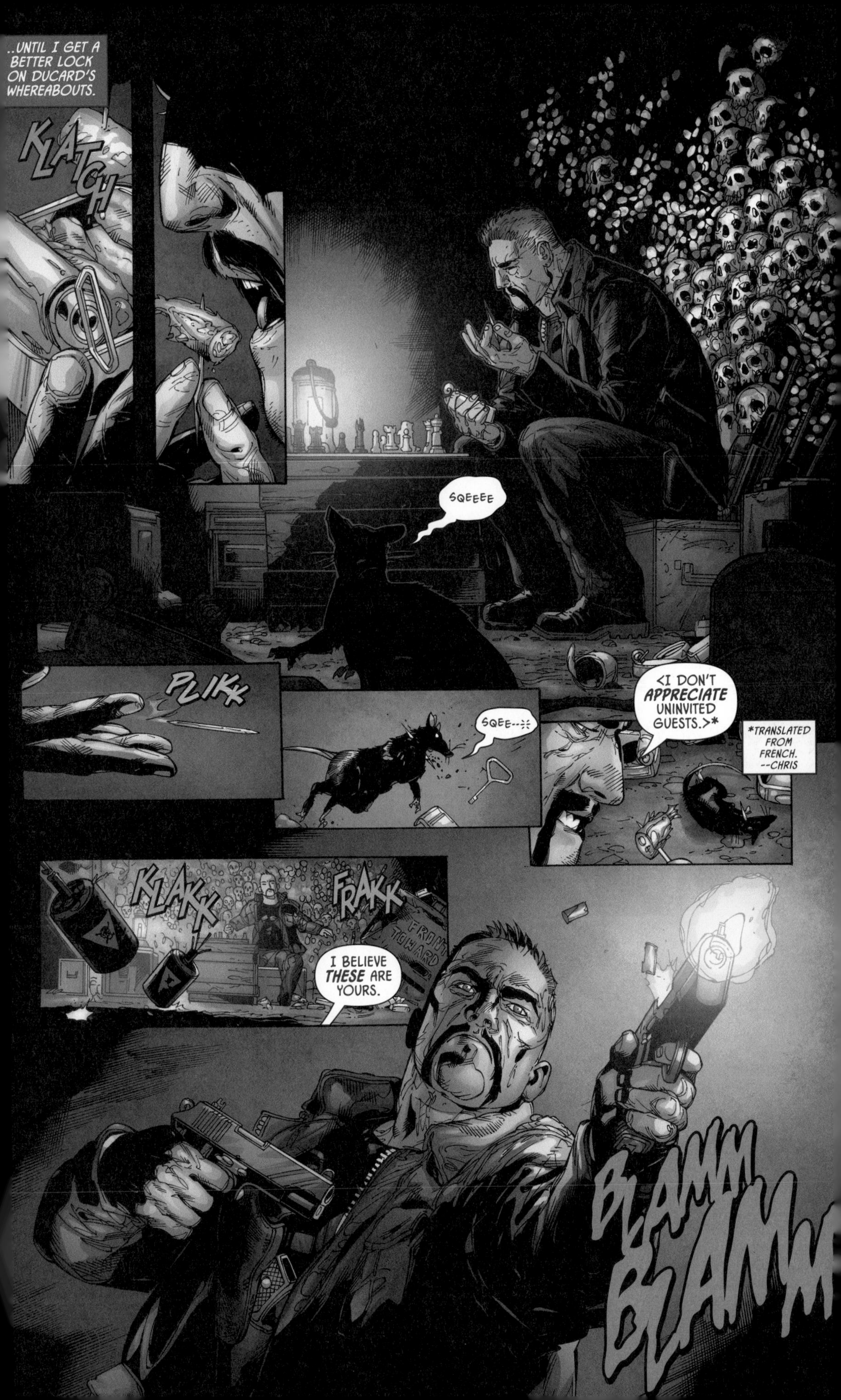
..UNTIL I GET A BETTER LOCK ON DUCARD'S WHEREABOUTS.
KLATCH
SQEEEE
PLIKK
SQEE--
<I DON'T **APPRECIATE** UNINVITED GUESTS.>*
*TRANSLATED FROM FRENCH. --CHRIS
KLAKK
FRAKK
I BELIEVE **THESE** ARE YOURS.
BLAMM
BLAMM

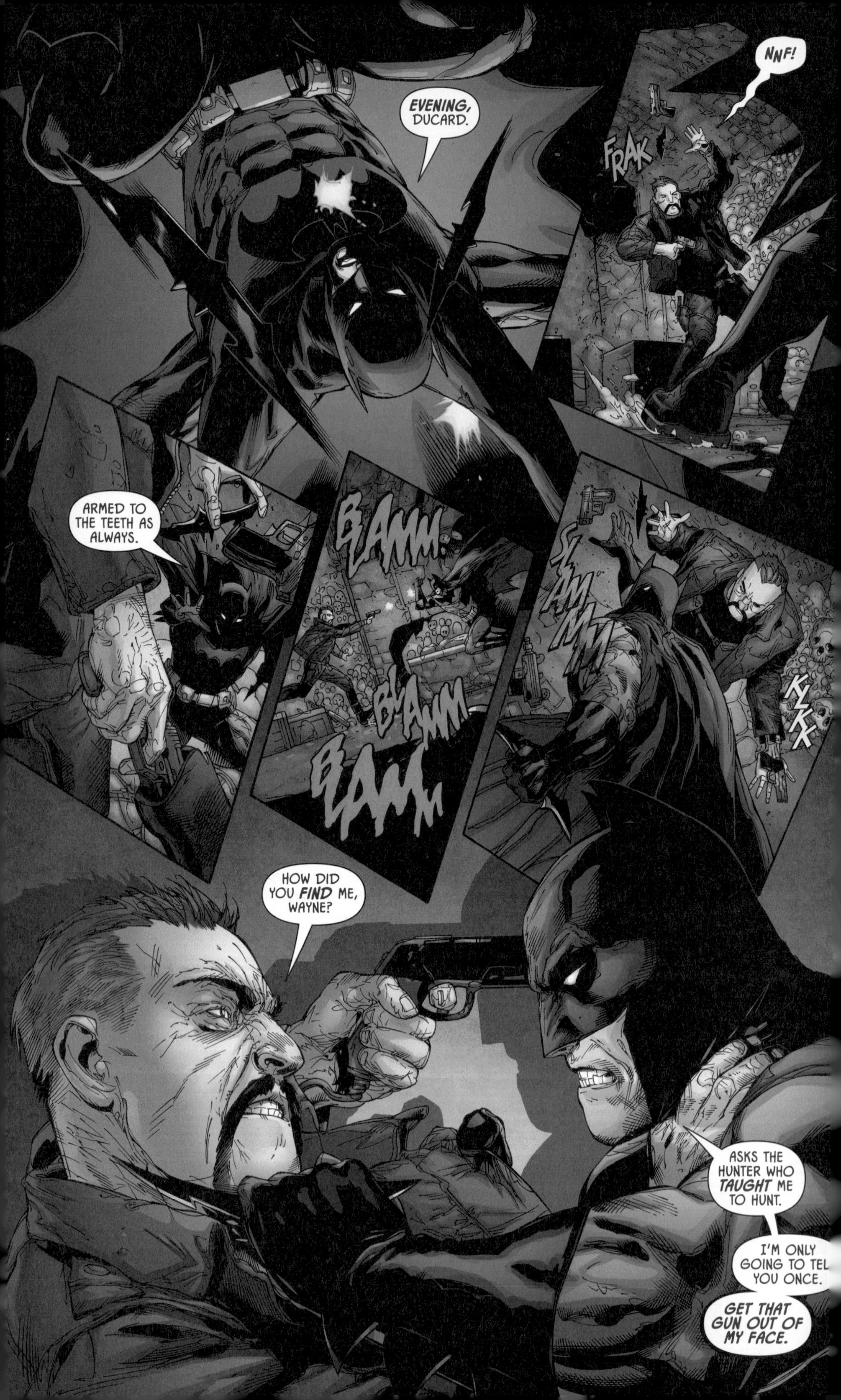
EVENING, DUCARD.
NNF!
FRAK
ARMED TO THE TEETH AS ALWAYS.
BLAMM
BLAMM
BLAM
KLAMM
KLKK
HOW DID YOU FIND ME, WAYNE?
ASKS THE HUNTER WHO TAUGHT ME TO HUNT.
I'M ONLY GOING TO TELL YOU ONCE.
GET THAT GUN OUT OF MY FACE.

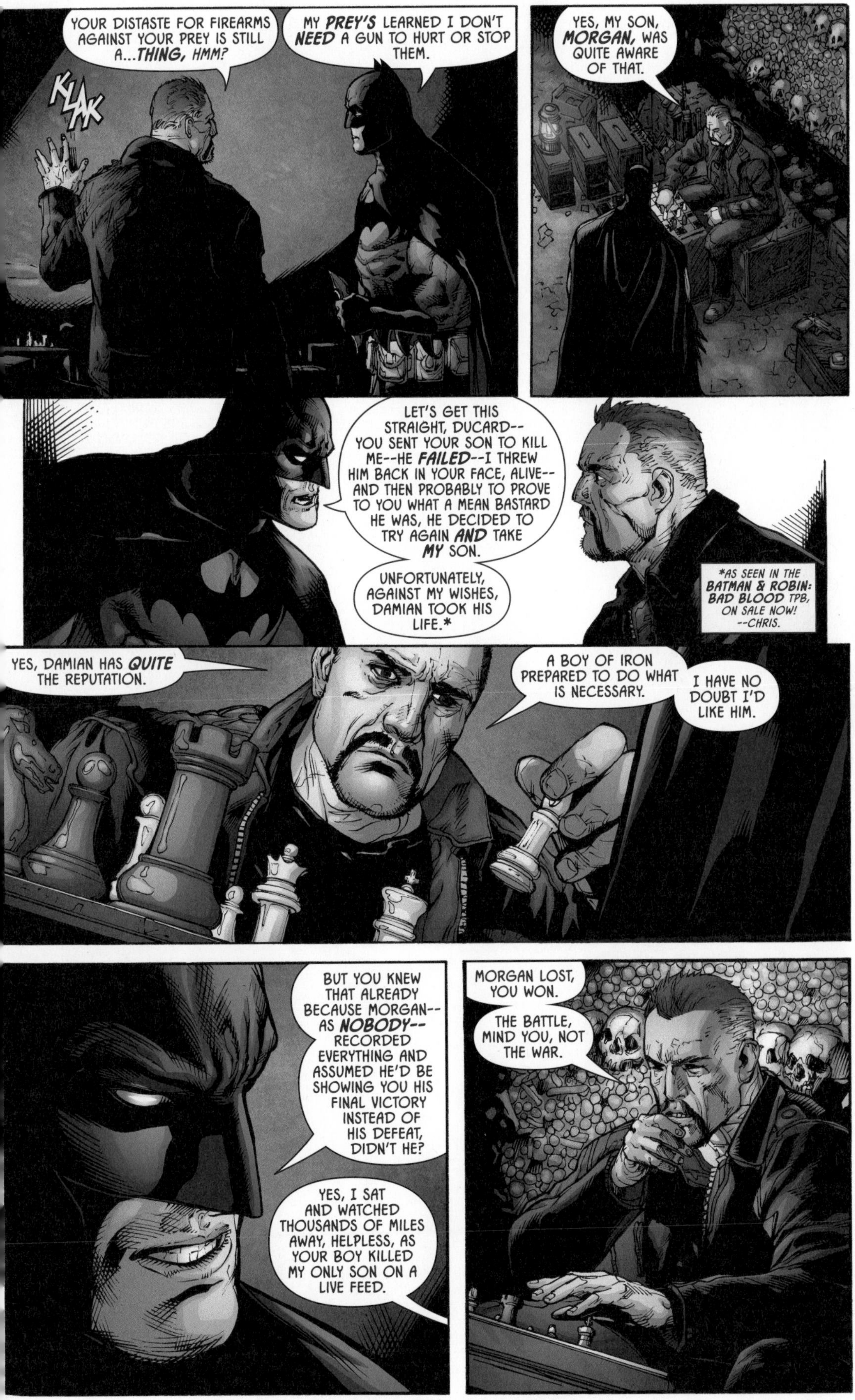
YOUR DISTASTE FOR FIREARMS AGAINST YOUR PREY IS STILL A...THING, HMM?
KLAK
MY PREY'S LEARNED I DON'T NEED A GUN TO HURT OR STOP THEM.
YES, MY SON, MORGAN, WAS QUITE AWARE OF THAT.
LET'S GET THIS STRAIGHT, DUCARD--YOU SENT YOUR SON TO KILL ME--HE FAILED--I THREW HIM BACK IN YOUR FACE, ALIVE--AND THEN PROBABLY TO PROVE TO YOU WHAT A MEAN BASTARD HE WAS, HE DECIDED TO TRY AGAIN AND TAKE MY SON.
UNFORTUNATELY, AGAINST MY WISHES, DAMIAN TOOK HIS LIFE.*
*AS SEEN IN THE BATMAN & ROBIN: BAD BLOOD TPB, ON SALE NOW! --CHRIS.
YES, DAMIAN HAS QUITE THE REPUTATION.
A BOY OF IRON PREPARED TO DO WHAT IS NECESSARY.
I HAVE NO DOUBT I'D LIKE HIM.
BUT YOU KNEW THAT ALREADY BECAUSE MORGAN--AS NOBODY--RECORDED EVERYTHING AND ASSUMED HE'D BE SHOWING YOU HIS FINAL VICTORY INSTEAD OF HIS DEFEAT, DIDN'T HE?
YES, I SAT AND WATCHED THOUSANDS OF MILES AWAY, HELPLESS, AS YOUR BOY KILLED MY ONLY SON ON A LIVE FEED.
MORGAN LOST, YOU WON.
THE BATTLE, MIND YOU, NOT THE WAR.

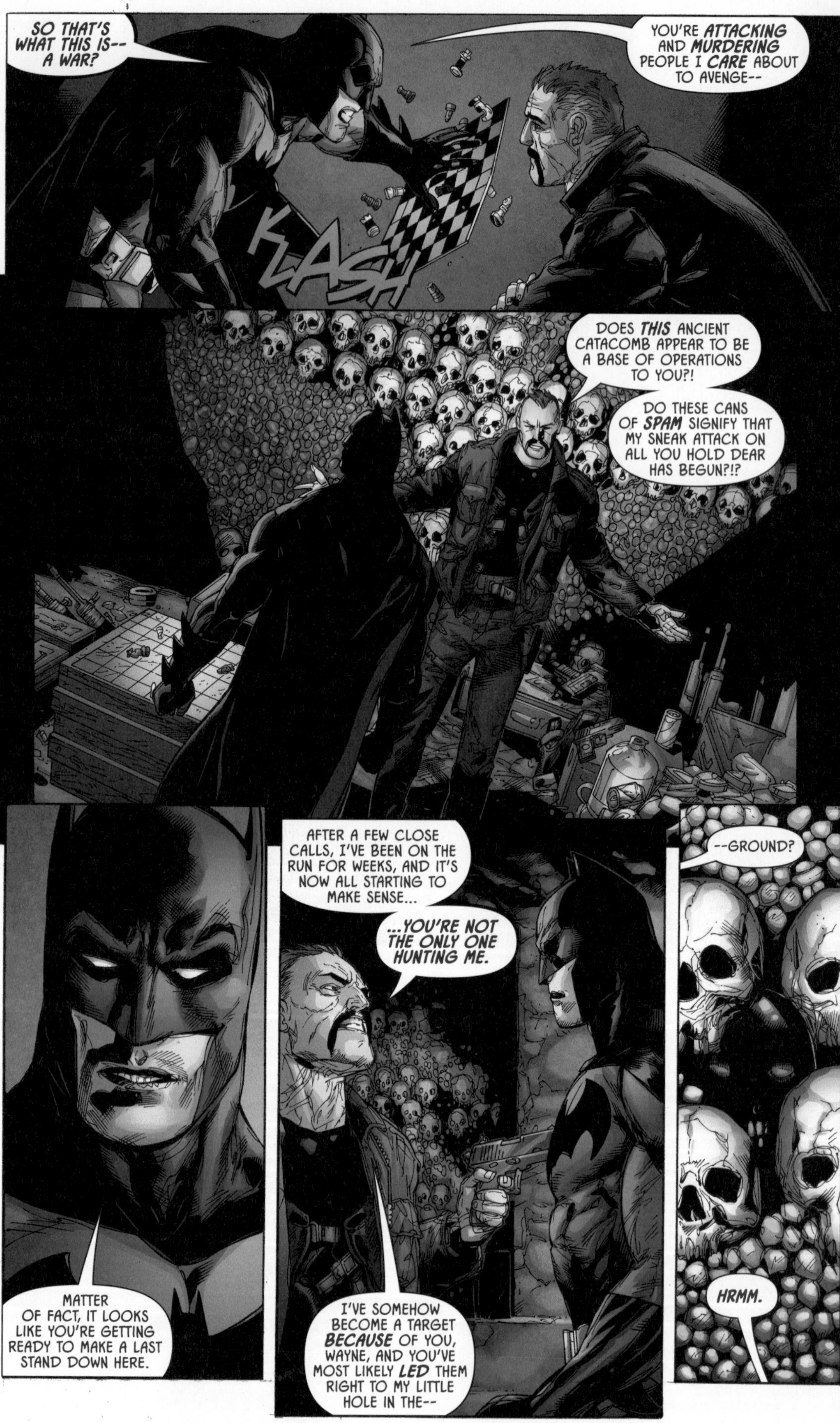
SO THAT'S WHAT THIS IS-- A WAR?
YOU'RE ATTACKING AND MURDERING PEOPLE I CARE ABOUT TO AVENGE--
KLASH
DOES THIS ANCIENT CATACOMB APPEAR TO BE A BASE OF OPERATIONS TO YOU?!
DO THESE CANS OF SPAM SIGNIFY THAT MY SNEAK ATTACK ON ALL YOU HOLD DEAR HAS BEGUN?!?
MATTER OF FACT, IT LOOKS LIKE YOU'RE GETTING READY TO MAKE A LAST STAND DOWN HERE.
AFTER A FEW CLOSE CALLS, I'VE BEEN ON THE RUN FOR WEEKS, AND IT'S NOW ALL STARTING TO MAKE SENSE...
...YOU'RE NOT THE ONLY ONE HUNTING ME.
I'VE SOMEHOW BECOME A TARGET BECAUSE OF YOU, WAYNE, AND YOU'VE MOST LIKELY LED THEM RIGHT TO MY LITTLE HOLE IN THE--
--GROUND?
HRMM.

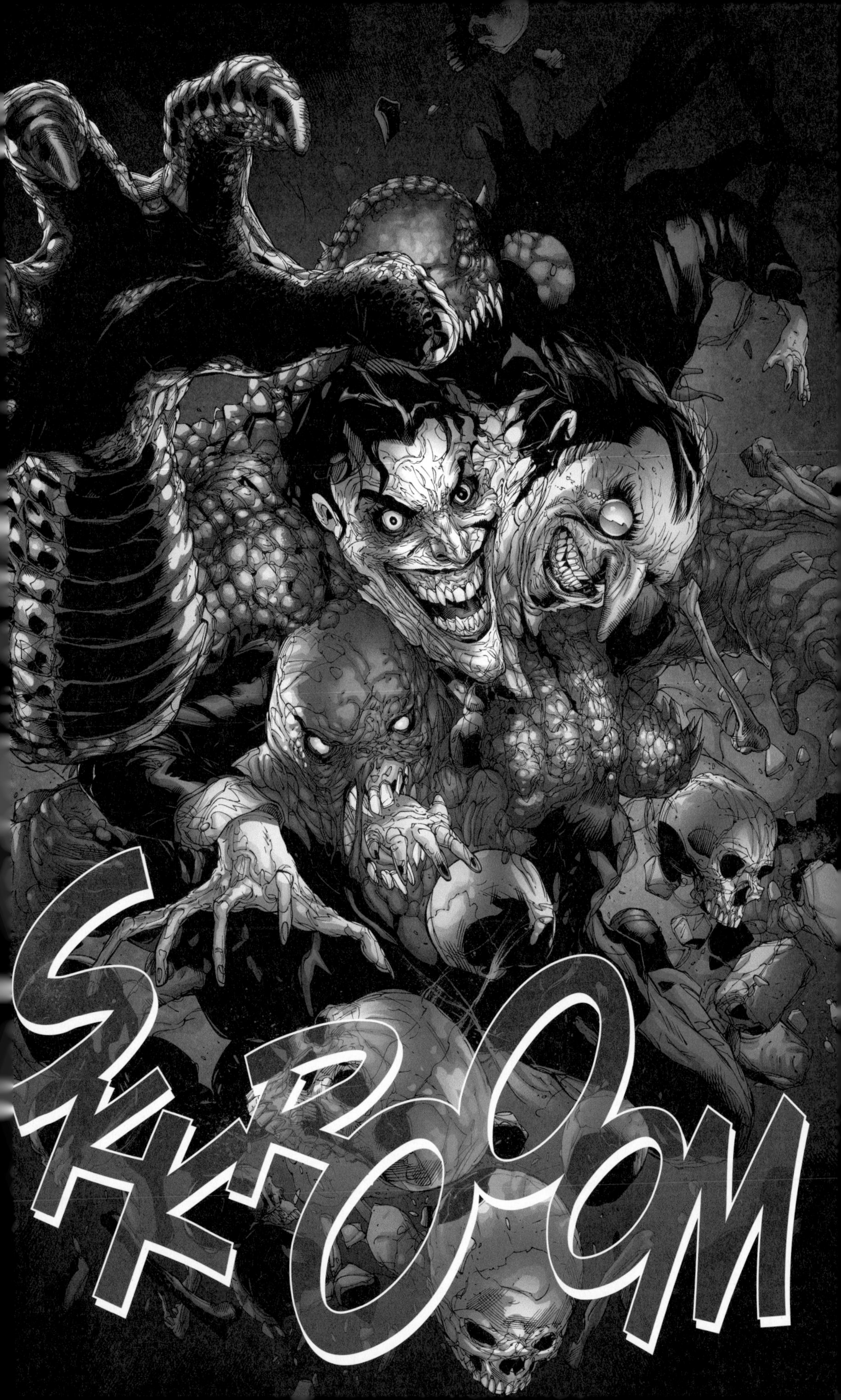
SKROOOM

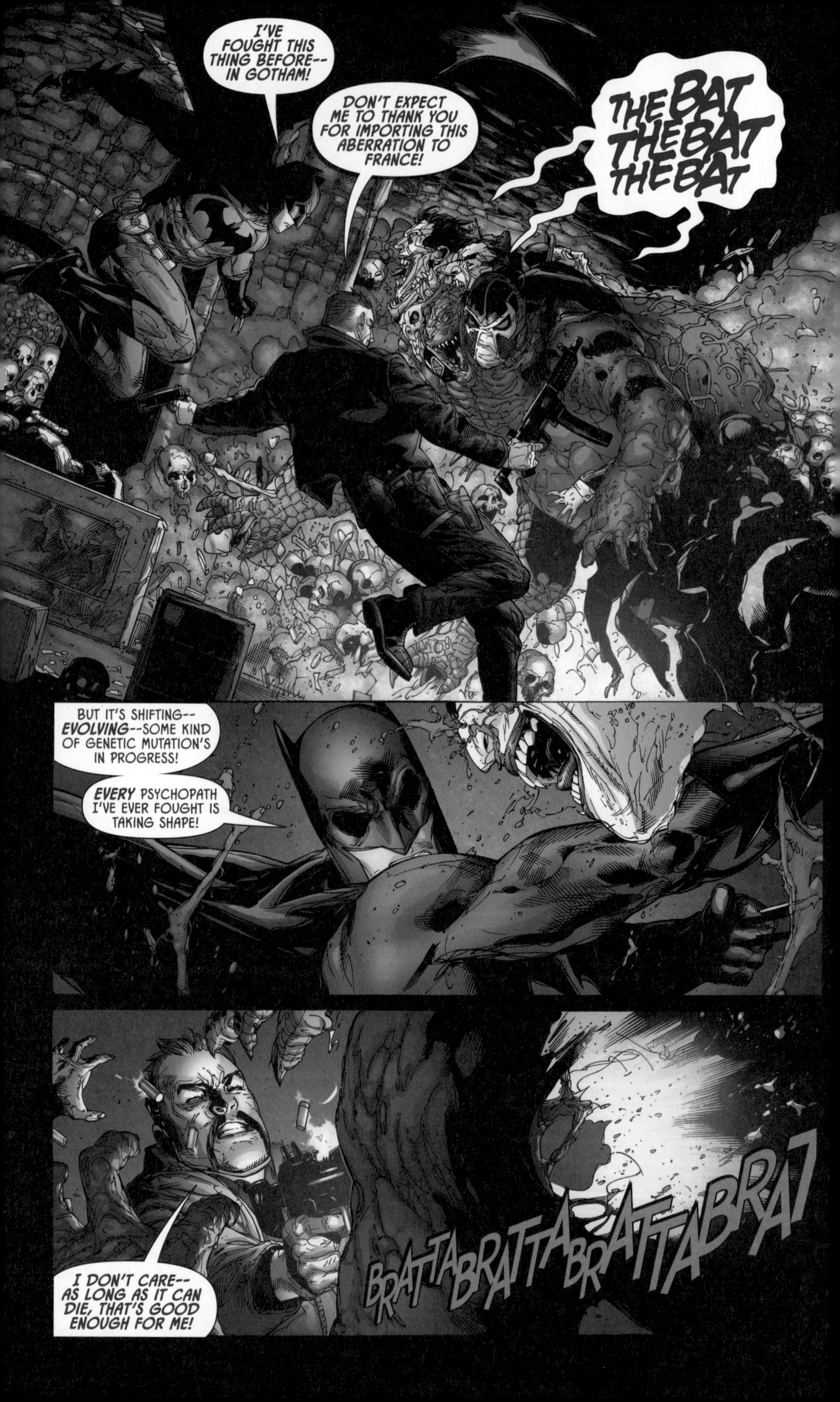

I'VE FOUGHT THIS THING BEFORE-- IN GOTHAM!
DON'T EXPECT ME TO THANK YOU FOR IMPORTING THIS ABERRATION TO FRANCE!
THE BAT THE BAT THE BAT
BUT IT'S SHIFTING-- EVOLVING--SOME KIND OF GENETIC MUTATION'S IN PROGRESS!
EVERY PSYCHOPATH I'VE EVER FOUGHT IS TAKING SHAPE!
I DON'T CARE-- AS LONG AS IT CAN DIE, THAT'S GOOD ENOUGH FOR ME!
BRATTABRATTABRATTABRAT

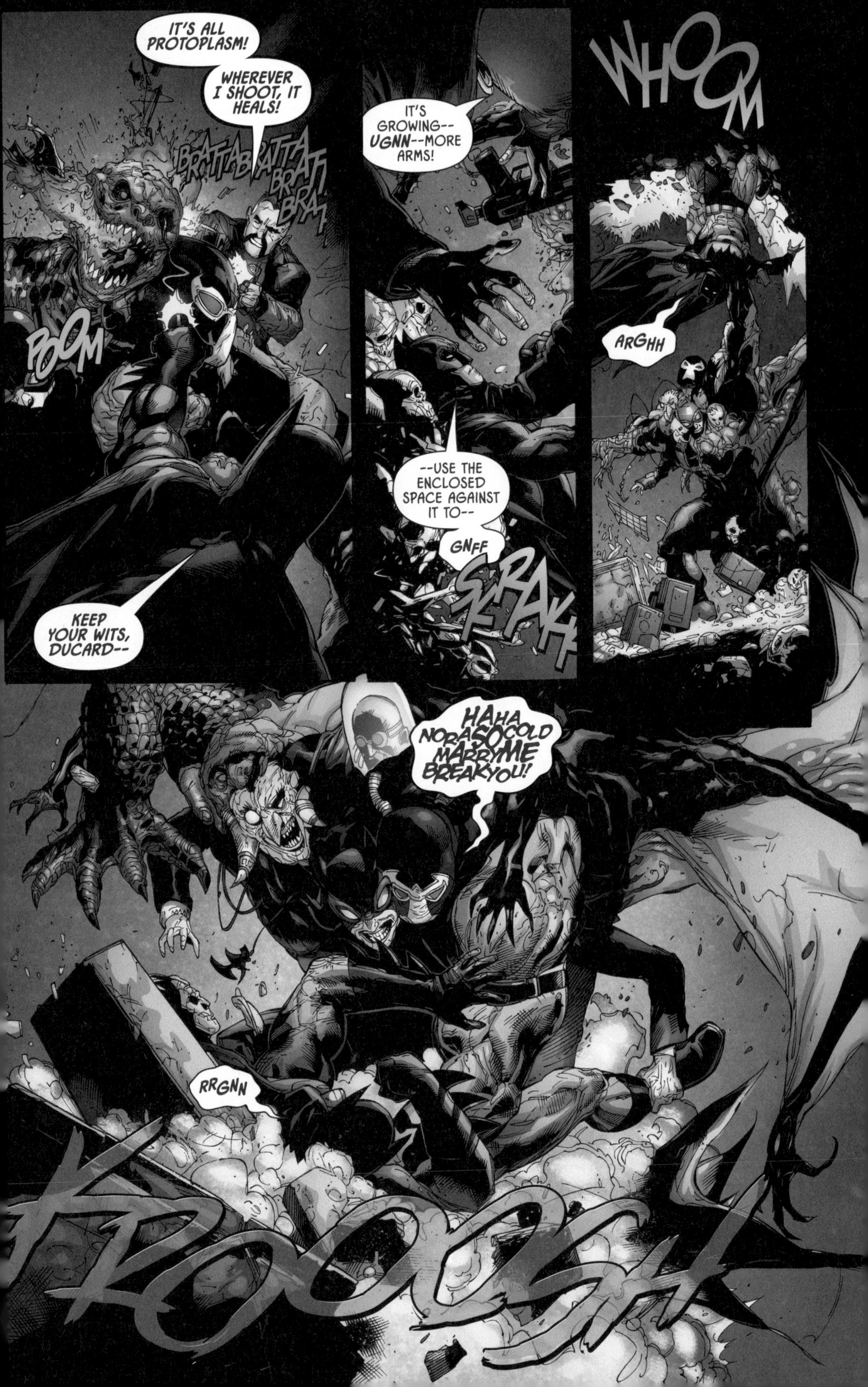
IT'S ALL PROTOPLASM!
WHEREVER I SHOOT, IT HEALS!
BRATTABRATTA BRAT BRAT
POOM
KEEP YOUR WITS, DUCARD--
IT'S GROWING--UGNN--MORE ARMS!
--USE THE ENCLOSED SPACE AGAINST IT TO--
GNFF
SKRAKK
WHOOM
ARGHH
HAHA NORA SO COLD MARRY ME BREAK YOU!
RRGNN
KROOSH

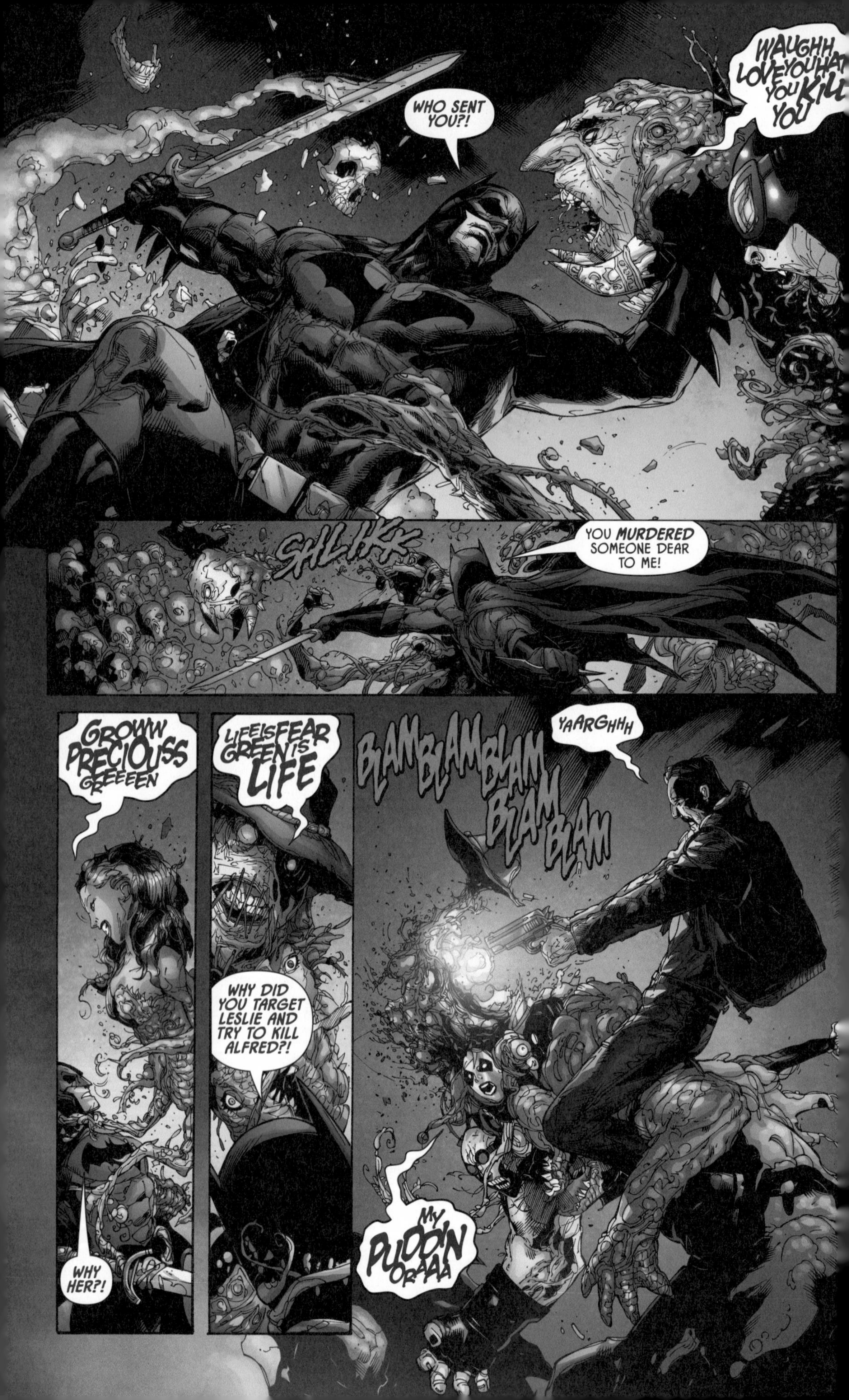

WHO SENT YOU?!
WAUGHH LOVE YOU HA YOU KILL YOU
SHLIKK
YOU MURDERED SOMEONE DEAR TO ME!
GROWW PRECIOUSS GREEEEN
WHY HER?!
LIFE IS FEAR GREEN IS LIFE
WHY DID YOU TARGET LESLIE AND TRY TO KILL ALFRED?!
BLAMBLAMBLAM BLAM BLAM
YAARGHHH
MY PUDDIN ORAAA

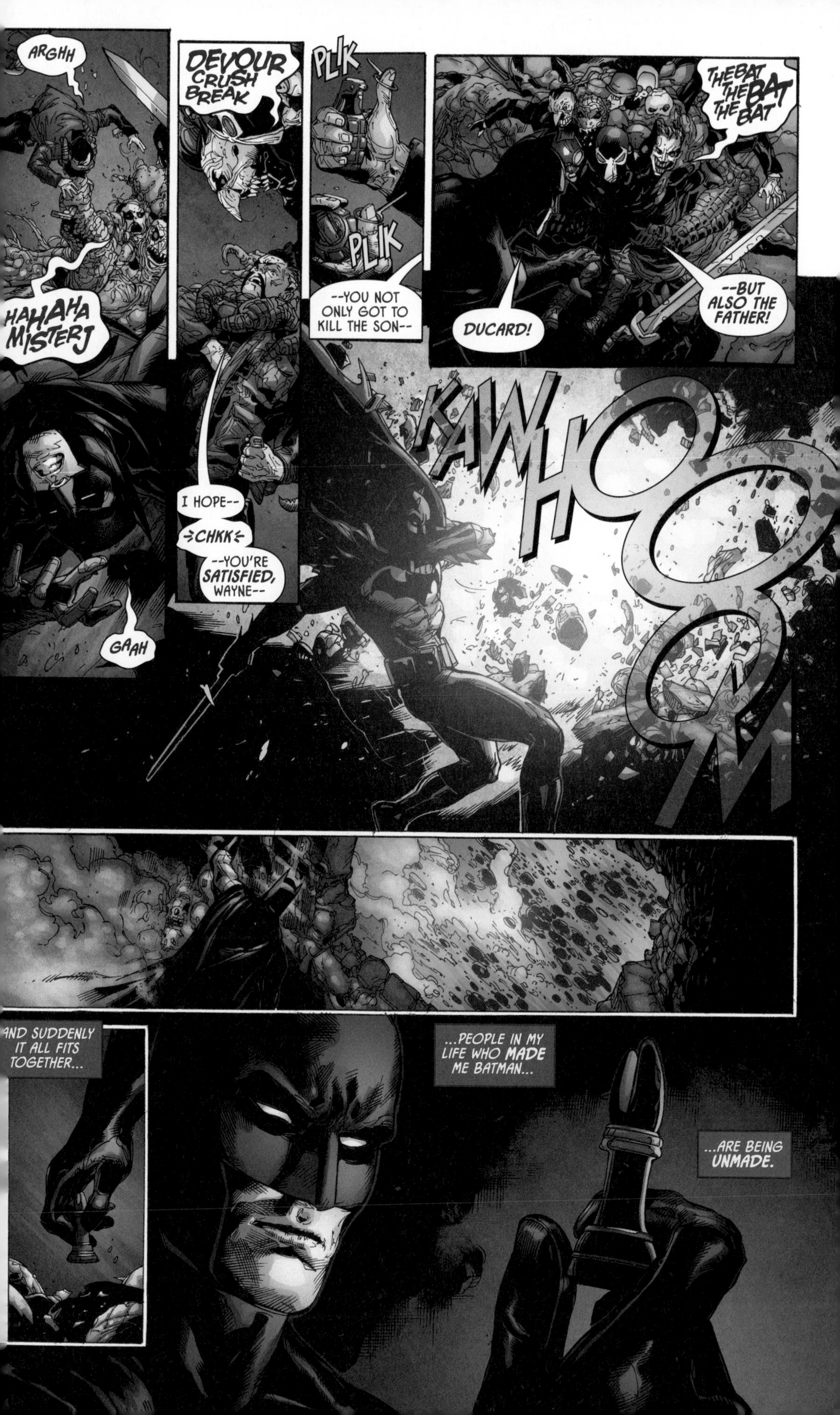
ARGHH
HAHAHA MISTER J
DEVOUR CRUSH BREAK
PLIK
PLIK
--YOU NOT ONLY GOT TO KILL THE SON--
THE BAT THE BAT THE BAT THE BAT
DUCARD!
--BUT ALSO THE FATHER!
I HOPE--
CHKK
--YOU'RE SATISFIED, WAYNE--
GAAH
KAWHOOOM
AND SUDDENLY IT ALL FITS TOGETHER...
...PEOPLE IN MY LIFE WHO MADE ME BATMAN...
...ARE BEING UNMADE.

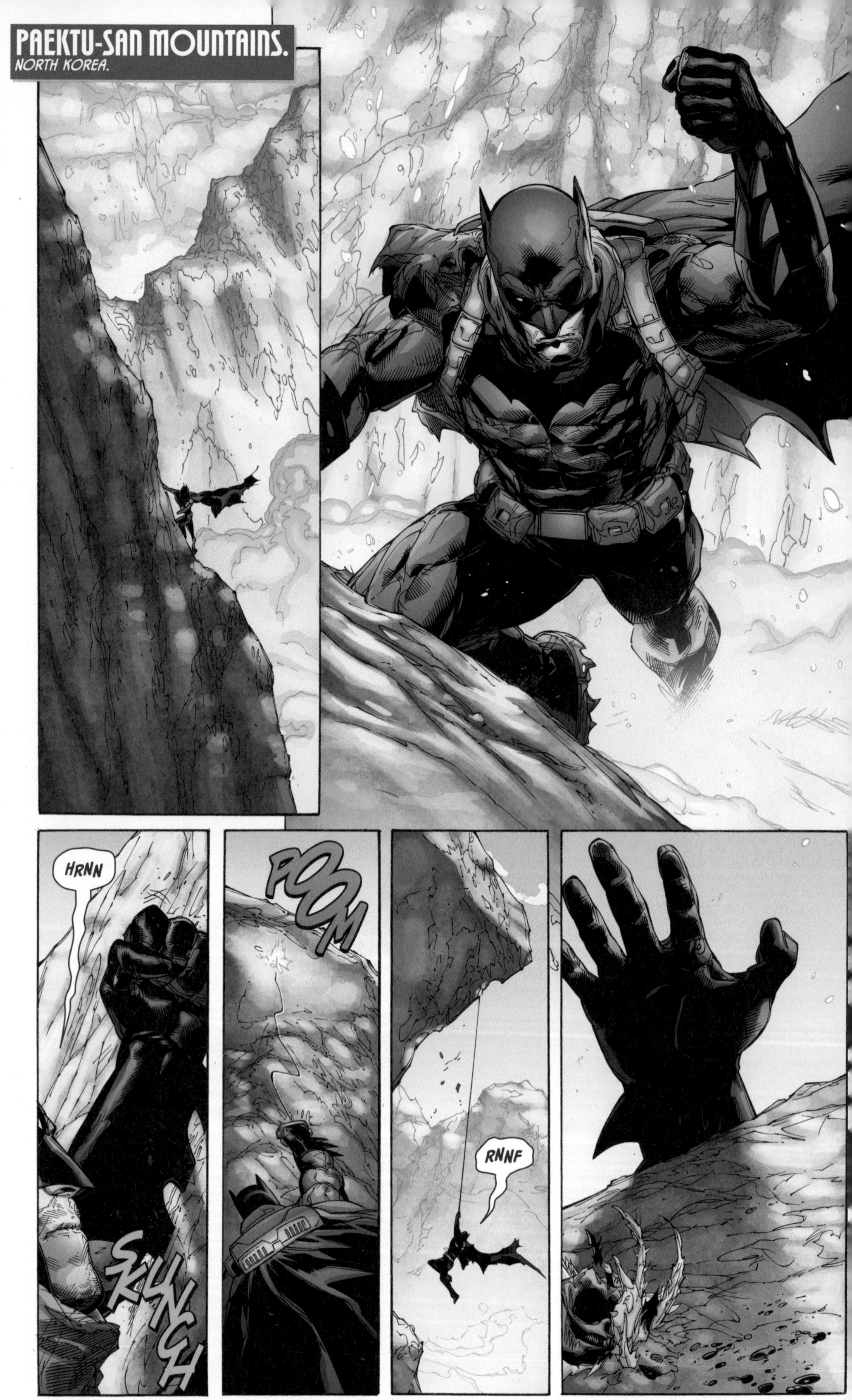
PAEKTU-SAN MOUNTAINS.
NORTH KOREA.
HRNN
SKUNCH
POOM
RNNF

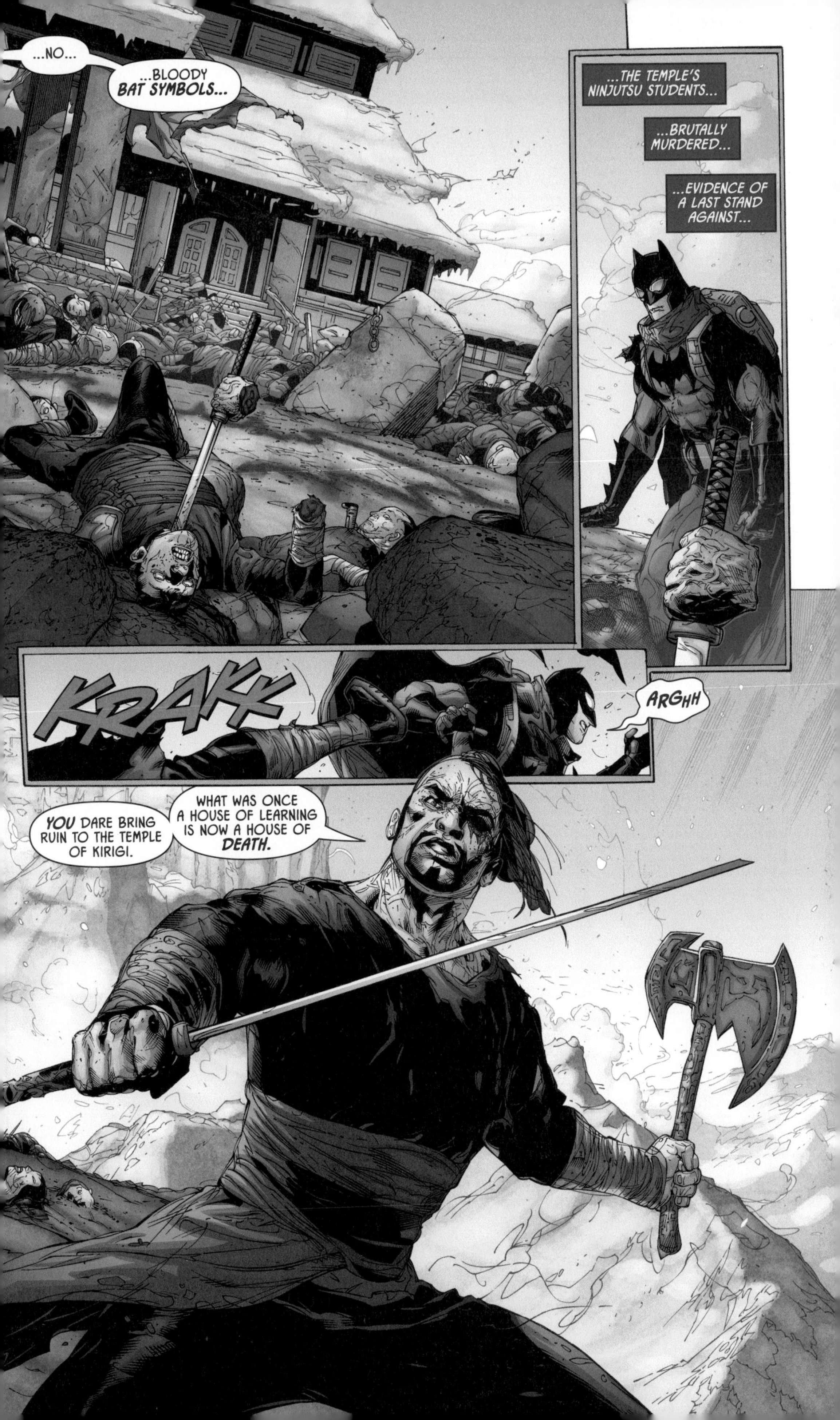
...NO...
...BLOODY BAT SYMBOLS...
...THE TEMPLE'S NINJUTSU STUDENTS...
...BRUTALLY MURDERED...
...EVIDENCE OF A LAST STAND AGAINST...
KRAKK
ARGHH
YOU DARE BRING RUIN TO THE TEMPLE OF KIRIGI.
WHAT WAS ONCE A HOUSE OF LEARNING IS NOW A HOUSE OF DEATH.

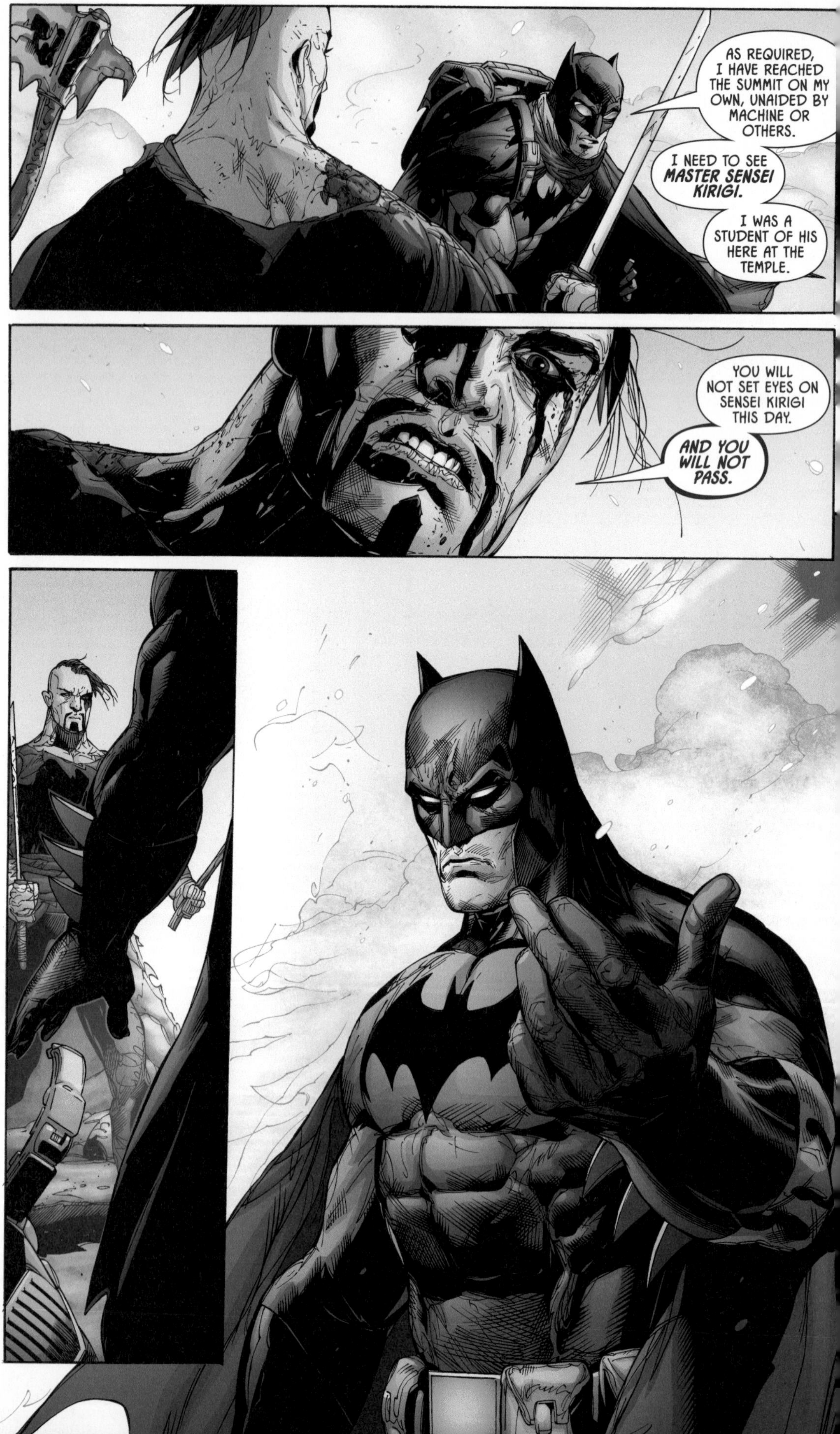
AS REQUIRED, I HAVE REACHED THE SUMMIT ON MY OWN, UNAIDED BY MACHINE OR OTHERS.
I NEED TO SEE MASTER SENSEI KIRIGI.
I WAS A STUDENT OF HIS HERE AT THE TEMPLE.
YOU WILL NOT SET EYES ON SENSEI KIRIGI THIS DAY.
AND YOU WILL NOT PASS.

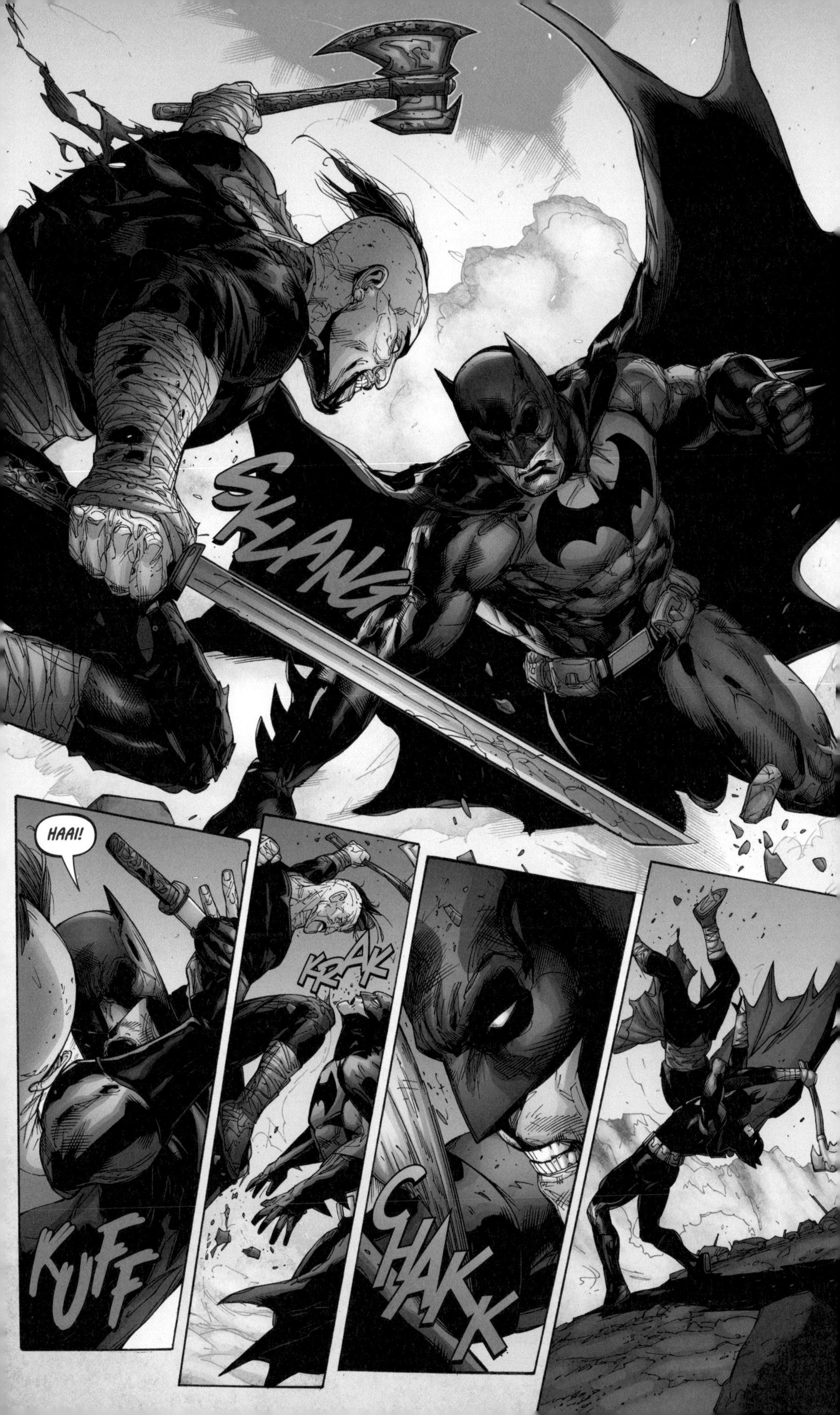
SHLANG
HAAI!
KUFF
KRAK
CHAKK

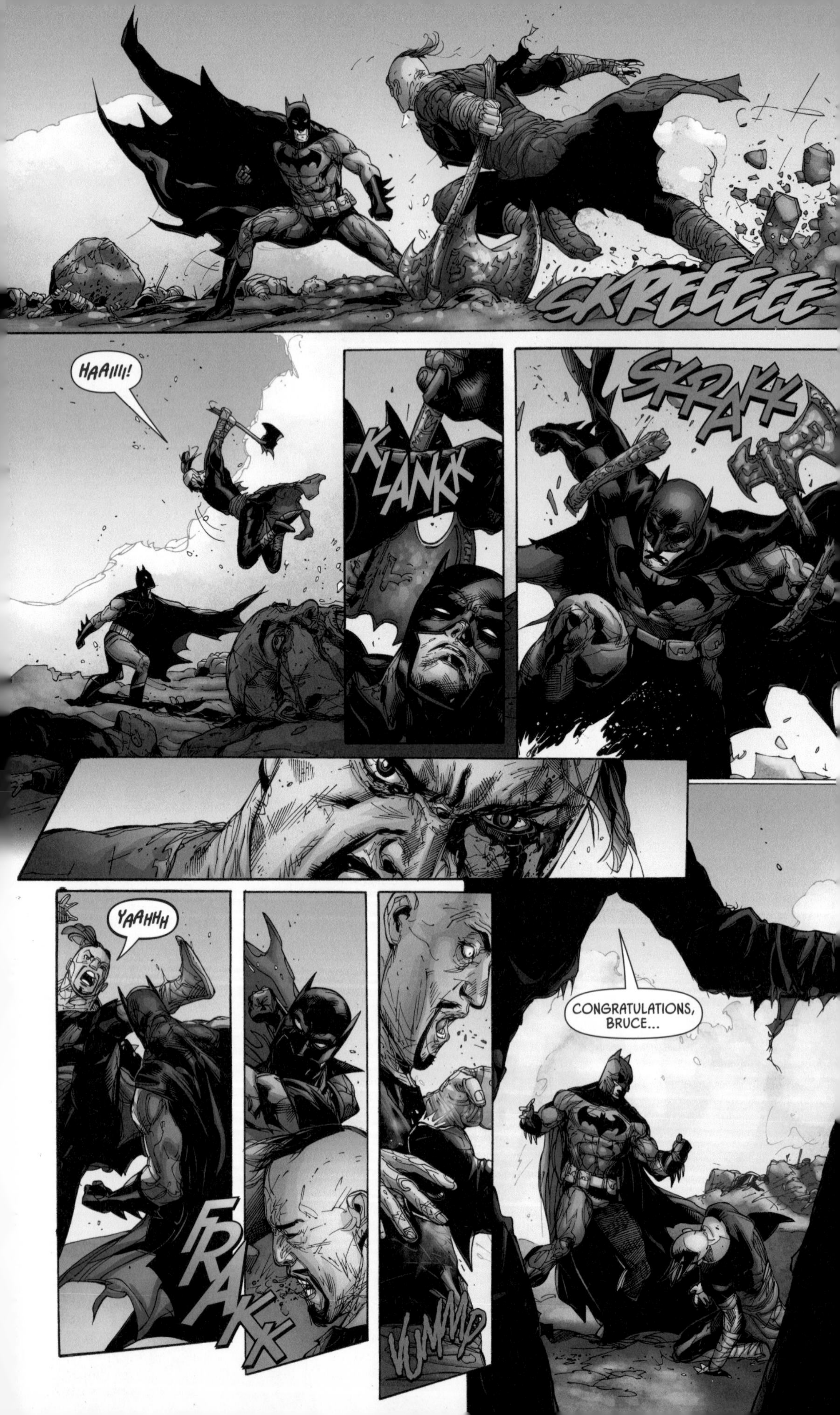
SKREEEEEE
HAAIIII!
KLANKK
SKRAKK
YAAHHH
FRAKK
VUMMP
CONGRATULATIONS, BRUCE...

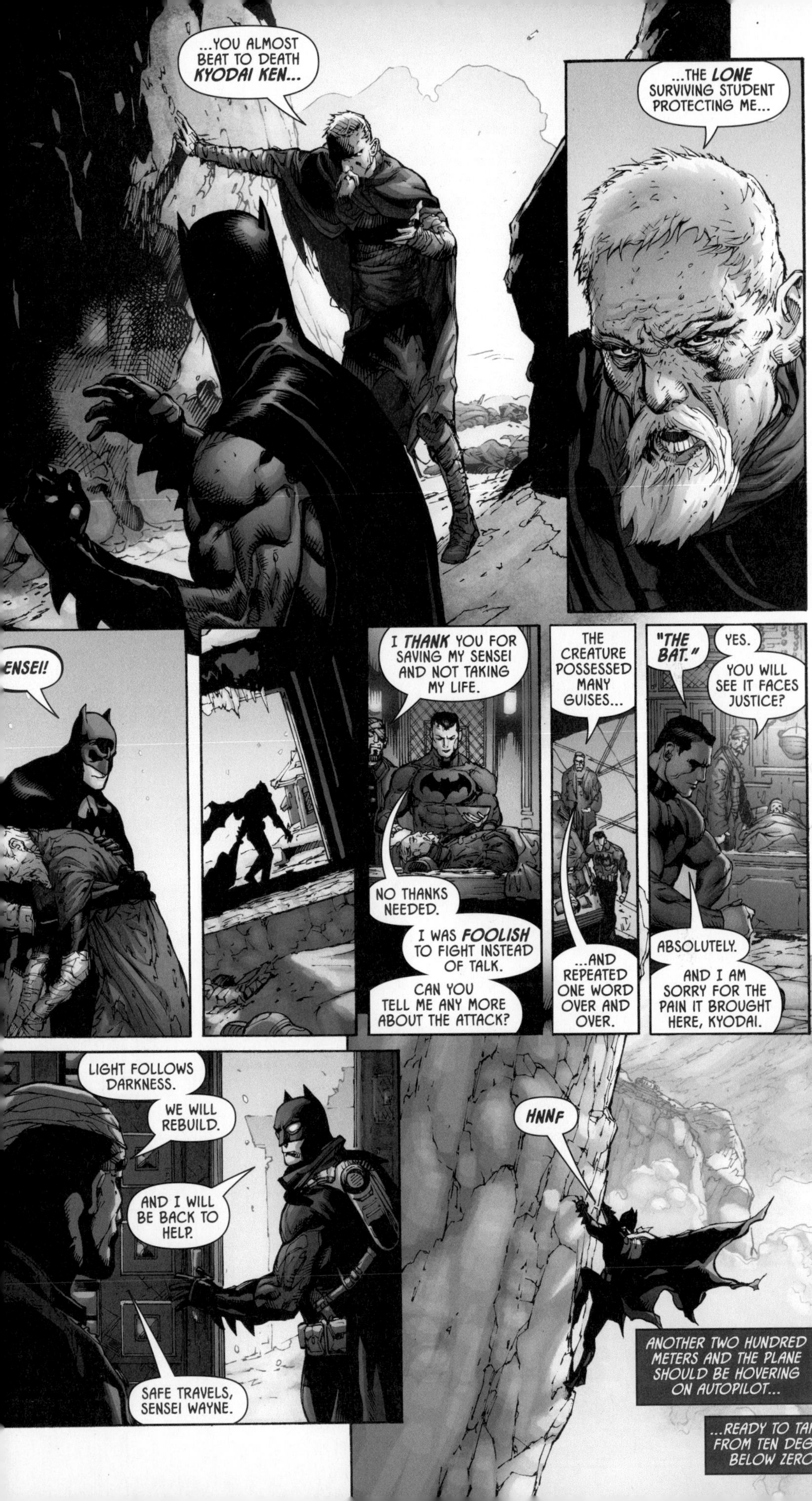
...YOU ALMOST BEAT TO DEATH KYODAI KEN...
...THE LONE SURVIVING STUDENT PROTECTING ME...
ENSEI!
I THANK YOU FOR SAVING MY SENSEI AND NOT TAKING MY LIFE.
NO THANKS NEEDED.
I WAS FOOLISH TO FIGHT INSTEAD OF TALK.
CAN YOU TELL ME ANY MORE ABOUT THE ATTACK?
THE CREATURE POSSESSED MANY GUISES...
...AND REPEATED ONE WORD OVER AND OVER.
"THE BAT."
YES.
YOU WILL SEE IT FACES JUSTICE?
ABSOLUTELY.
AND I AM SORRY FOR THE PAIN IT BROUGHT HERE, KYODAI.
LIGHT FOLLOWS DARKNESS.
WE WILL REBUILD.
AND I WILL BE BACK TO HELP.
SAFE TRAVELS, SENSEI WAYNE.
HNNF
ANOTHER TWO HUNDRED METERS AND THE PLANE SHOULD BE HOVERING ON AUTOPILOT...
...READY TO TAKE ME FROM TEN DEGREES BELOW ZERO...

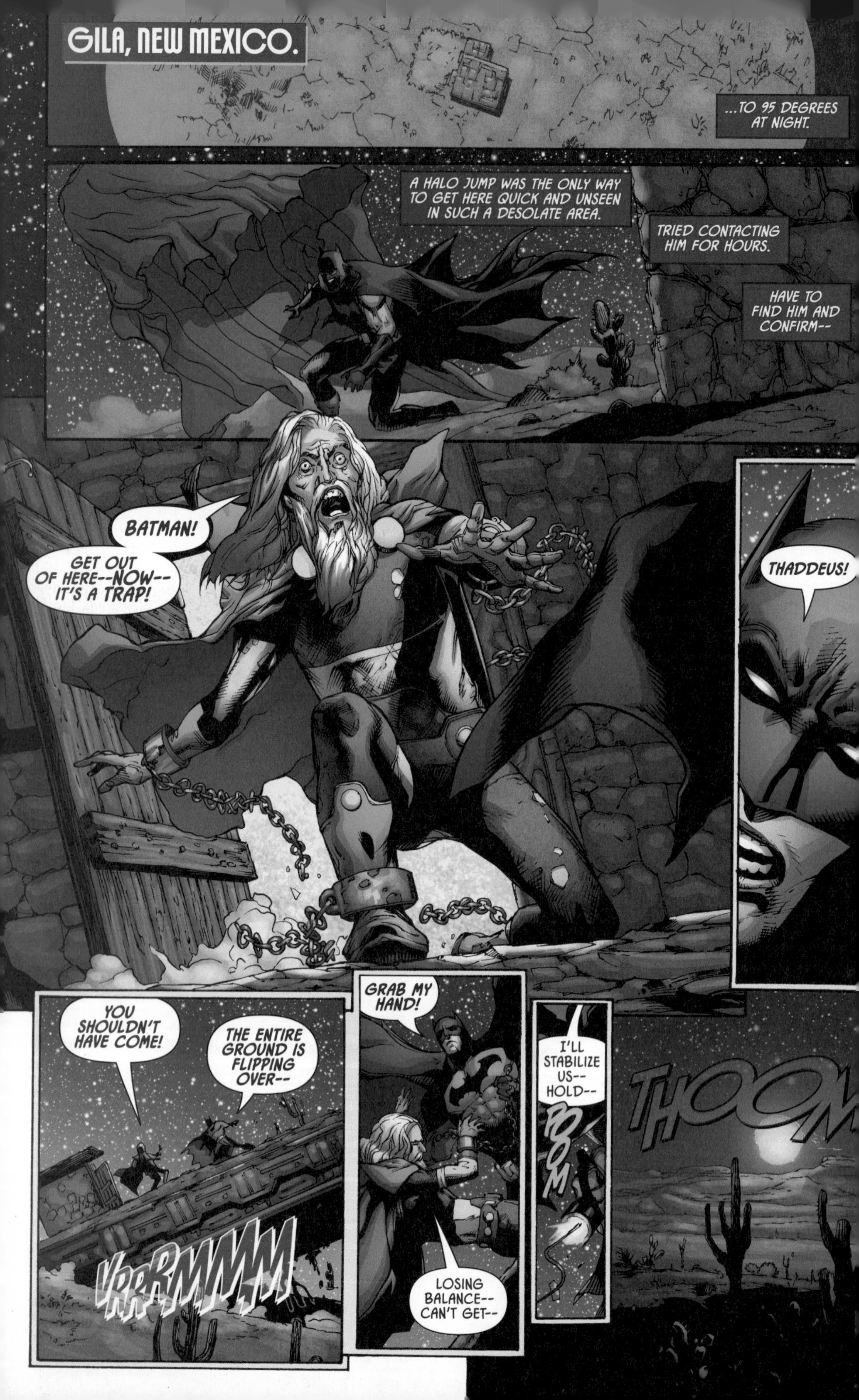
GILA, NEW MEXICO.
...TO 95 DEGREES AT NIGHT.
A HALO JUMP WAS THE ONLY WAY TO GET HERE QUICK AND UNSEEN IN SUCH A DESOLATE AREA.
TRIED CONTACTING HIM FOR HOURS.
HAVE TO FIND HIM AND CONFIRM--
BATMAN!
GET OUT OF HERE--NOW--IT'S A TRAP!
THADDEUS!
YOU SHOULDN'T HAVE COME!
THE ENTIRE GROUND IS FLIPPING OVER--
VRRRMMMM
GRAB MY HAND!
LOSING BALANCE--CAN'T GET--
I'LL STABILIZE US--HOLD--
BOOM
THOOM

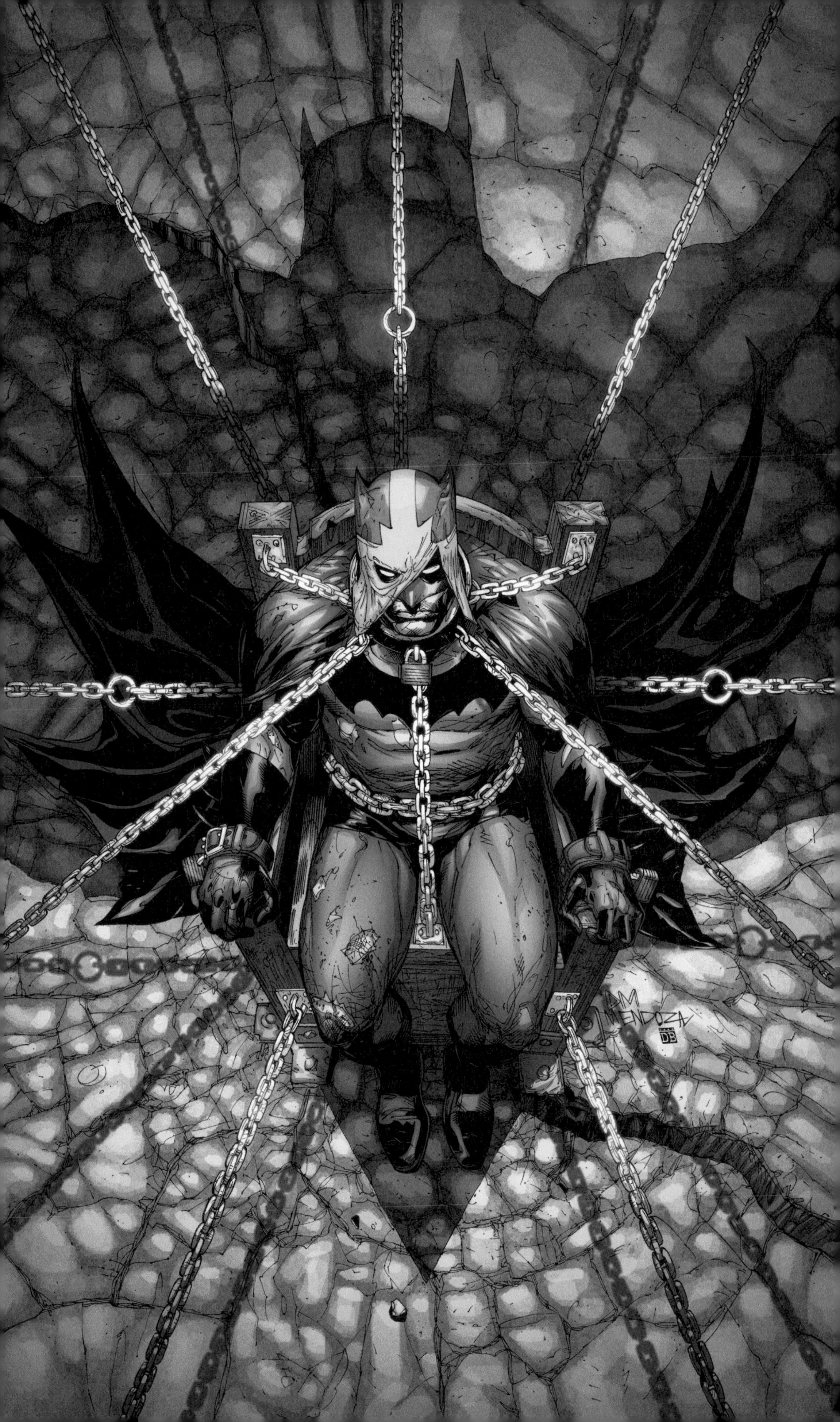
DM
MENDOZA
DB

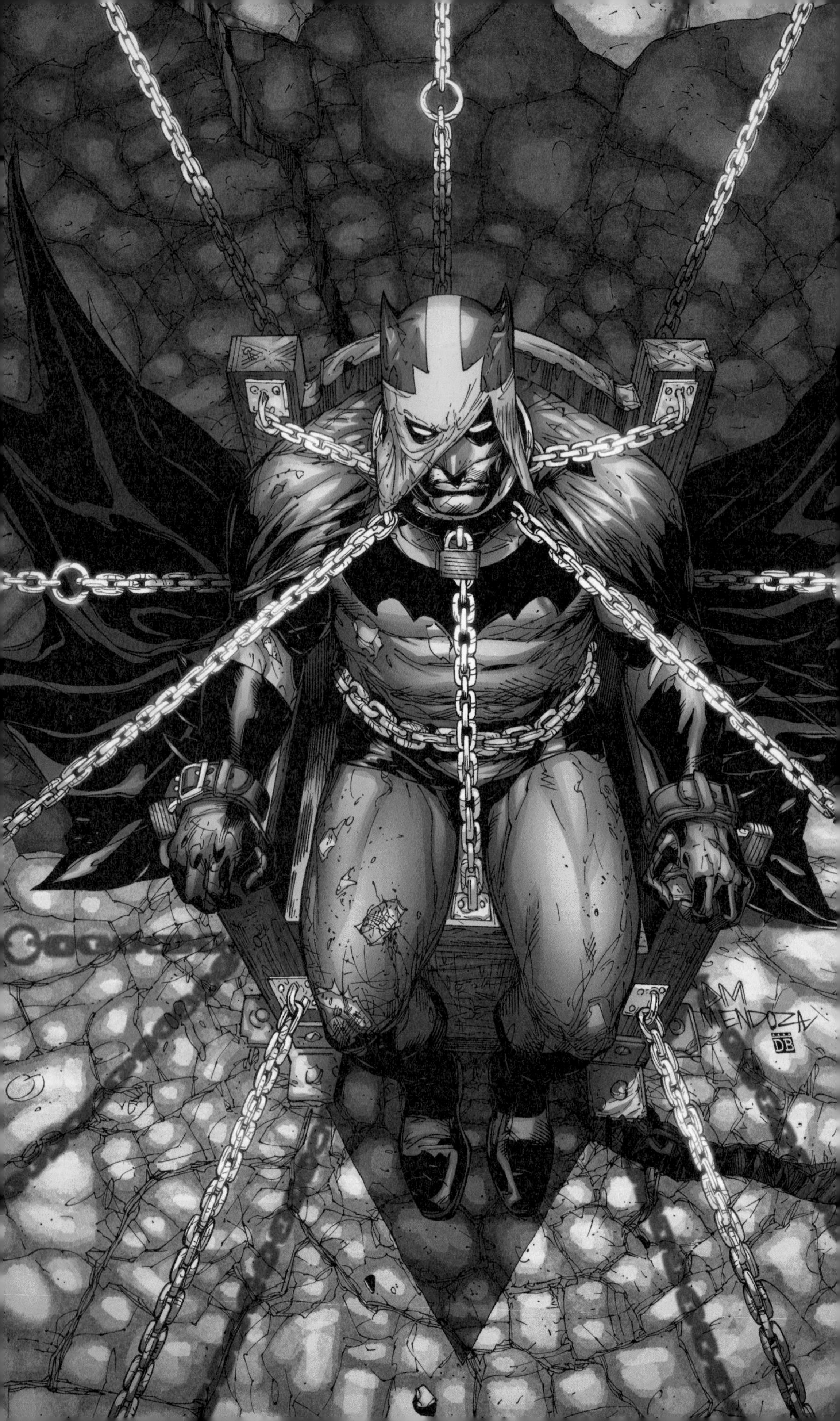
DM
MENDOZA
DB

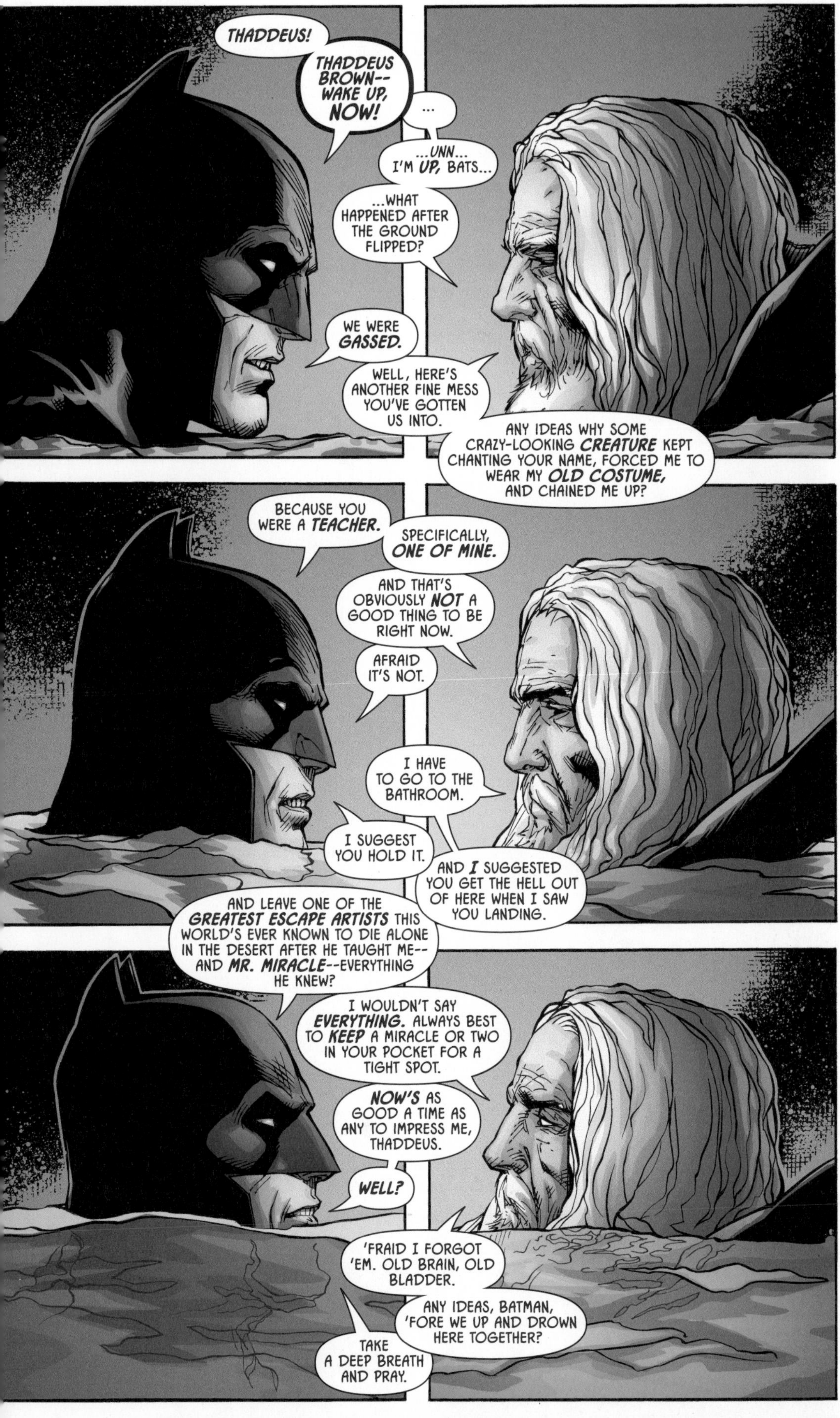
THADDEUS!
THADDEUS BROWN-- WAKE UP, NOW!
...
...UNN... I'M UP, BATS...
...WHAT HAPPENED AFTER THE GROUND FLIPPED?
WE WERE GASSED.
WELL, HERE'S ANOTHER FINE MESS YOU'VE GOTTEN US INTO.
ANY IDEAS WHY SOME CRAZY-LOOKING CREATURE KEPT CHANTING YOUR NAME, FORCED ME TO WEAR MY OLD COSTUME, AND CHAINED ME UP?
BECAUSE YOU WERE A TEACHER.
SPECIFICALLY, ONE OF MINE.
AND THAT'S OBVIOUSLY NOT A GOOD THING TO BE RIGHT NOW.
AFRAID IT'S NOT.
I HAVE TO GO TO THE BATHROOM.
I SUGGEST YOU HOLD IT.
AND I SUGGESTED YOU GET THE HELL OUT OF HERE WHEN I SAW YOU LANDING.
AND LEAVE ONE OF THE GREATEST ESCAPE ARTISTS THIS WORLD'S EVER KNOWN TO DIE ALONE IN THE DESERT AFTER HE TAUGHT ME-- AND MR. MIRACLE--EVERYTHING HE KNEW?
I WOULDN'T SAY EVERYTHING. ALWAYS BEST TO KEEP A MIRACLE OR TWO IN YOUR POCKET FOR A TIGHT SPOT.
NOW'S AS GOOD A TIME AS ANY TO IMPRESS ME, THADDEUS.
WELL?
'FRAID I FORGOT 'EM. OLD BRAIN, OLD BLADDER.
ANY IDEAS, BATMAN, 'FORE WE UP AND DROWN HERE TOGETHER?
TAKE A DEEP BREATH AND PRAY.

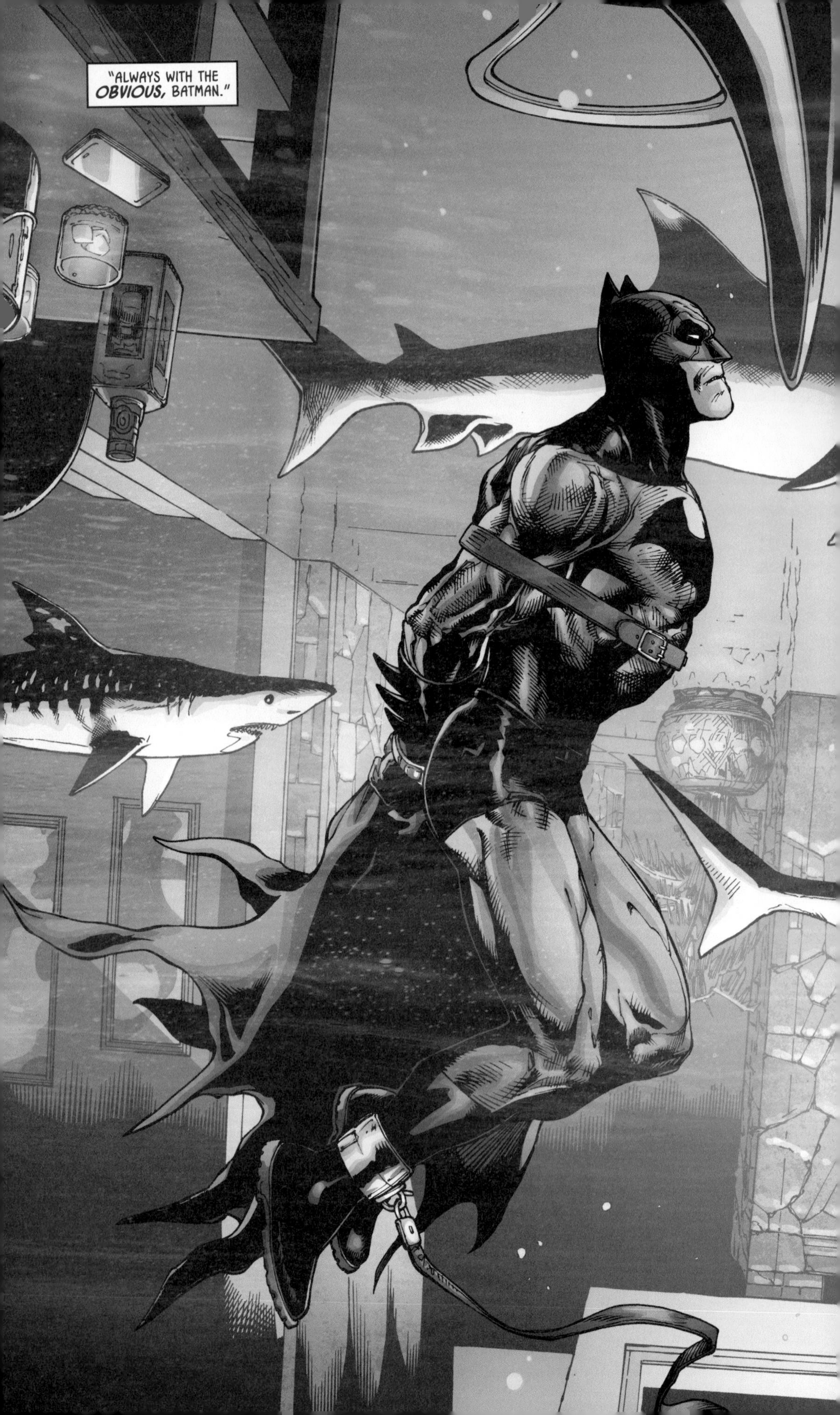
"ALWAYS WITH THE *OBVIOUS,* BATMAN."

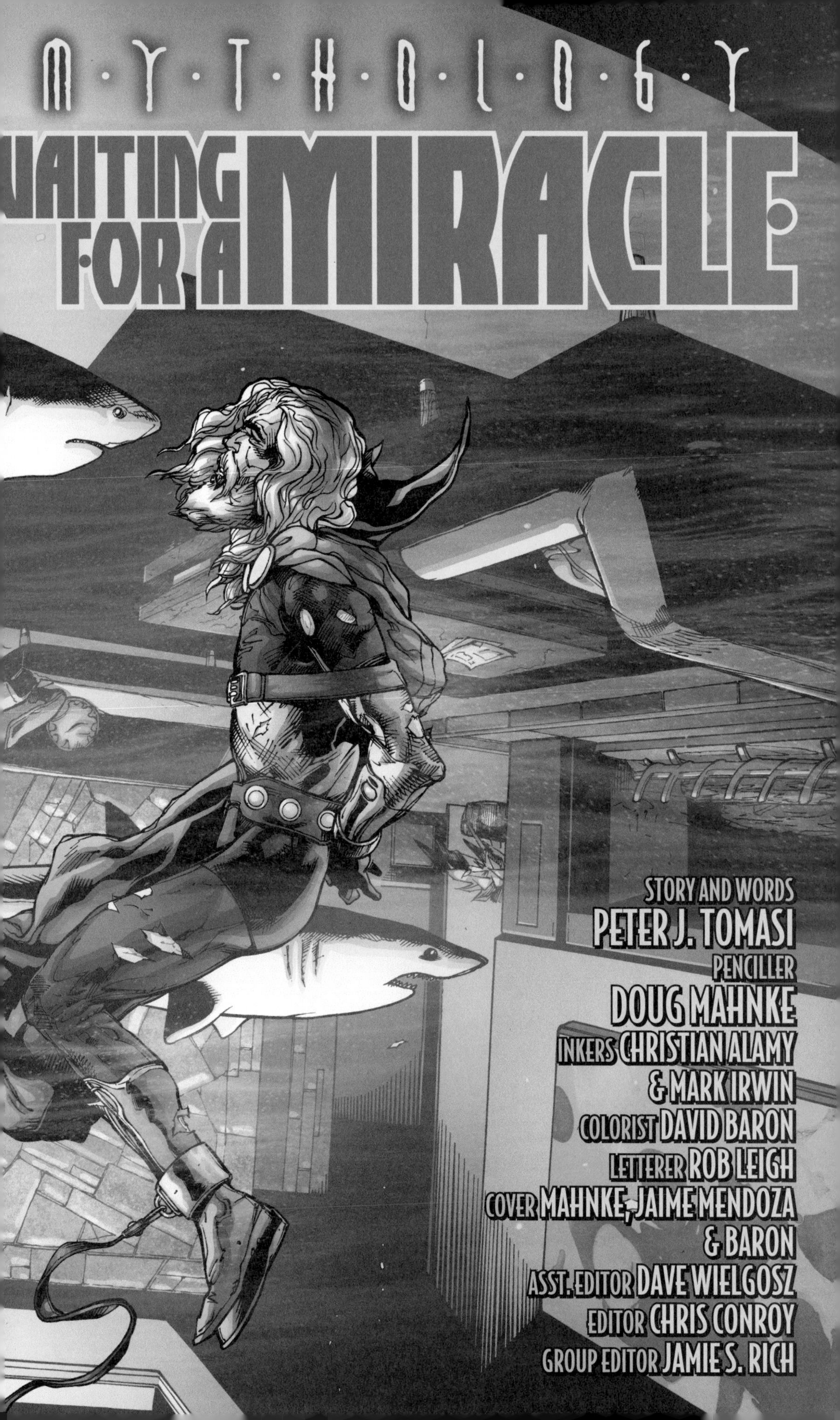
M·Y·T·H·O·L·O·G·Y
WAITING FOR A MIRACLE
STORY AND WORDS PETER J. TOMASI
PENCILLER DOUG MAHNKE
INKERS CHRISTIAN ALAMY & MARK IRWIN
COLORIST DAVID BARON
LETTERER ROB LEIGH
COVER MAHNKE, JAIME MENDOZA & BARON
ASST. EDITOR DAVE WIELGOSZ
EDITOR CHRIS CONROY
GROUP EDITOR JAMIE S. RICH

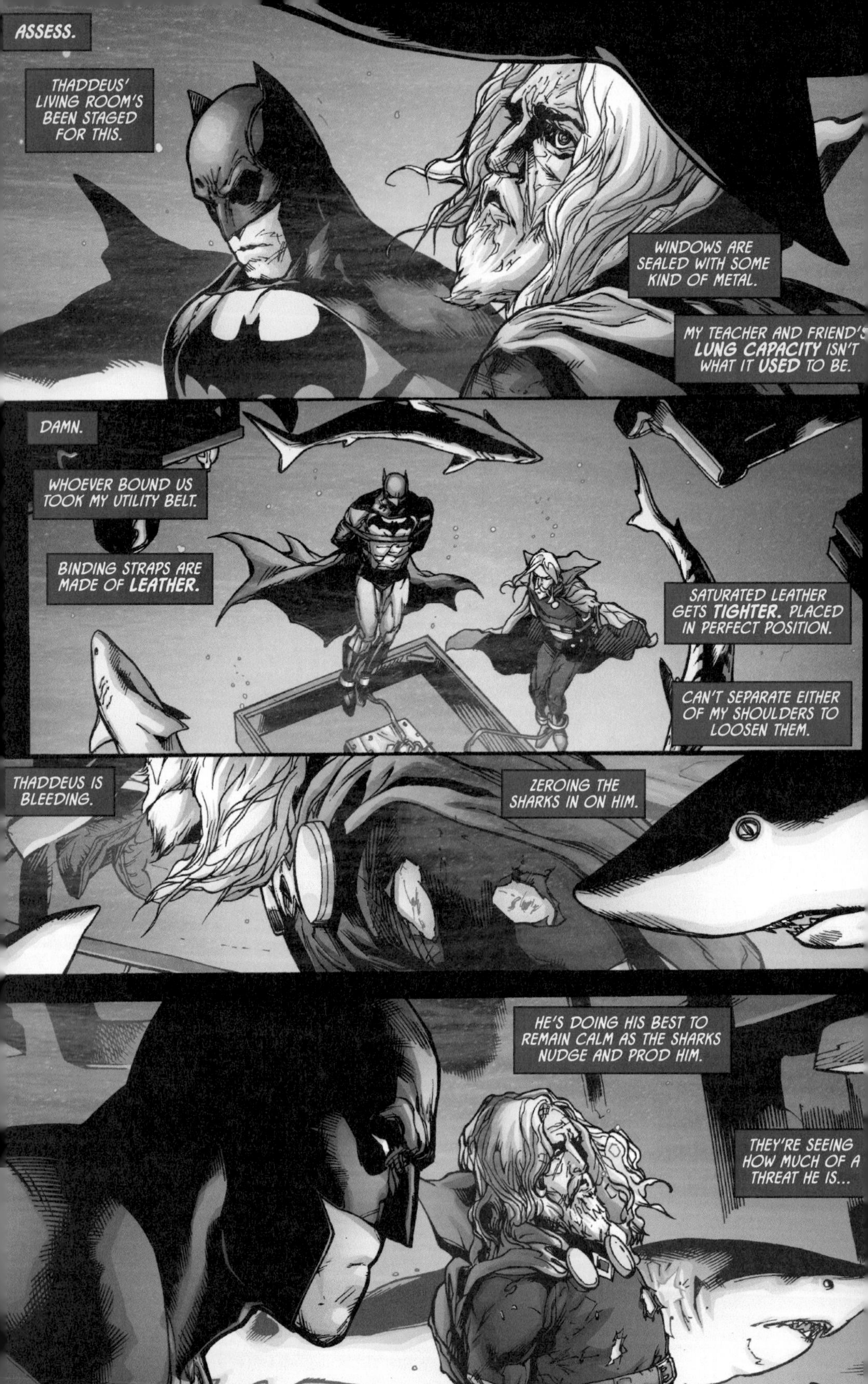
ASSESS.
THADDEUS' LIVING ROOM'S BEEN STAGED FOR THIS.
WINDOWS ARE SEALED WITH SOME KIND OF METAL.
MY TEACHER AND FRIEND'S **LUNG CAPACITY** ISN'T WHAT IT **USED** TO BE.
DAMN.
WHOEVER BOUND US TOOK MY UTILITY BELT.
BINDING STRAPS ARE MADE OF **LEATHER.**
SATURATED LEATHER GETS **TIGHTER.** PLACED IN PERFECT POSITION.
CAN'T SEPARATE EITHER OF MY SHOULDERS TO LOOSEN THEM.
THADDEUS IS BLEEDING.
ZEROING THE SHARKS IN ON HIM.
HE'S DOING HIS BEST TO REMAIN CALM AS THE SHARKS NUDGE AND PROD HIM.
THEY'RE SEEING HOW MUCH OF A THREAT HE IS...

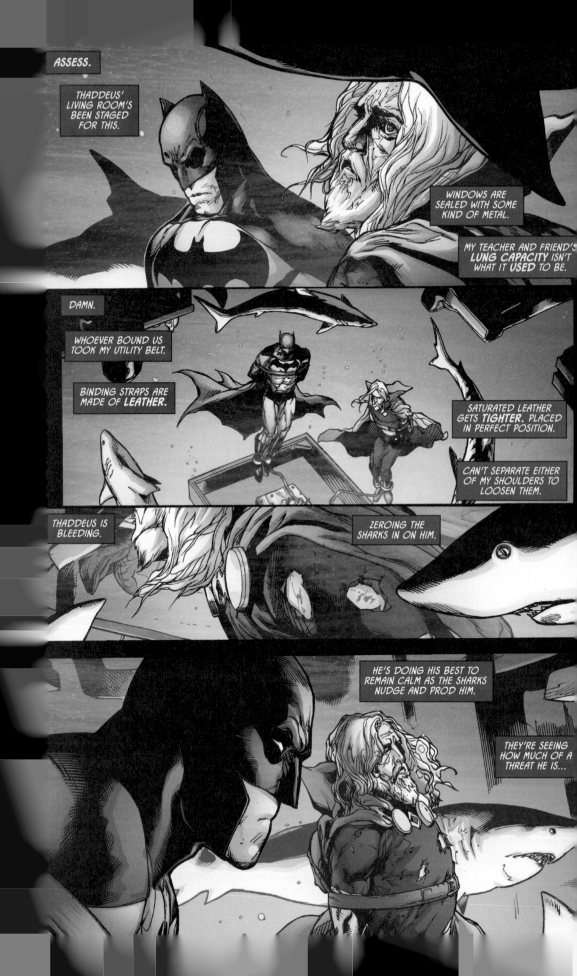

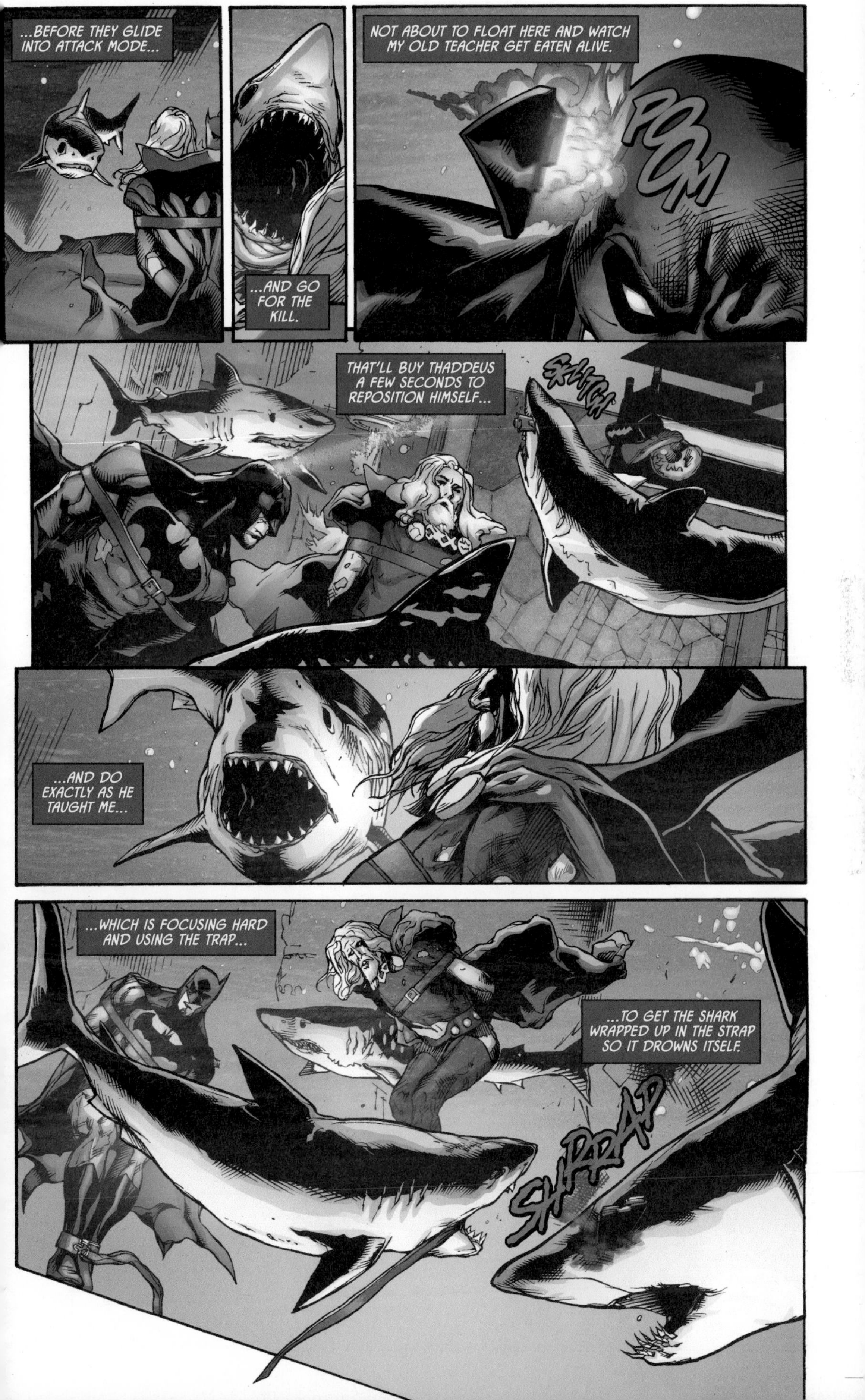

...BEFORE THEY GLIDE INTO ATTACK MODE...
...AND GO FOR THE KILL.
NOT ABOUT TO FLOAT HERE AND WATCH MY OLD TEACHER GET EATEN ALIVE.
POOM
THAT'LL BUY THADDEUS A FEW SECONDS TO REPOSITION HIMSELF...
SKLITCH
...AND DO EXACTLY AS HE TAUGHT ME...
...WHICH IS FOCUSING HARD AND USING THE TRAP...
...TO GET THE SHARK WRAPPED UP IN THE STRAP SO IT DROWNS ITSELF.
SHRRAP

THAT'S IT.

PAY ATTENTION TO ME.

USE THE SHARK'S MOMENTUM AGAINST IT...

...AND LET THE GLOVE SCALLOPS DO THE WORK...

...ON THE SHARK'S SOFT UNDERBELLY.

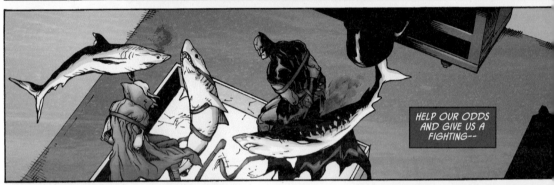

HELP OUR ODDS AND GIVE US A FIGHTING--

MORE BUBBLES.

THADDEUS IS RUNNING OUT OF AIR...

...AND THAT METAL WINDOW BEHIND US IS OPENING...

SO MUCH FOR OUR ODDS GETTING BETTER.

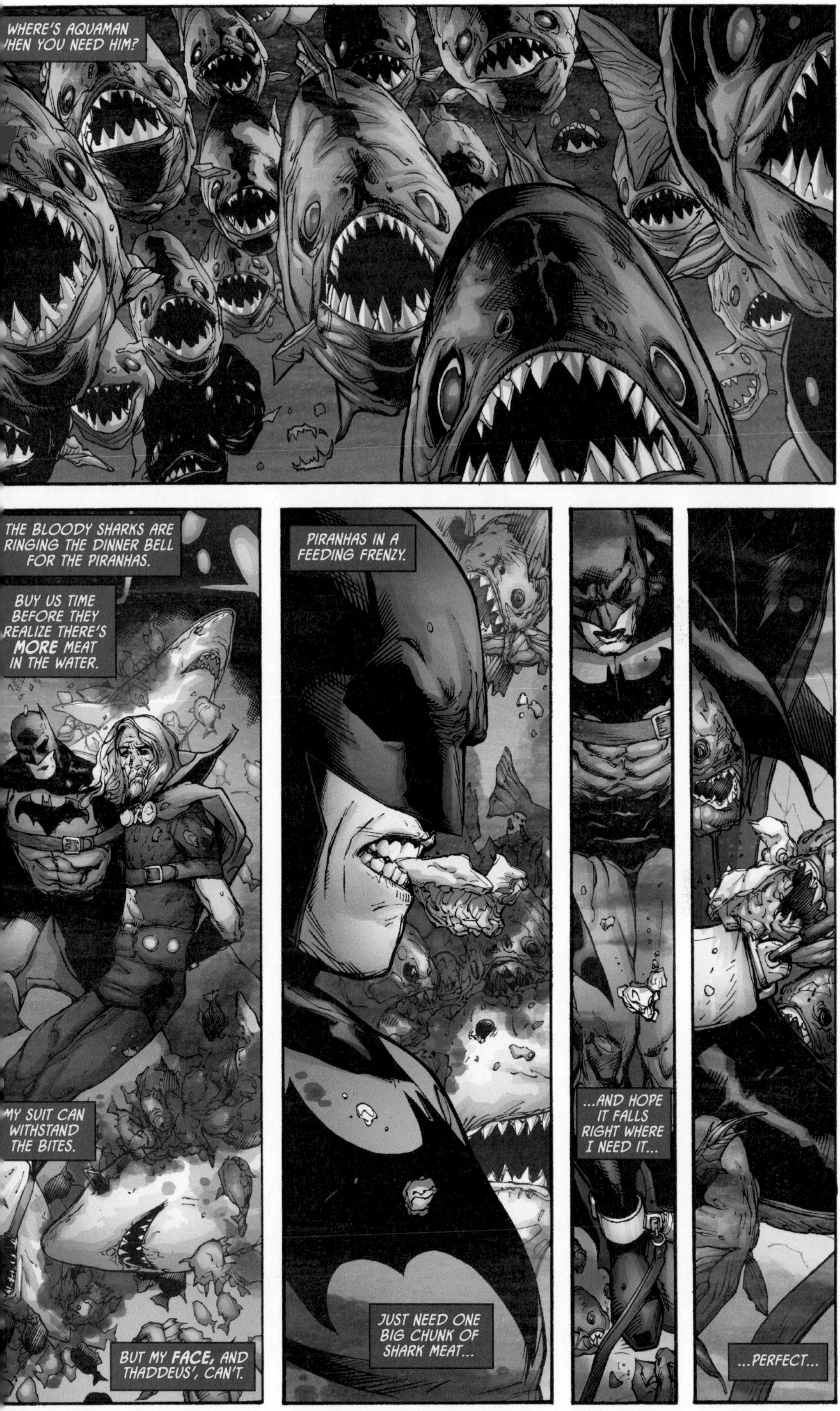
WHERE'S AQUAMAN
WHEN YOU NEED HIM?
THE BLOODY SHARKS ARE RINGING THE DINNER BELL FOR THE PIRANHAS.
BUY US TIME BEFORE THEY REALIZE THERE'S MORE MEAT IN THE WATER.
MY SUIT CAN WITHSTAND THE BITES.
BUT MY FACE, AND THADDEUS', CAN'T.
PIRANHAS IN A FEEDING FRENZY.
JUST NEED ONE BIG CHUNK OF SHARK MEAT...
...AND HOPE IT FALLS RIGHT WHERE I NEED IT...
...PERFECT...

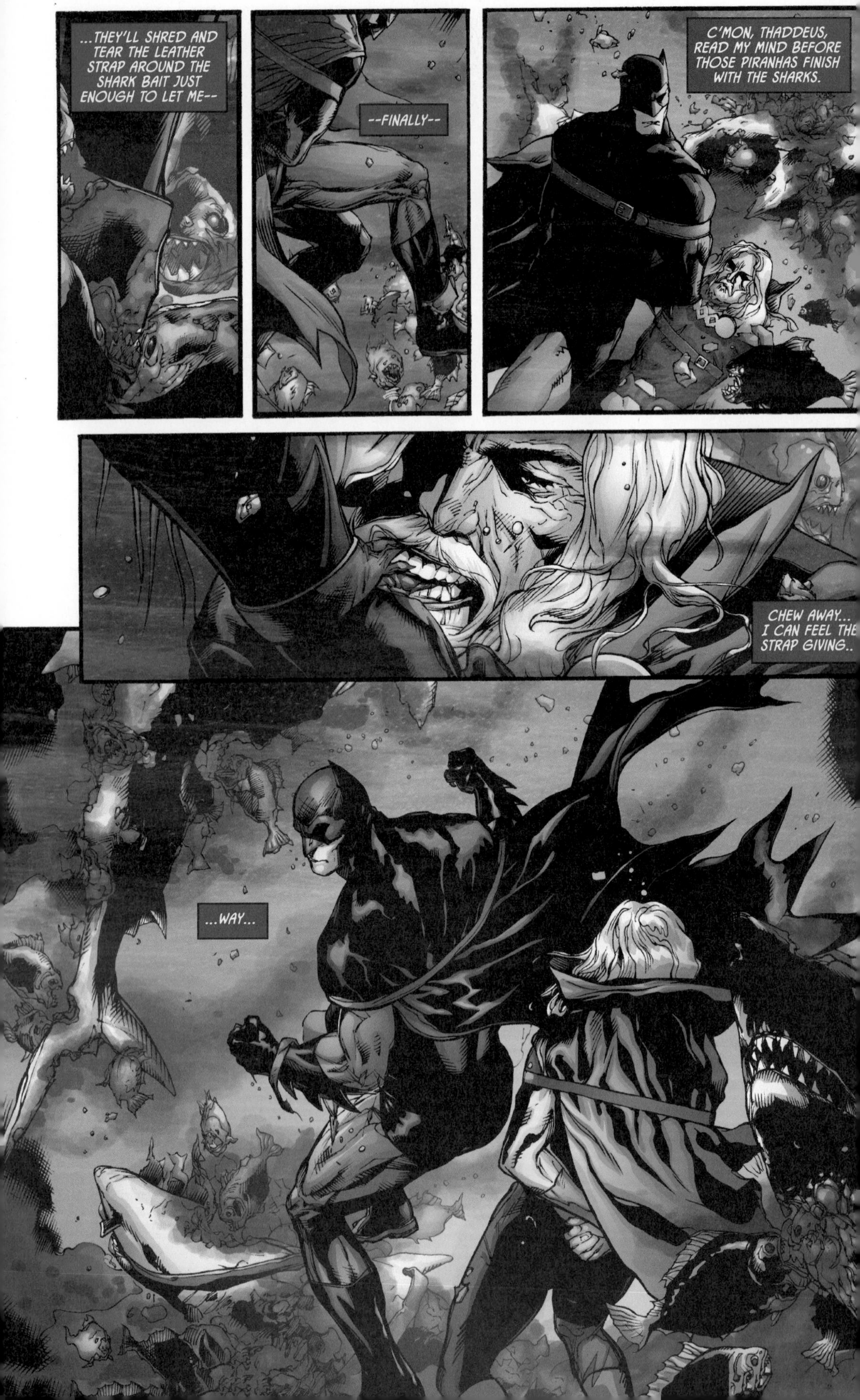
...THEY'LL SHRED AND TEAR THE LEATHER STRAP AROUND THE SHARK BAIT JUST ENOUGH TO LET ME--
--FINALLY--
C'MON, THADDEUS, READ MY MIND BEFORE THOSE PIRANHAS FINISH WITH THE SHARKS.
CHEW AWAY... I CAN FEEL THE STRAP GIVING..
...WAY...

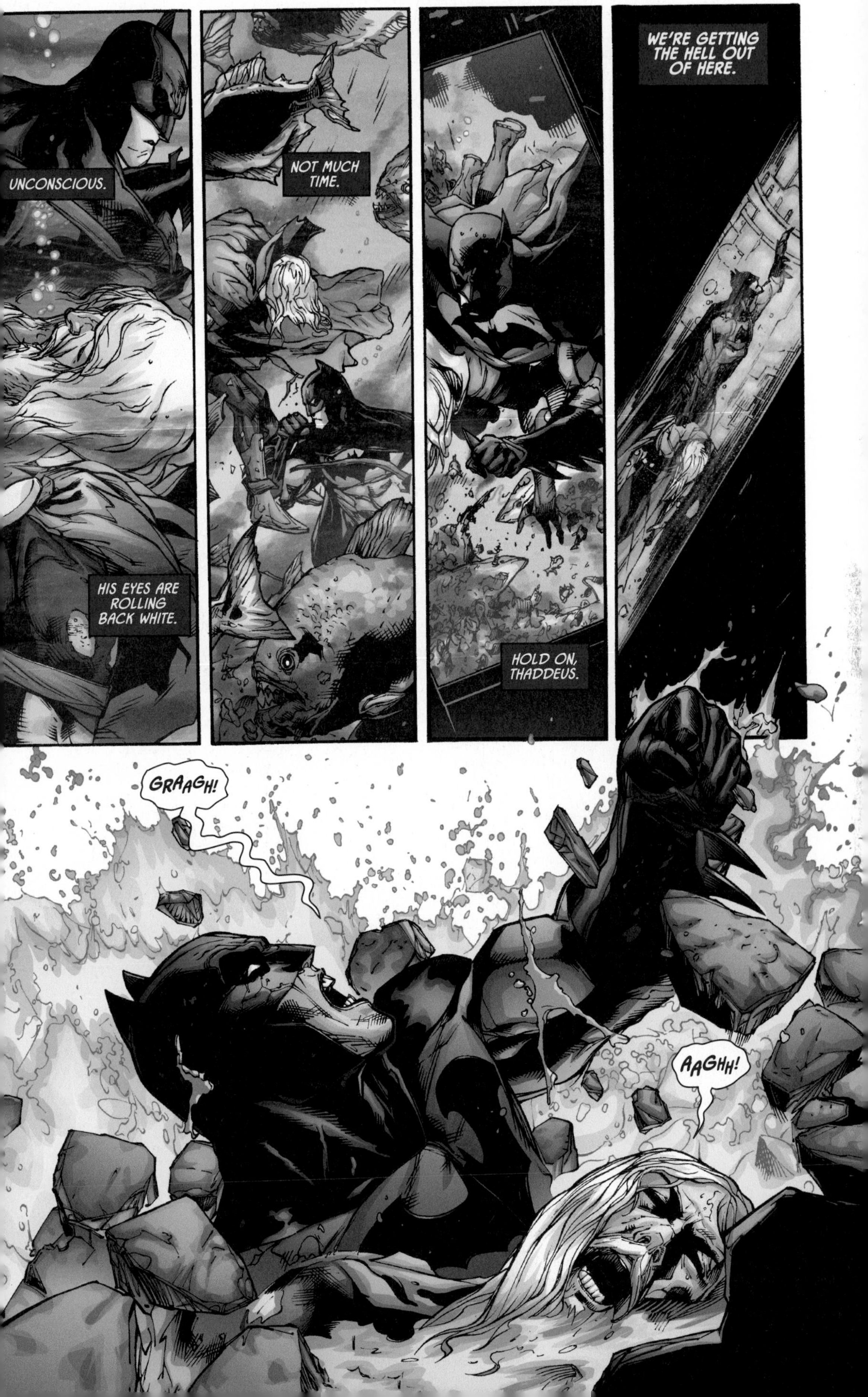
UNCONSCIOUS.
HIS EYES ARE ROLLING BACK WHITE.
NOT MUCH TIME.
HOLD ON, THADDEUS.
WE'RE GETTING THE HELL OUT OF HERE.
GRAAGH!
AAGHH!

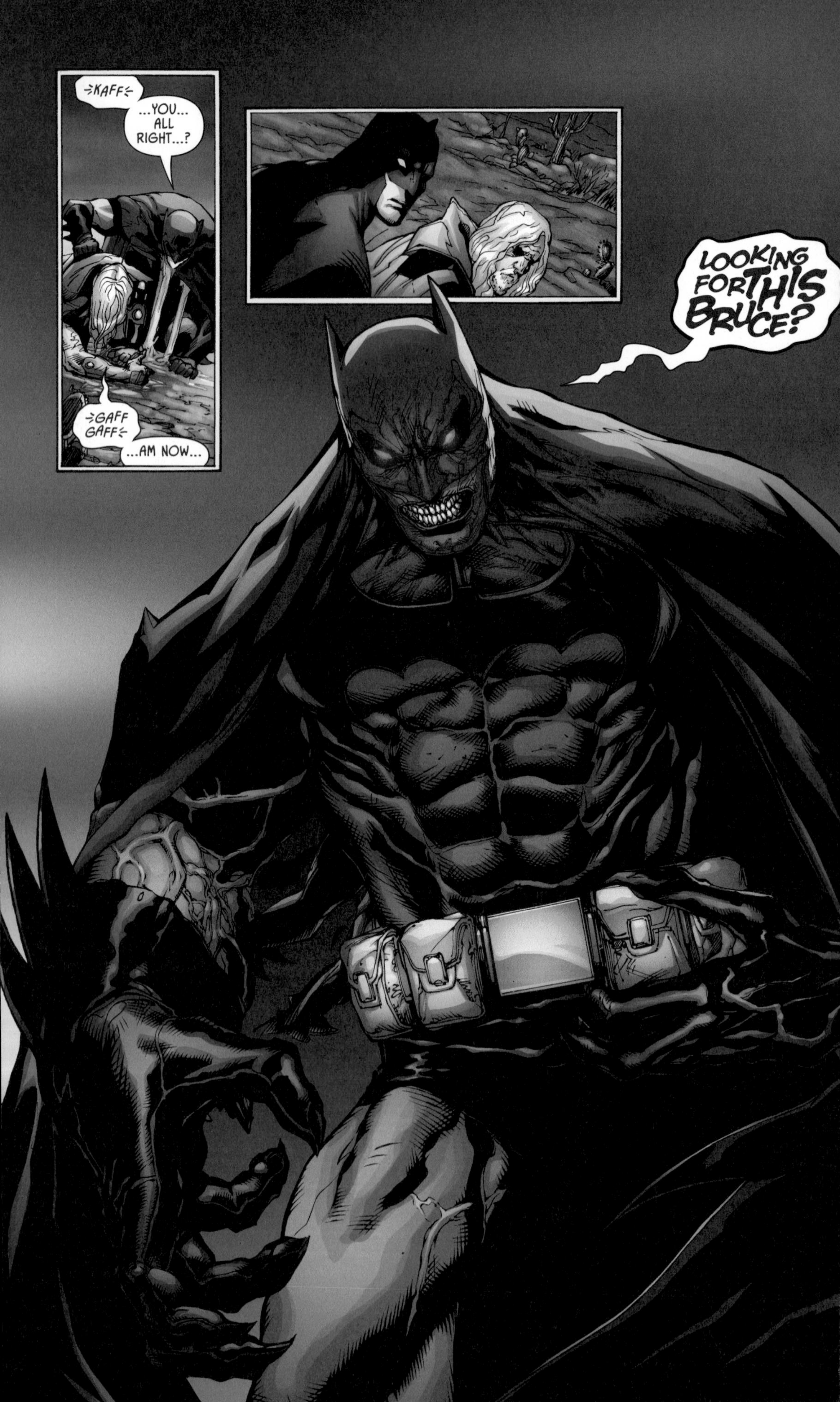

>KAFF<
...YOU... ALL RIGHT...?
>GAFF GAFF<
...AM NOW...
LOOKING FOR THIS BRUCE?

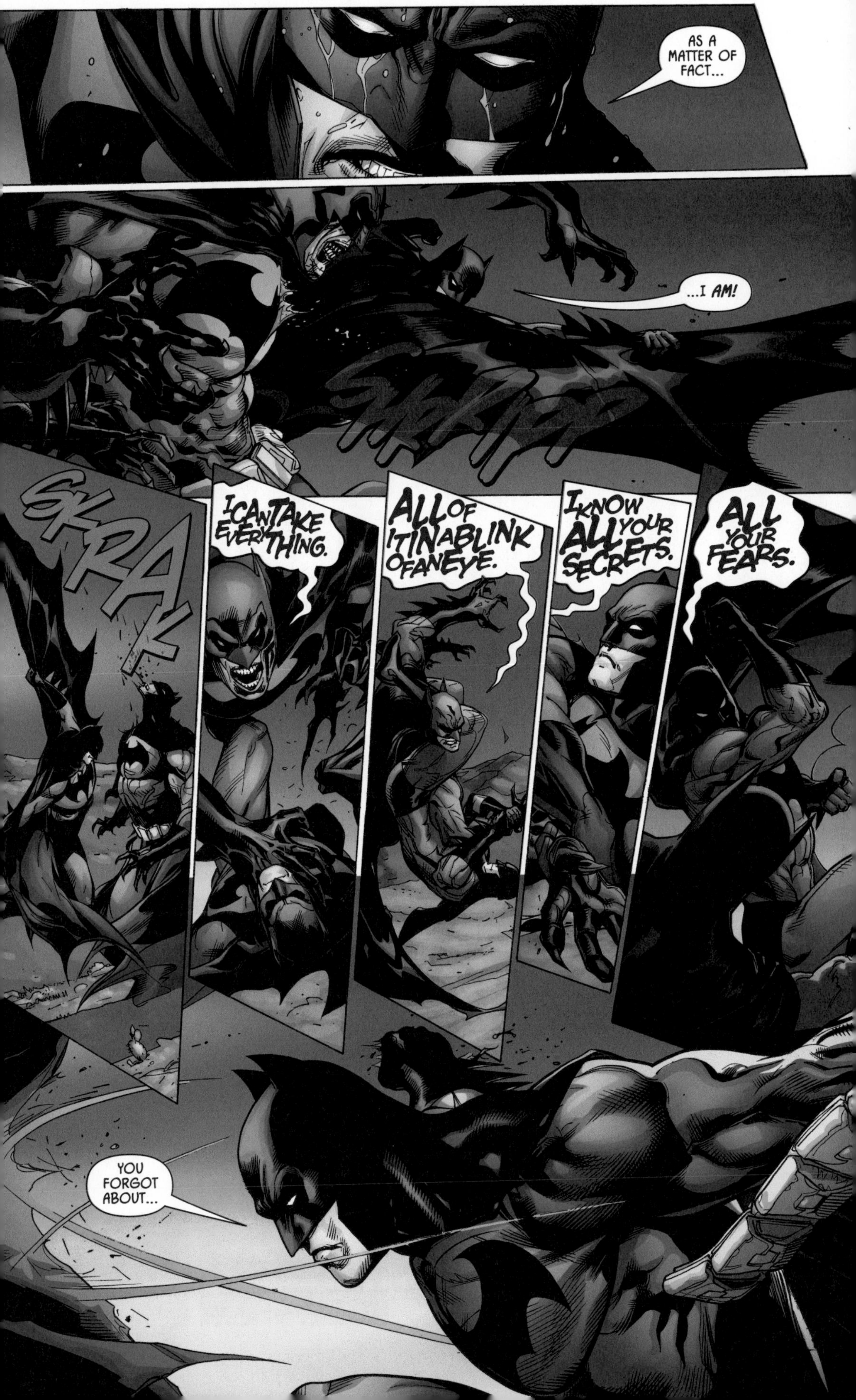

AS A MATTER OF FACT...
...I AM!
SKRAK
I CAN TAKE EVERYTHING.
ALL OF IT IN A BLINK OF AN EYE.
I KNOW ALL YOUR SECRETS.
ALL YOUR FEARS.
YOU FORGOT ABOUT...

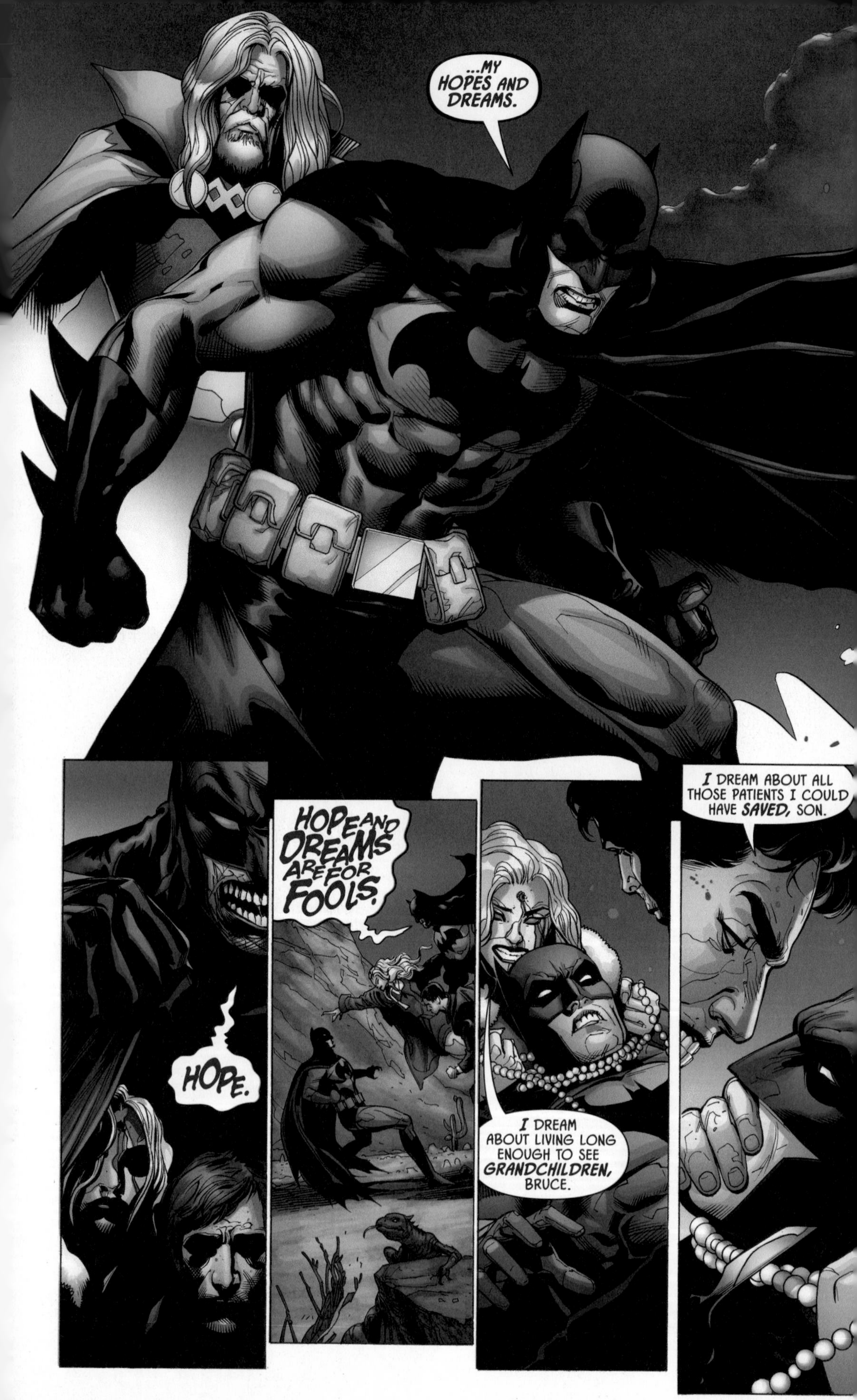
...MY HOPES AND DREAMS.
HOPE.
HOPE AND DREAMS ARE FOR FOOLS.
I DREAM ABOUT LIVING LONG ENOUGH TO SEE GRANDCHILDREN, BRUCE.
I DREAM ABOUT ALL THOSE PATIENTS I COULD HAVE SAVED, SON.

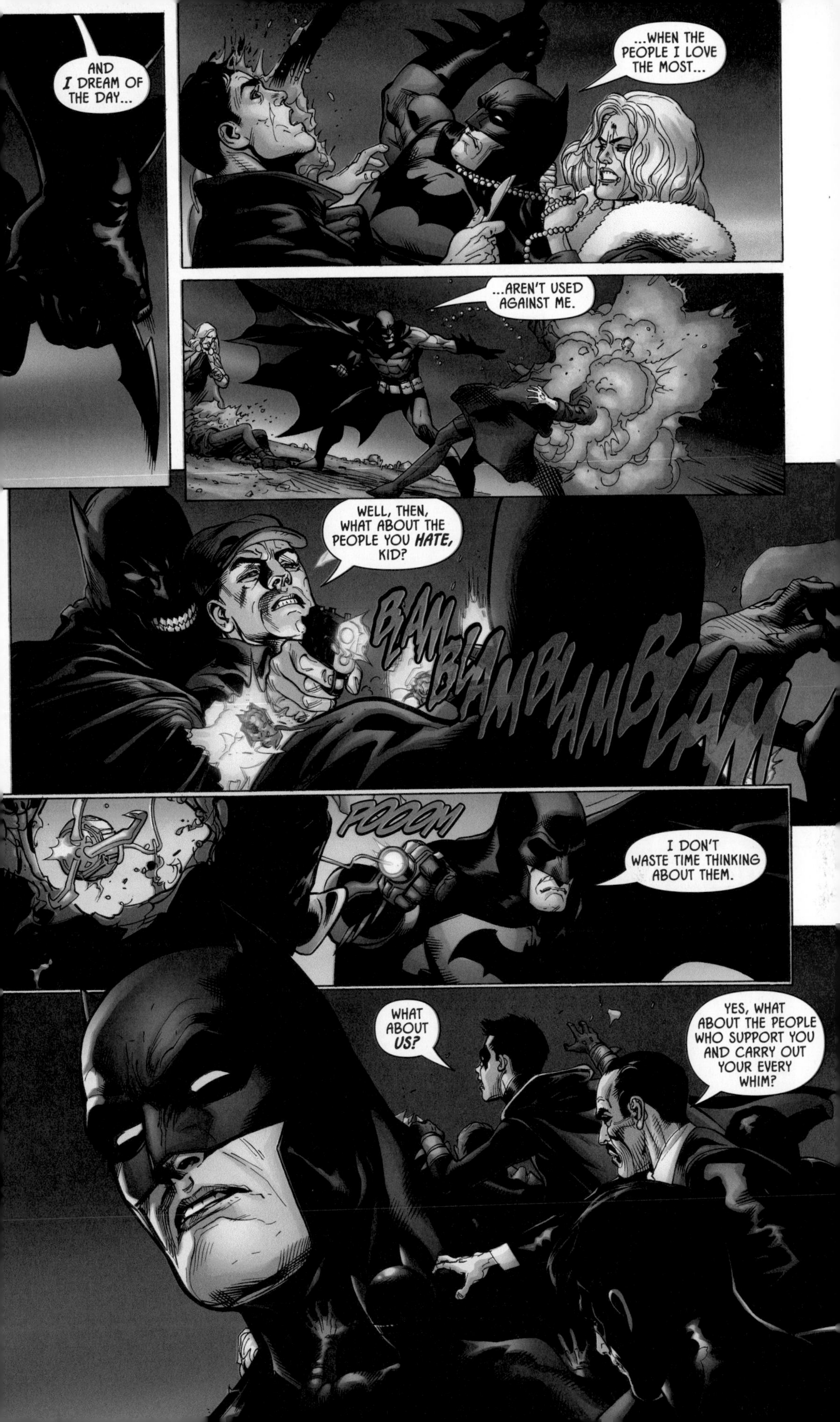
AND *I* DREAM OF THE DAY...
...WHEN THE PEOPLE I LOVE THE MOST...
...AREN'T USED AGAINST ME.
WELL, THEN, WHAT ABOUT THE PEOPLE YOU *HATE,* KID?
BLAM BLAM BLAM BLAM
FOOOM
I DON'T WASTE TIME THINKING ABOUT THEM.
WHAT ABOUT *US?*
YES, WHAT ABOUT THE PEOPLE WHO SUPPORT YOU AND CARRY OUT YOUR EVERY WHIM?

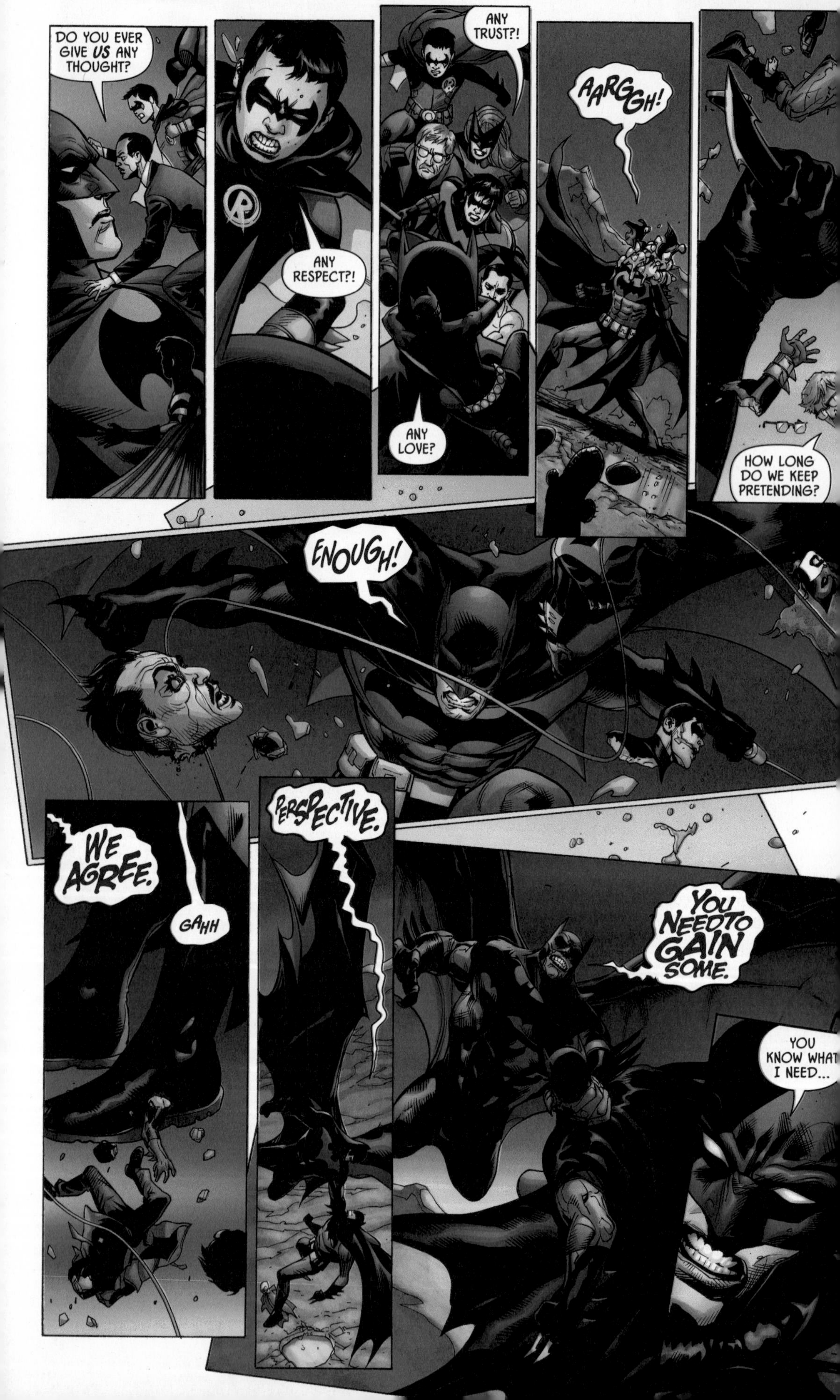
DO YOU EVER GIVE US ANY THOUGHT?
ANY RESPECT?!
ANY TRUST?!
ANY LOVE?
AARGGH!
HOW LONG DO WE KEEP PRETENDING?
ENOUGH!
WE AGREE.
GAHH
PERSPECTIVE.
YOU NEED TO GAIN SOME.
YOU KNOW WHAT I NEED...

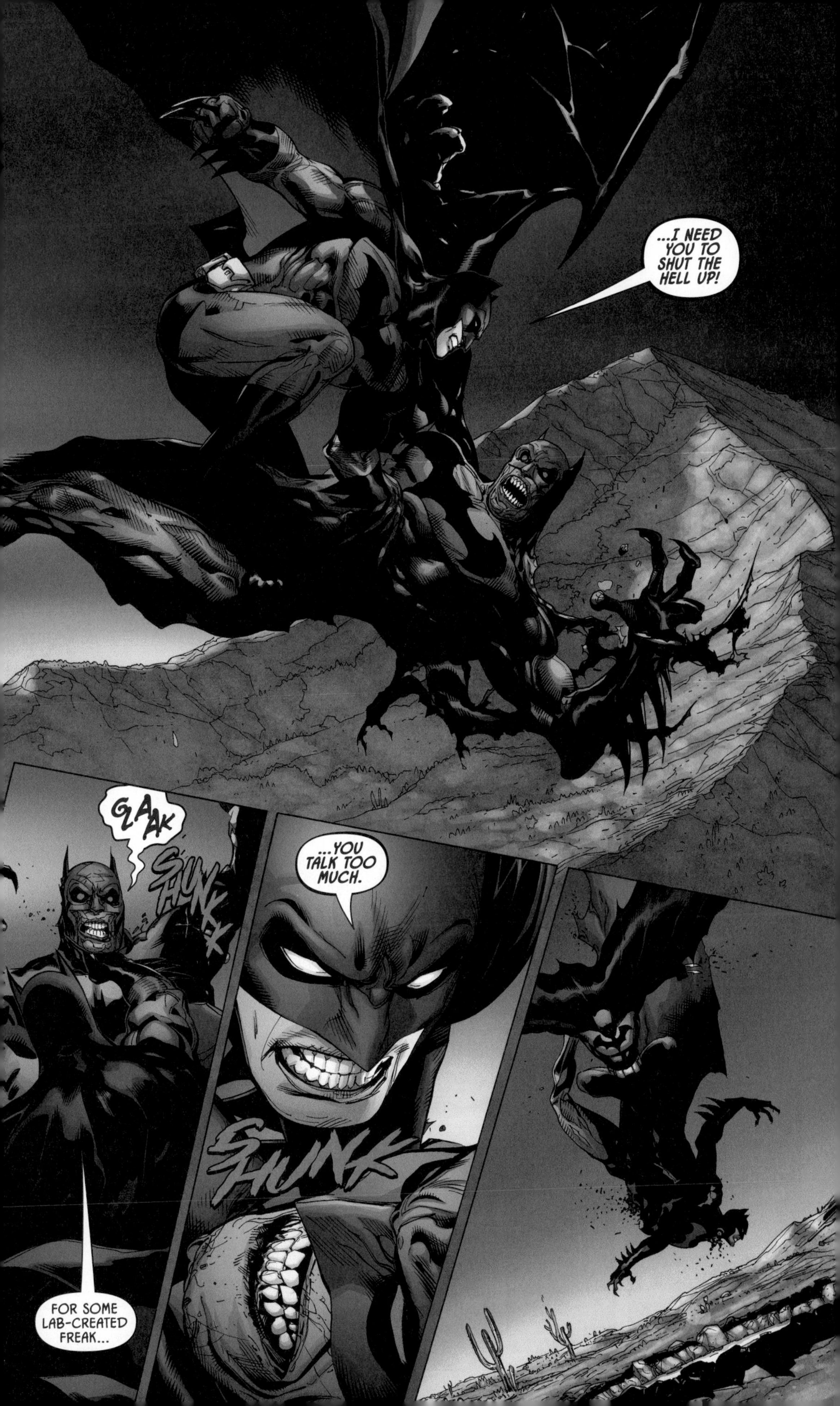

...I NEED YOU TO SHUT THE HELL UP!
GLAAK
SHUNK
FOR SOME LAB-CREATED FREAK...
...YOU TALK TOO MUCH.
SHUNK

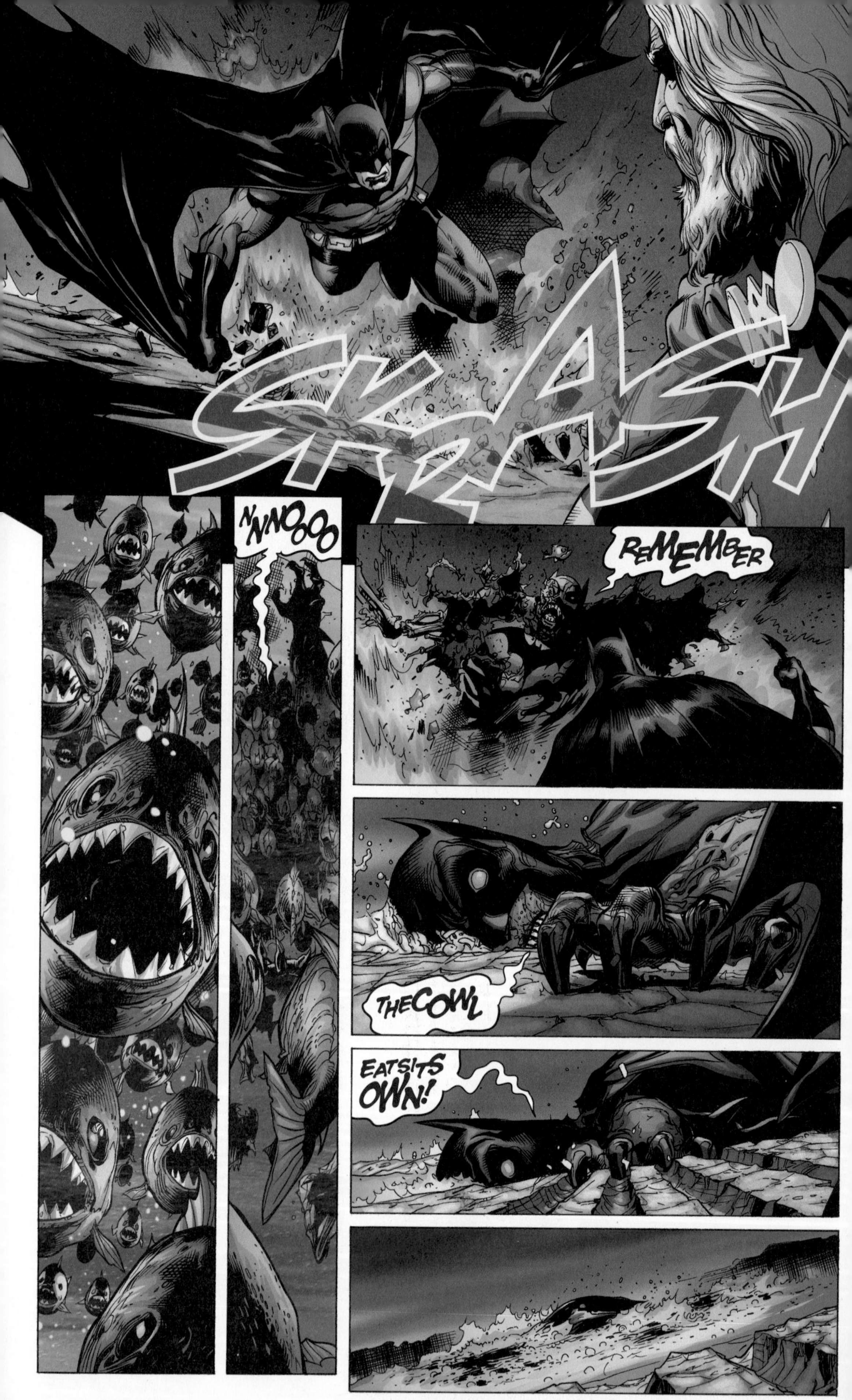
SKRASH
NNNOOOO
REMEMBER
THE COWL
EATS ITS OWN!

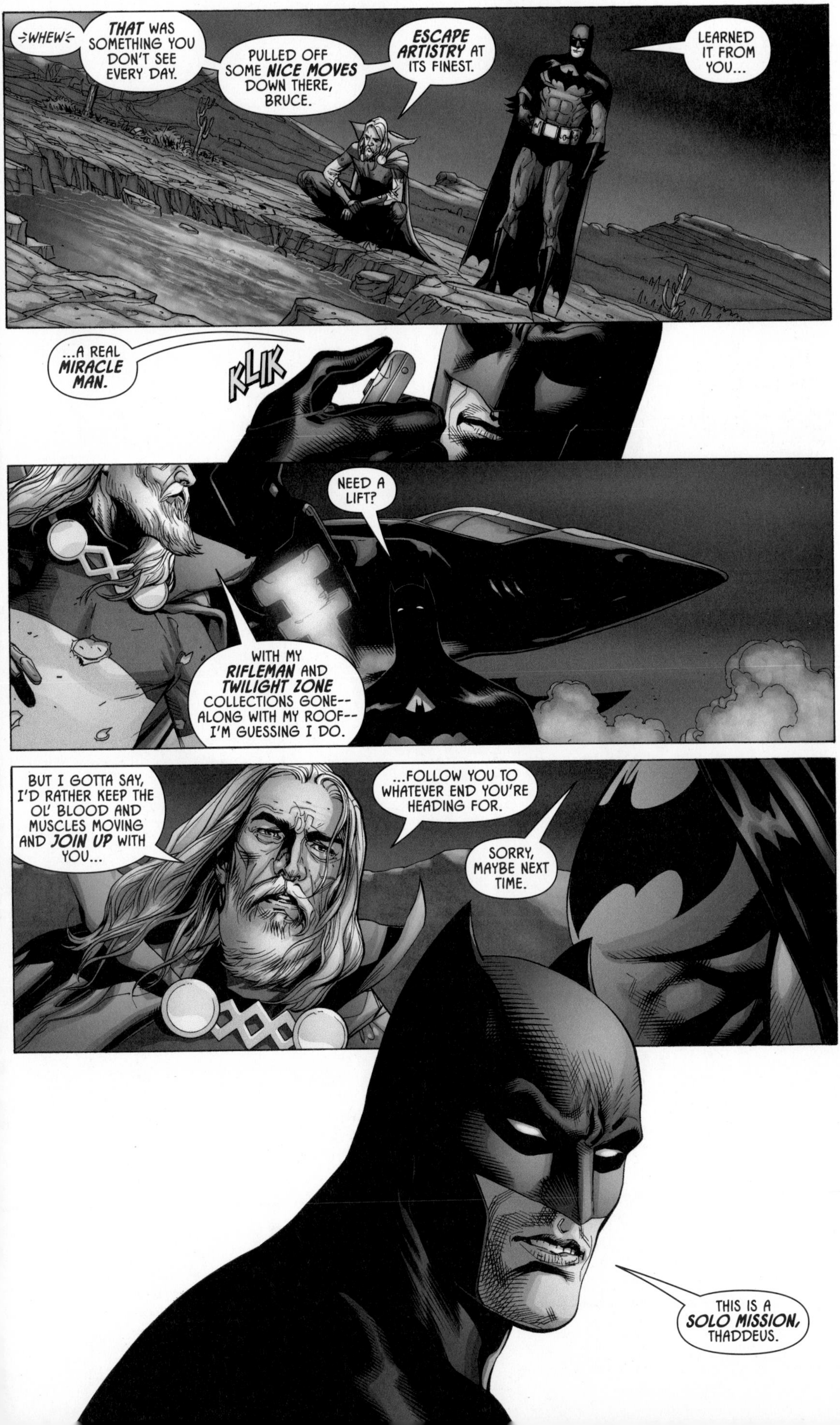
WHEW
THAT WAS SOMETHING YOU DON'T SEE EVERY DAY.
PULLED OFF SOME NICE MOVES DOWN THERE, BRUCE.
ESCAPE ARTISTRY AT ITS FINEST.
LEARNED IT FROM YOU...
...A REAL MIRACLE MAN.
KLIK
NEED A LIFT?
WITH MY RIFLEMAN AND TWILIGHT ZONE COLLECTIONS GONE-- ALONG WITH MY ROOF-- I'M GUESSING I DO.
BUT I GOTTA SAY, I'D RATHER KEEP THE OL' BLOOD AND MUSCLES MOVING AND JOIN UP WITH YOU...
...FOLLOW YOU TO WHATEVER END YOU'RE HEADING FOR.
SORRY, MAYBE NEXT TIME.
THIS IS A SOLO MISSION, THADDEUS.

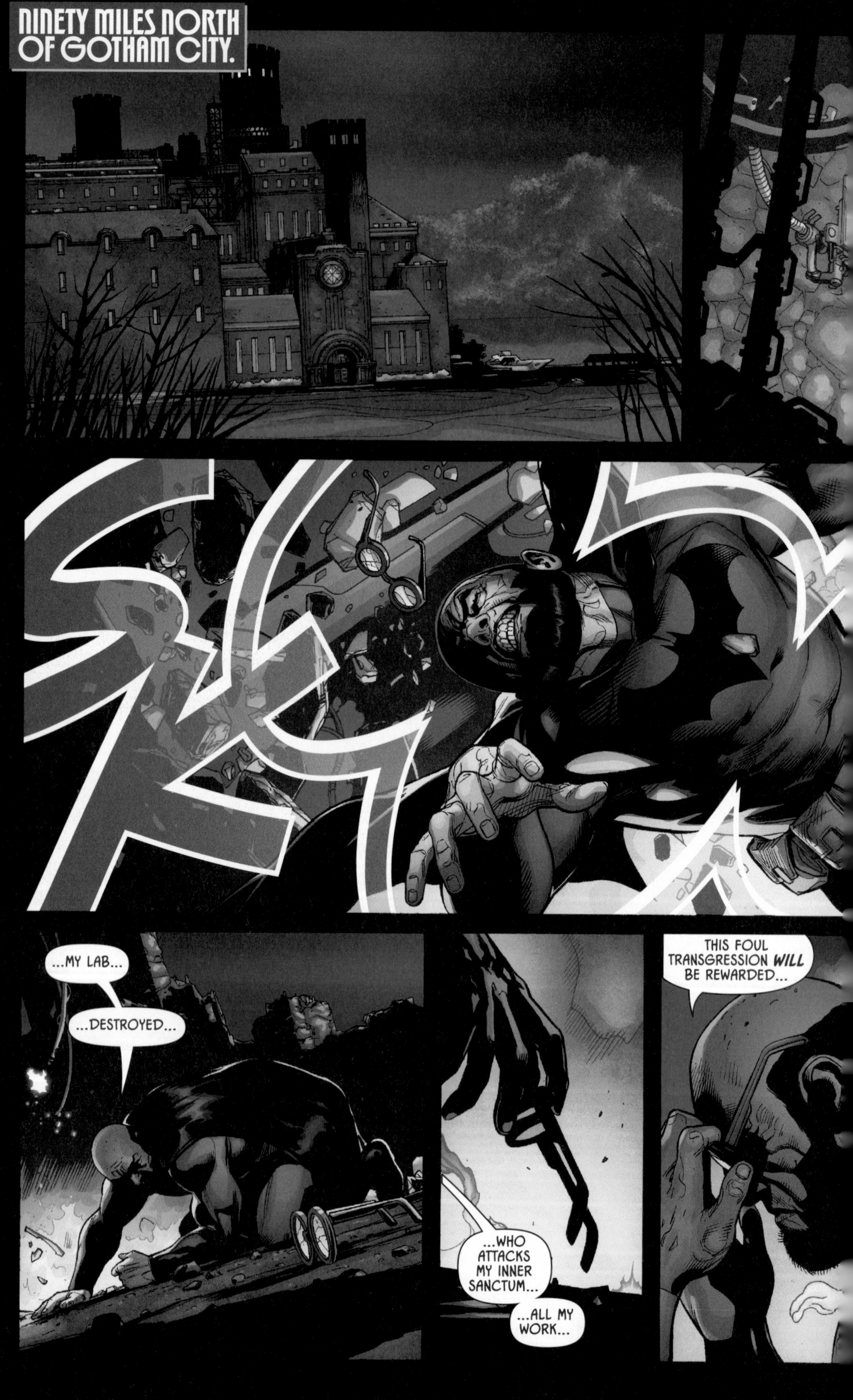
NINETY MILES NORTH OF GOTHAM CITY.
...MY LAB...
...DESTROYED...
...WHO ATTACKS MY INNER SANCTUM...
...ALL MY WORK...
THIS FOUL TRANSGRESSION WILL BE REWARDED...

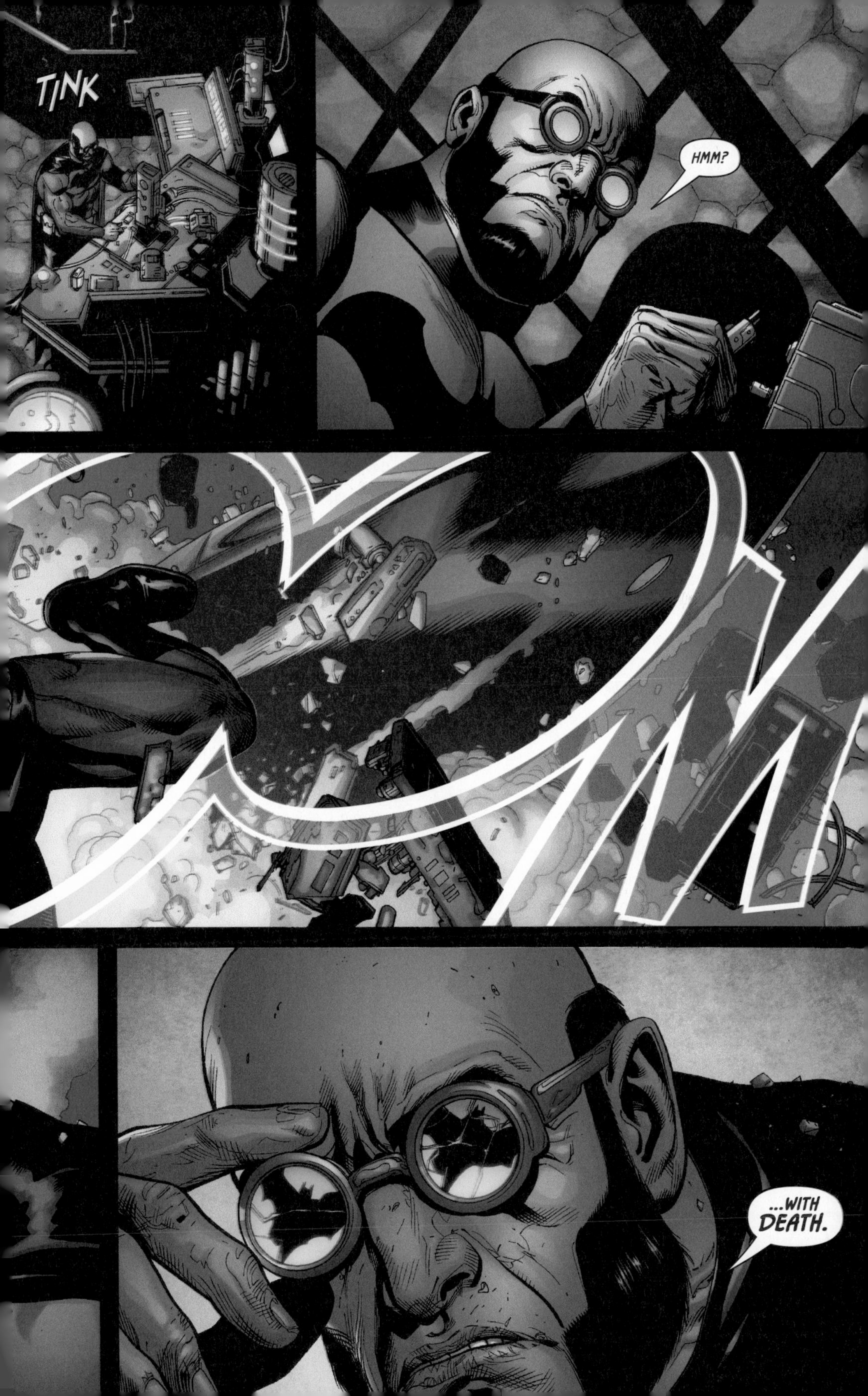
TINK
HMM?
...WITH DEATH.

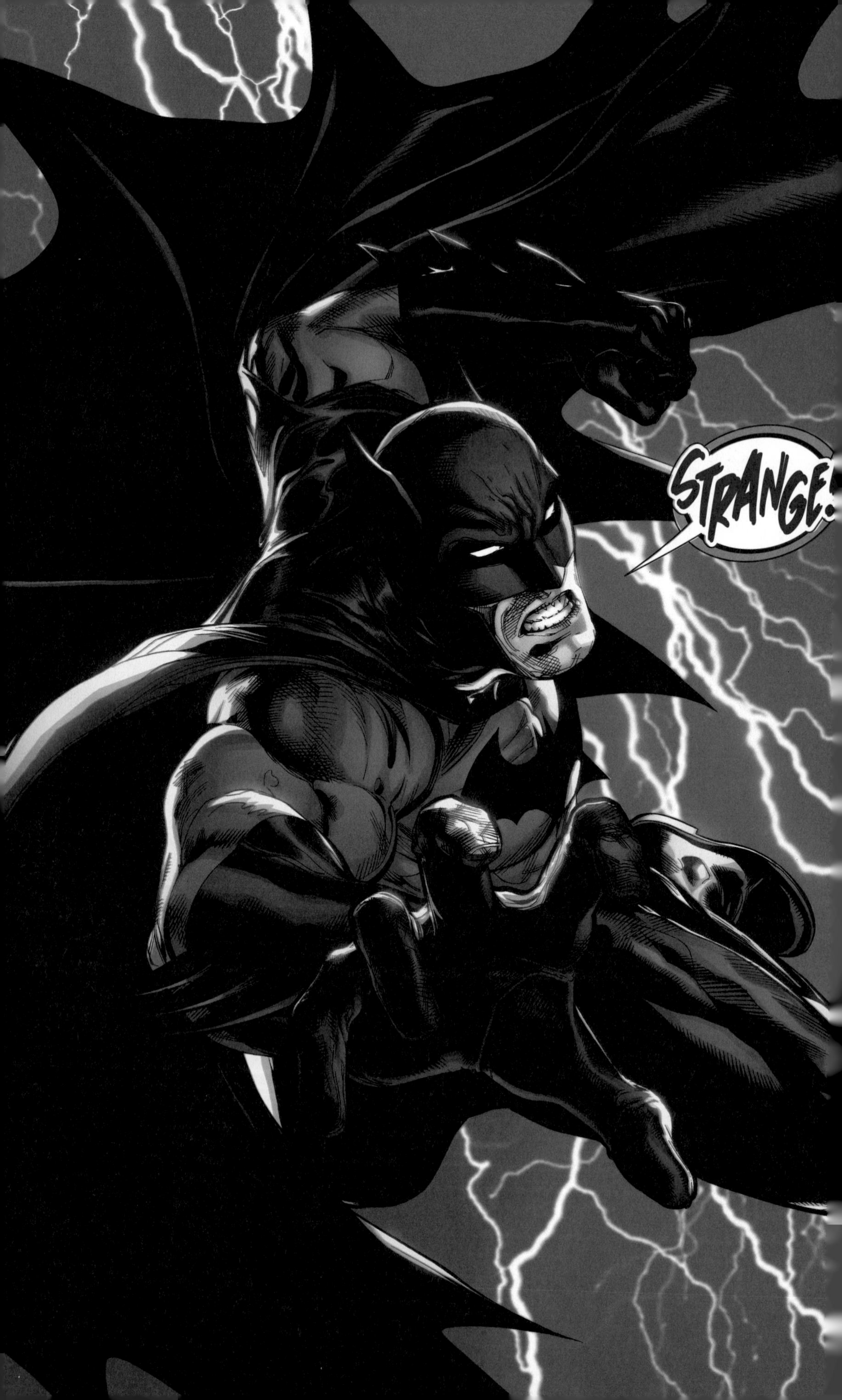
STRANGE!

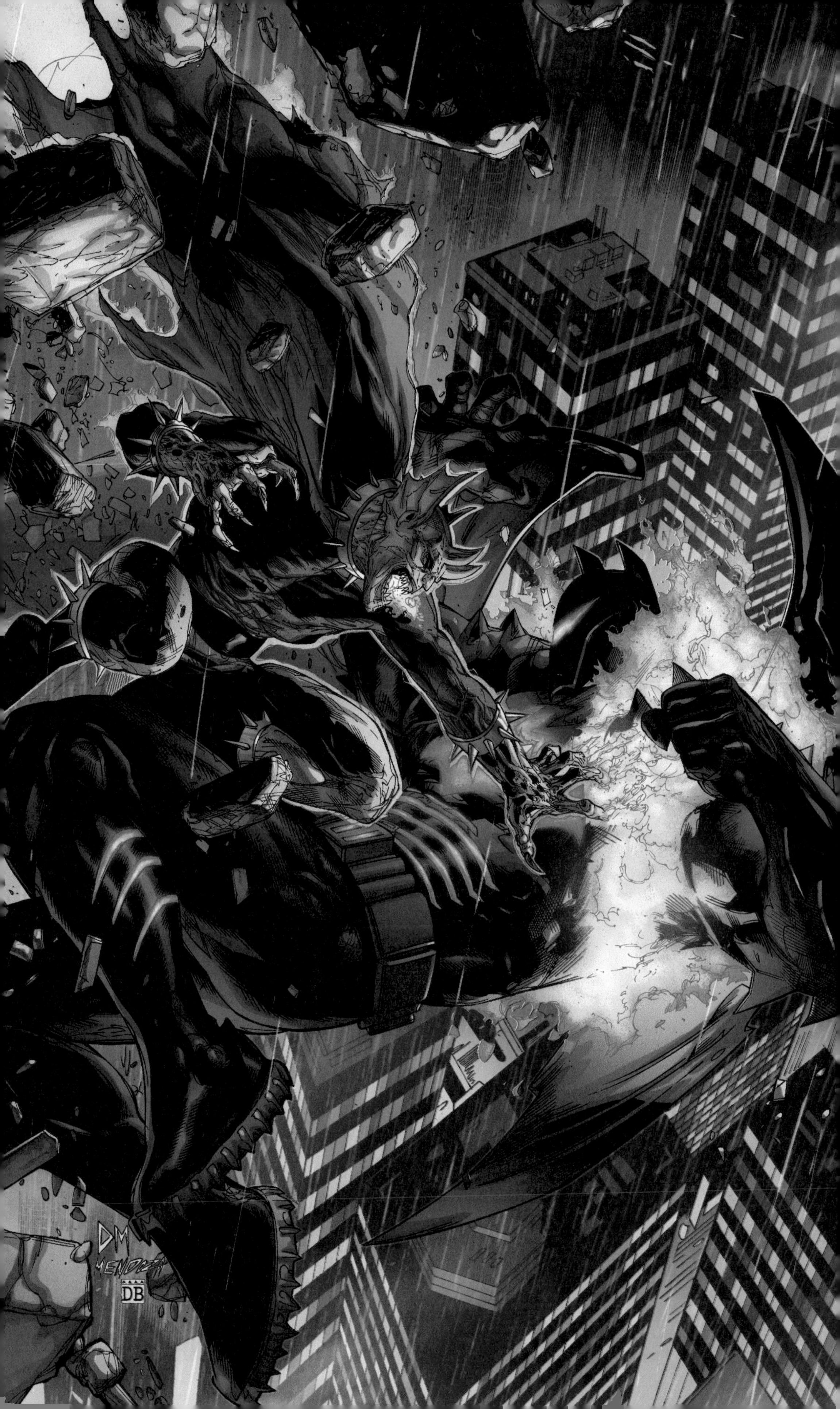
DM
MENDOZA
DB

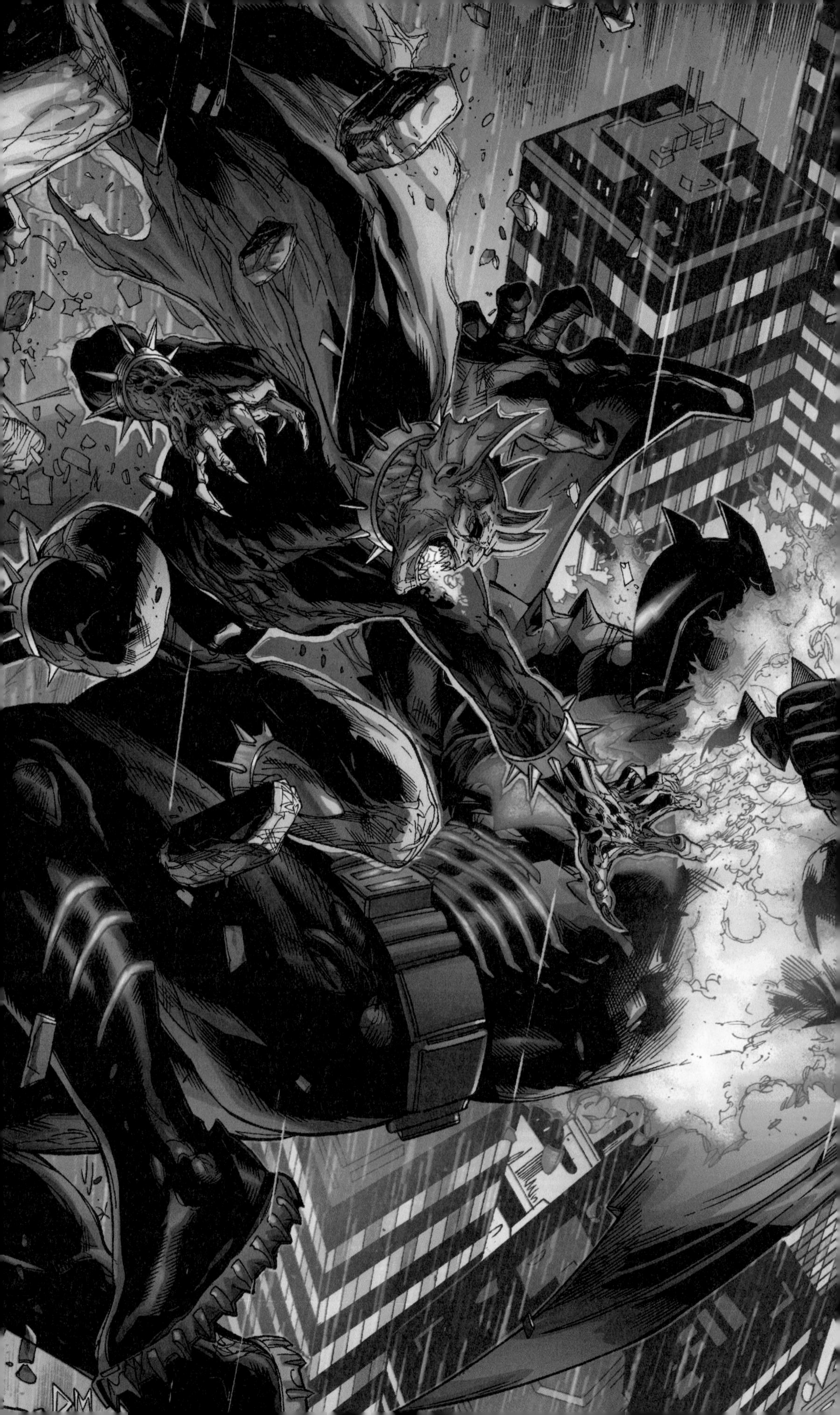

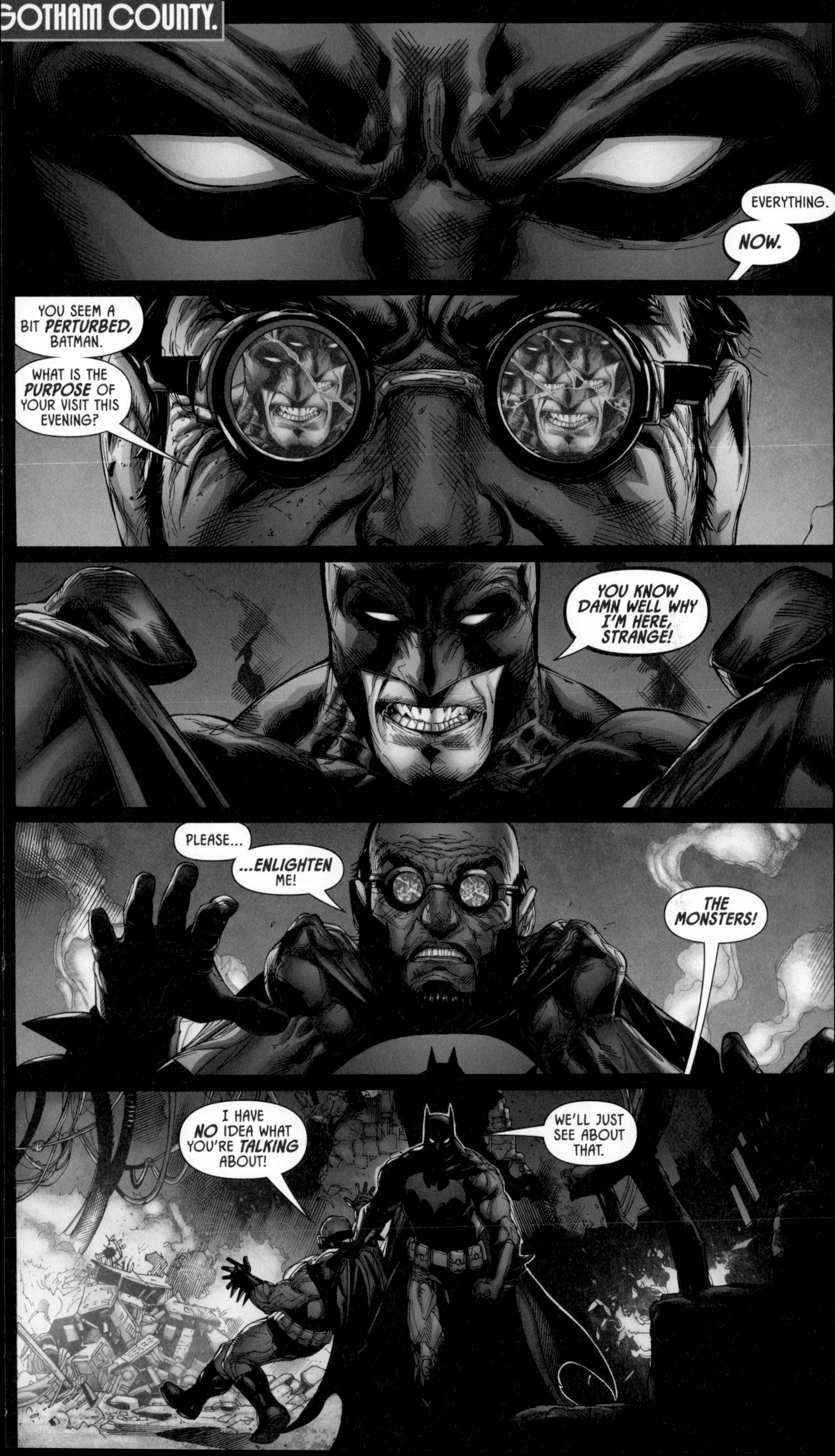

GOTHAM COUNTY.
EVERYTHING.
NOW.
YOU SEEM A BIT PERTURBED, BATMAN.
WHAT IS THE PURPOSE OF YOUR VISIT THIS EVENING?
YOU KNOW DAMN WELL WHY I'M HERE, STRANGE!
PLEASE...
...ENLIGHTEN ME!
THE MONSTERS!
I HAVE NO IDEA WHAT YOU'RE TALKING ABOUT!
WE'LL JUST SEE ABOUT THAT.

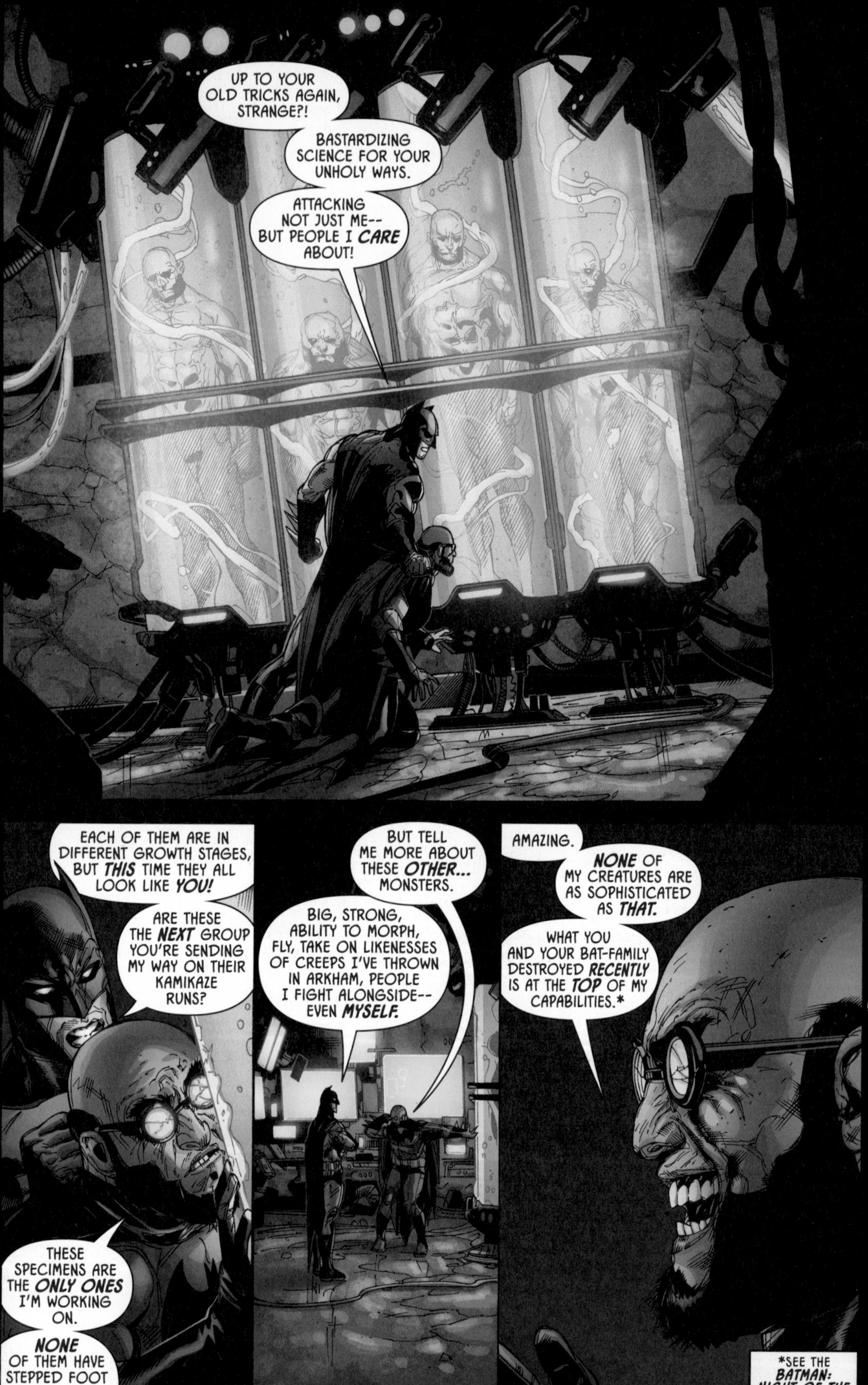
UP TO YOUR OLD TRICKS AGAIN, STRANGE?!
BASTARDIZING SCIENCE FOR YOUR UNHOLY WAYS.
ATTACKING NOT JUST ME-- BUT PEOPLE I CARE ABOUT!
EACH OF THEM ARE IN DIFFERENT GROWTH STAGES, BUT THIS TIME THEY ALL LOOK LIKE YOU!
ARE THESE THE NEXT GROUP YOU'RE SENDING MY WAY ON THEIR KAMIKAZE RUNS?
THESE SPECIMENS ARE THE ONLY ONES I'M WORKING ON.
NONE OF THEM HAVE STEPPED FOOT OFF THE GROUNDS.
BUT TELL ME MORE ABOUT THESE OTHER... MONSTERS.
BIG, STRONG, ABILITY TO MORPH, FLY, TAKE ON LIKENESSES OF CREEPS I'VE THROWN IN ARKHAM, PEOPLE I FIGHT ALONGSIDE-- EVEN MYSELF.
AMAZING.
NONE OF MY CREATURES ARE AS SOPHISTICATED AS THAT.
WHAT YOU AND YOUR BAT-FAMILY DESTROYED RECENTLY IS AT THE TOP OF MY CAPABILITIES.*
*SEE THE BATMAN: NIGHT OF THE MONSTER MEN TPB! --CHRIS

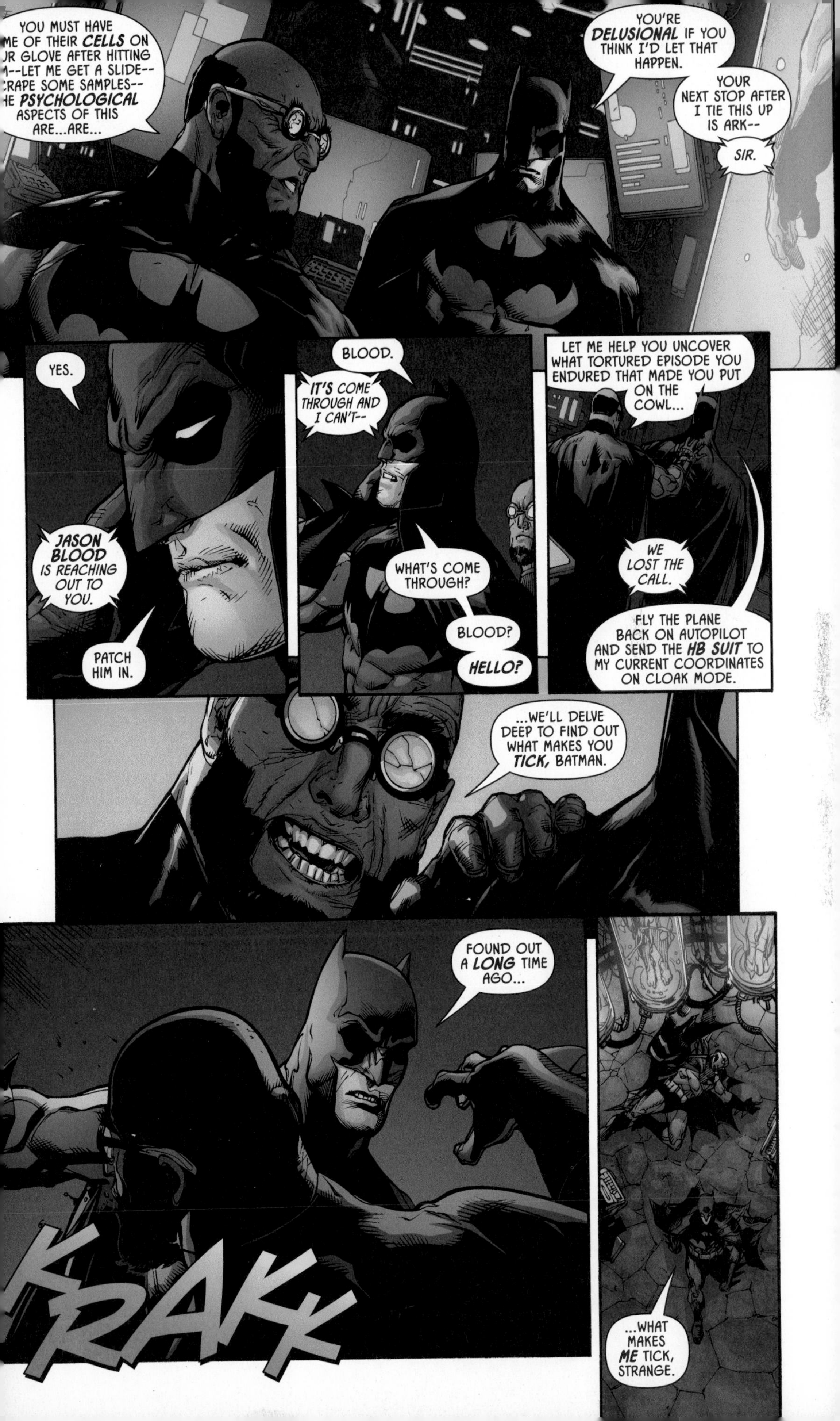
YOU MUST HAVE ME OF THEIR CELLS ON UR GLOVE AFTER HITTING M--LET ME GET A SLIDE-- RAPE SOME SAMPLES-- HE PSYCHOLOGICAL ASPECTS OF THIS ARE...ARE...
YOU'RE DELUSIONAL IF YOU THINK I'D LET THAT HAPPEN.
YOUR NEXT STOP AFTER I TIE THIS UP IS ARK--
SIR.
YES.
JASON BLOOD IS REACHING OUT TO YOU.
PATCH HIM IN.
BLOOD.
IT'S COME THROUGH AND I CAN'T--
WHAT'S COME THROUGH?
BLOOD?
HELLO?
LET ME HELP YOU UNCOVER WHAT TORTURED EPISODE YOU ENDURED THAT MADE YOU PUT ON THE COWL...
WE LOST THE CALL.
FLY THE PLANE BACK ON AUTOPILOT AND SEND THE HB SUIT TO MY CURRENT COORDINATES ON CLOAK MODE.
...WE'LL DELVE DEEP TO FIND OUT WHAT MAKES YOU TICK, BATMAN.
FOUND OUT A LONG TIME AGO...
KRAKK
...WHAT MAKES ME TICK, STRANGE.

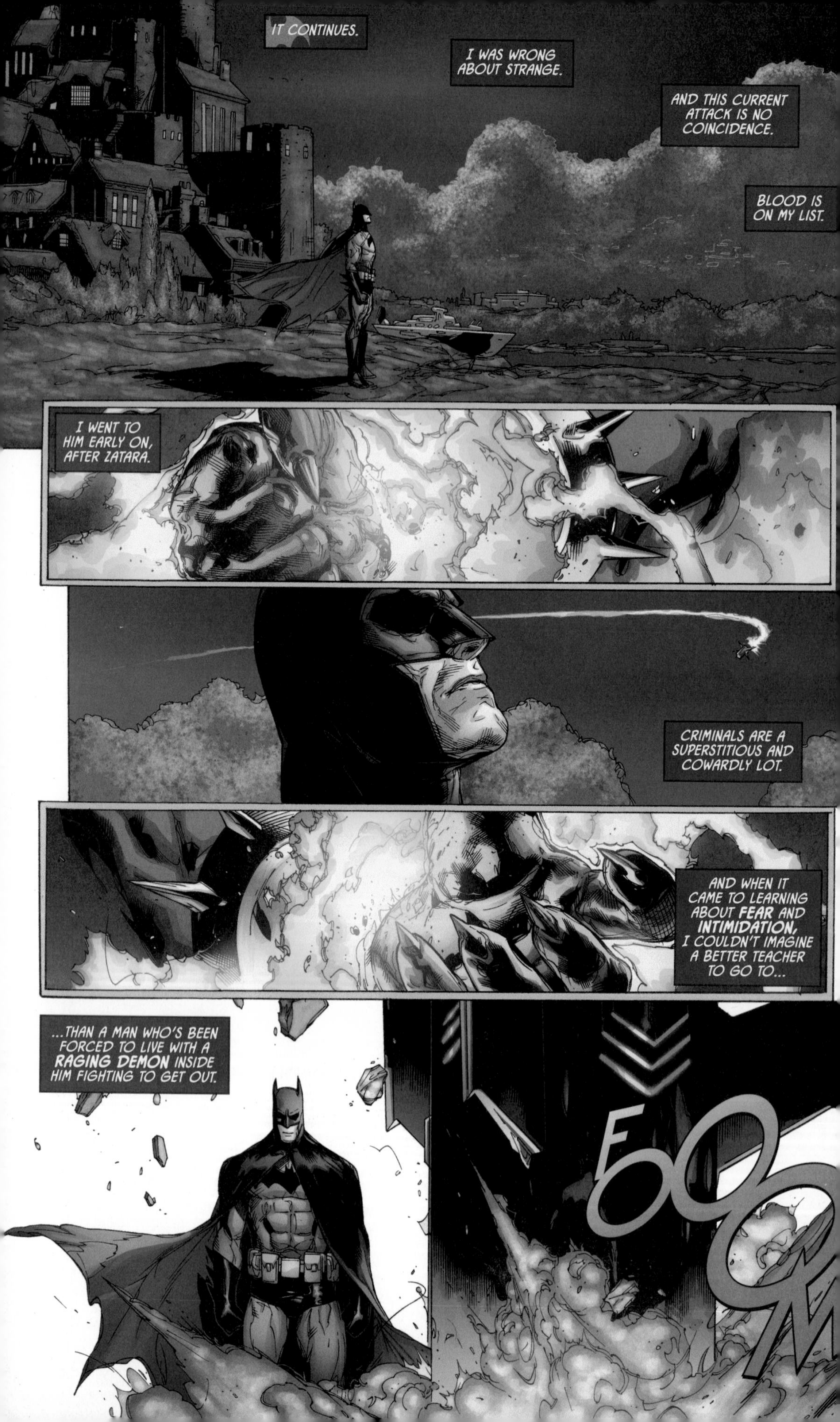
IT CONTINUES.
I WAS WRONG ABOUT STRANGE.
AND THIS CURRENT ATTACK IS NO COINCIDENCE.
BLOOD IS ON MY LIST.
I WENT TO HIM EARLY ON, AFTER ZATARA.
CRIMINALS ARE A SUPERSTITIOUS AND COWARDLY LOT.
AND WHEN IT CAME TO LEARNING ABOUT **FEAR** AND **INTIMIDATION,** I COULDN'T IMAGINE A BETTER TEACHER TO GO TO...
...THAN A MAN WHO'S BEEN FORCED TO LIVE WITH A **RAGING DEMON** INSIDE HIM FIGHTING TO GET OUT.
FOOOM

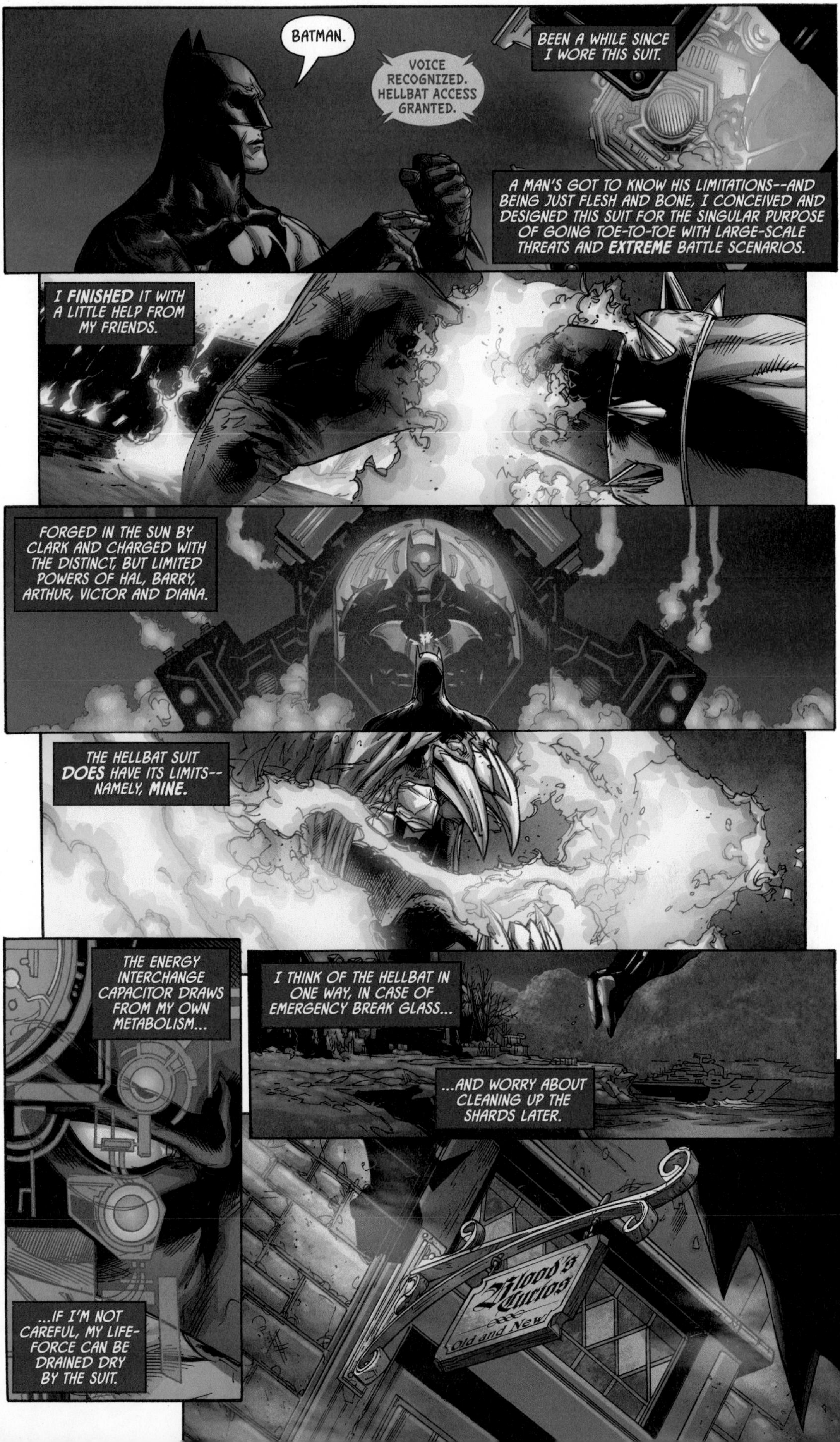

BATMAN.
VOICE RECOGNIZED. HELLBAT ACCESS GRANTED.
BEEN A WHILE SINCE I WORE THIS SUIT.
A MAN'S GOT TO KNOW HIS LIMITATIONS--AND BEING JUST FLESH AND BONE, I CONCEIVED AND DESIGNED THIS SUIT FOR THE SINGULAR PURPOSE OF GOING TOE-TO-TOE WITH LARGE-SCALE THREATS AND **EXTREME** BATTLE SCENARIOS.
I **FINISHED** IT WITH A LITTLE HELP FROM MY FRIENDS.
FORGED IN THE SUN BY CLARK AND CHARGED WITH THE DISTINCT, BUT LIMITED POWERS OF HAL, BARRY, ARTHUR, VICTOR AND DIANA.
THE HELLBAT SUIT **DOES** HAVE ITS LIMITS--NAMELY, **MINE.**
THE ENERGY INTERCHANGE CAPACITOR DRAWS FROM MY OWN METABOLISM...
I THINK OF THE HELLBAT IN ONE WAY, IN CASE OF EMERGENCY BREAK GLASS...
...AND WORRY ABOUT CLEANING UP THE SHARDS LATER.
...IF I'M NOT CAREFUL, MY LIFE-FORCE CAN BE DRAINED DRY BY THE SUIT.
Blood's Curios
Old and New

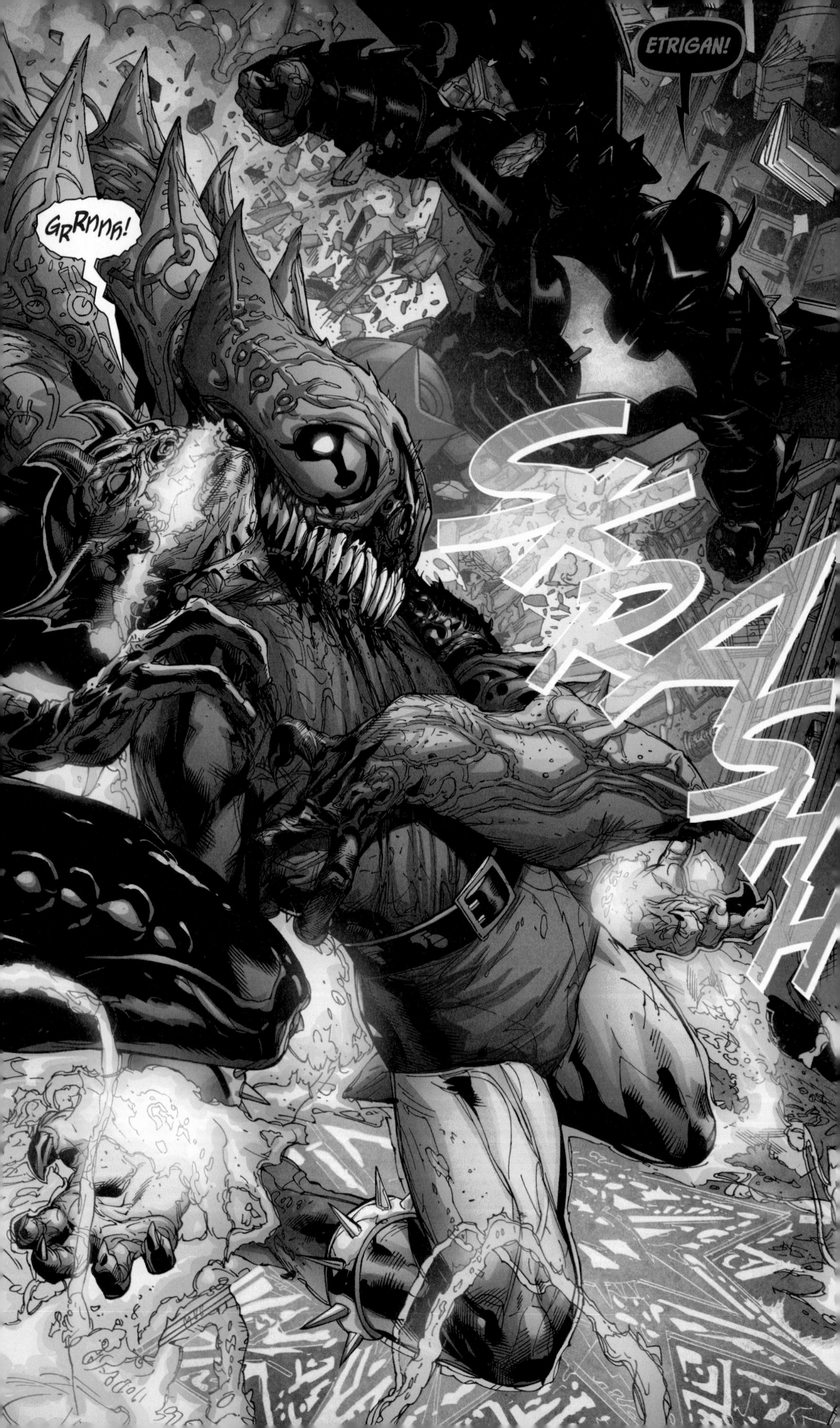
ETRIGAN!
GRRNNA!
SKRASSH

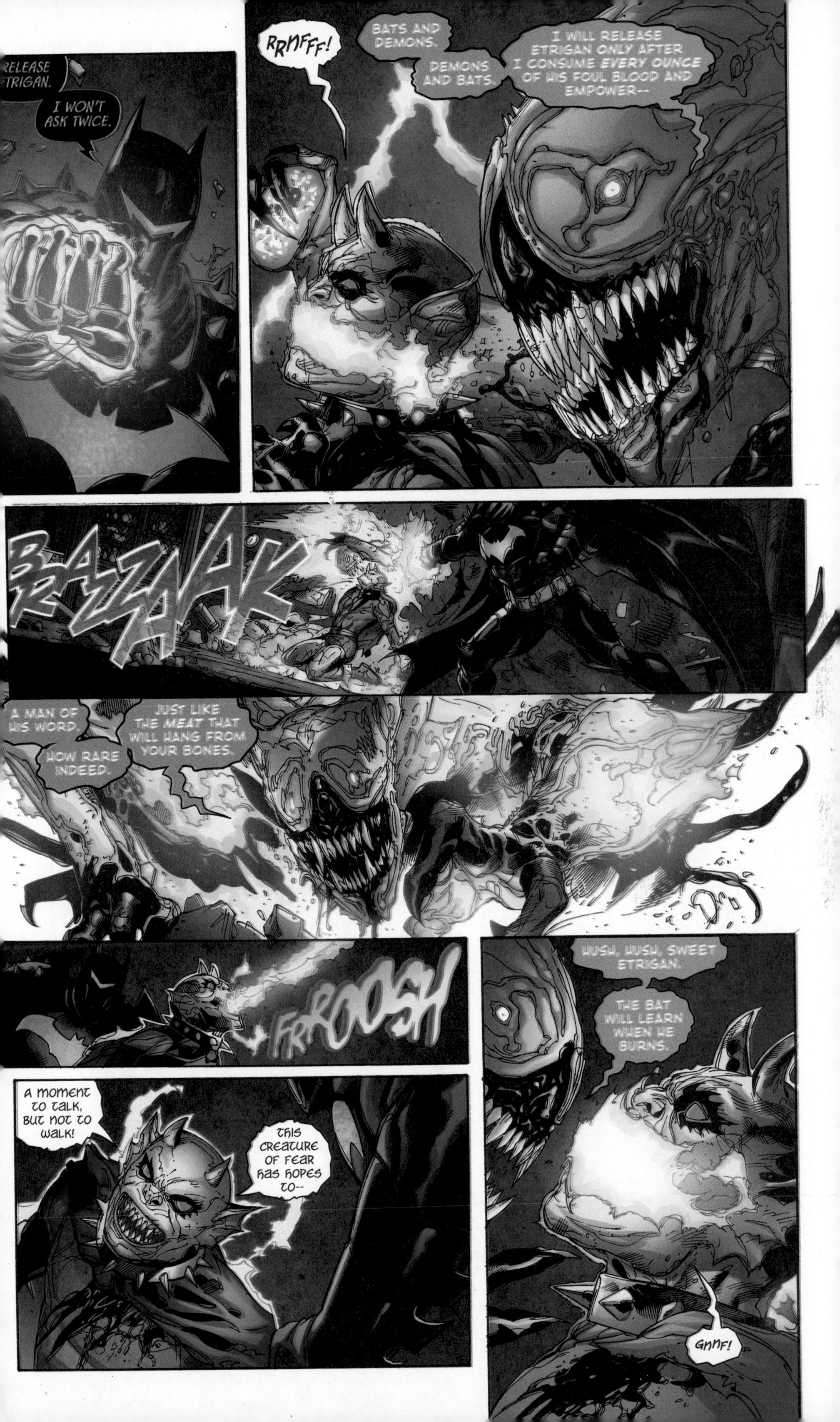

RELEASE ETRIGAN.
I WON'T ASK TWICE.
RRNFFF!
BATS AND DEMONS.
DEMONS AND BATS.
I WILL RELEASE ETRIGAN ONLY AFTER I CONSUME *EVERY OUNCE* OF HIS FOUL BLOOD AND EMPOWER--
BRAZZAK
A MAN OF HIS WORD.
HOW RARE INDEED.
JUST LIKE THE *MEAT* THAT WILL HANG FROM YOUR BONES.
FFRROOSH
HUSH, HUSH, SWEET ETRIGAN.
THE BAT WILL LEARN WHEN HE BURNS.
A MOMENT TO TALK, BUT NOT TO WALK!
THIS CREATURE OF FEAR HAS HOPES TO--
GNNF!

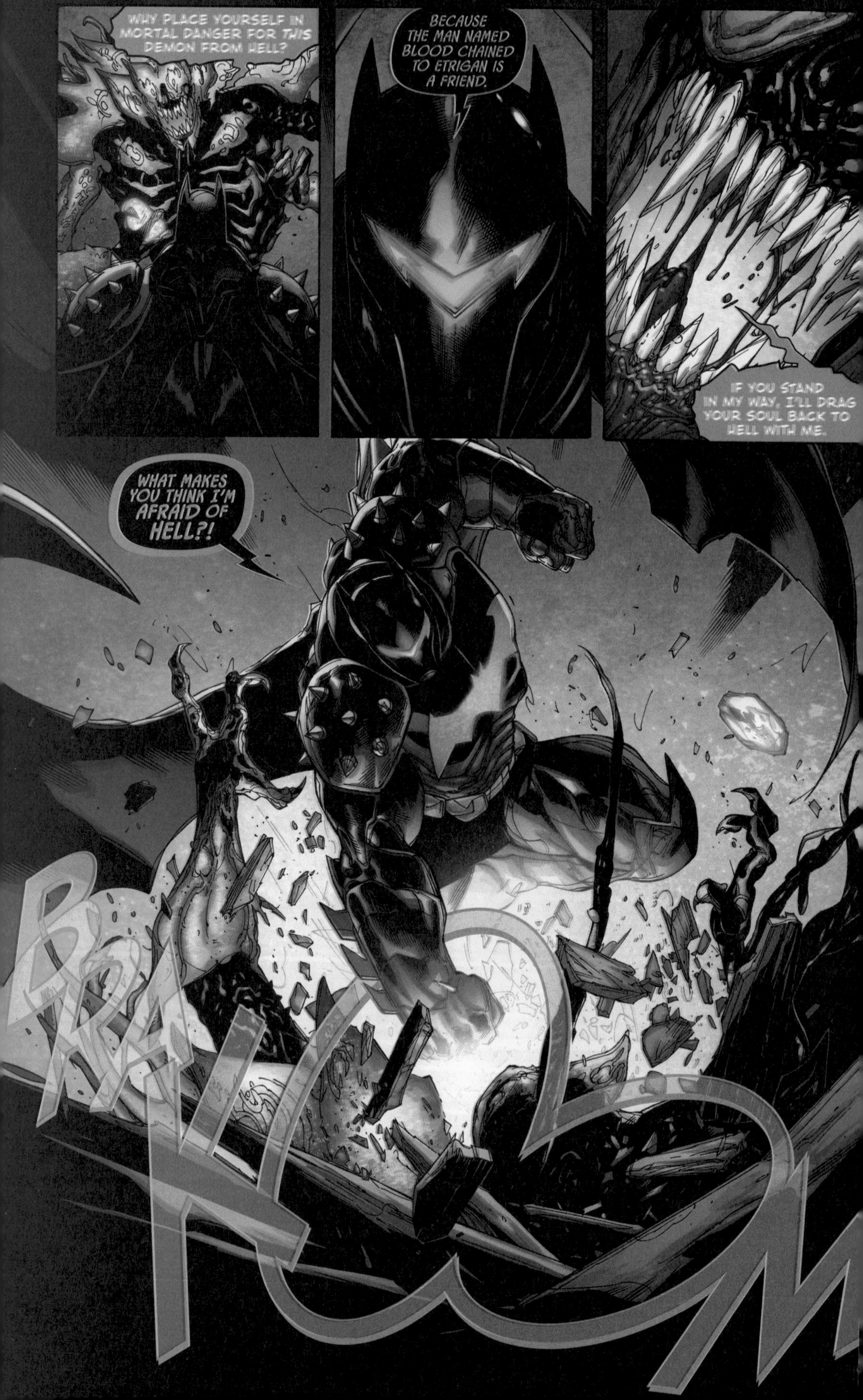
WHY PLACE YOURSELF IN MORTAL DANGER FOR THIS DEMON FROM HELL?
BECAUSE THE MAN NAMED BLOOD CHAINED TO ETRIGAN IS A FRIEND.
IF YOU STAND IN MY WAY, I'LL DRAG YOUR SOUL BACK TO HELL WITH ME.
WHAT MAKES YOU THINK I'M AFRAID OF HELL?!

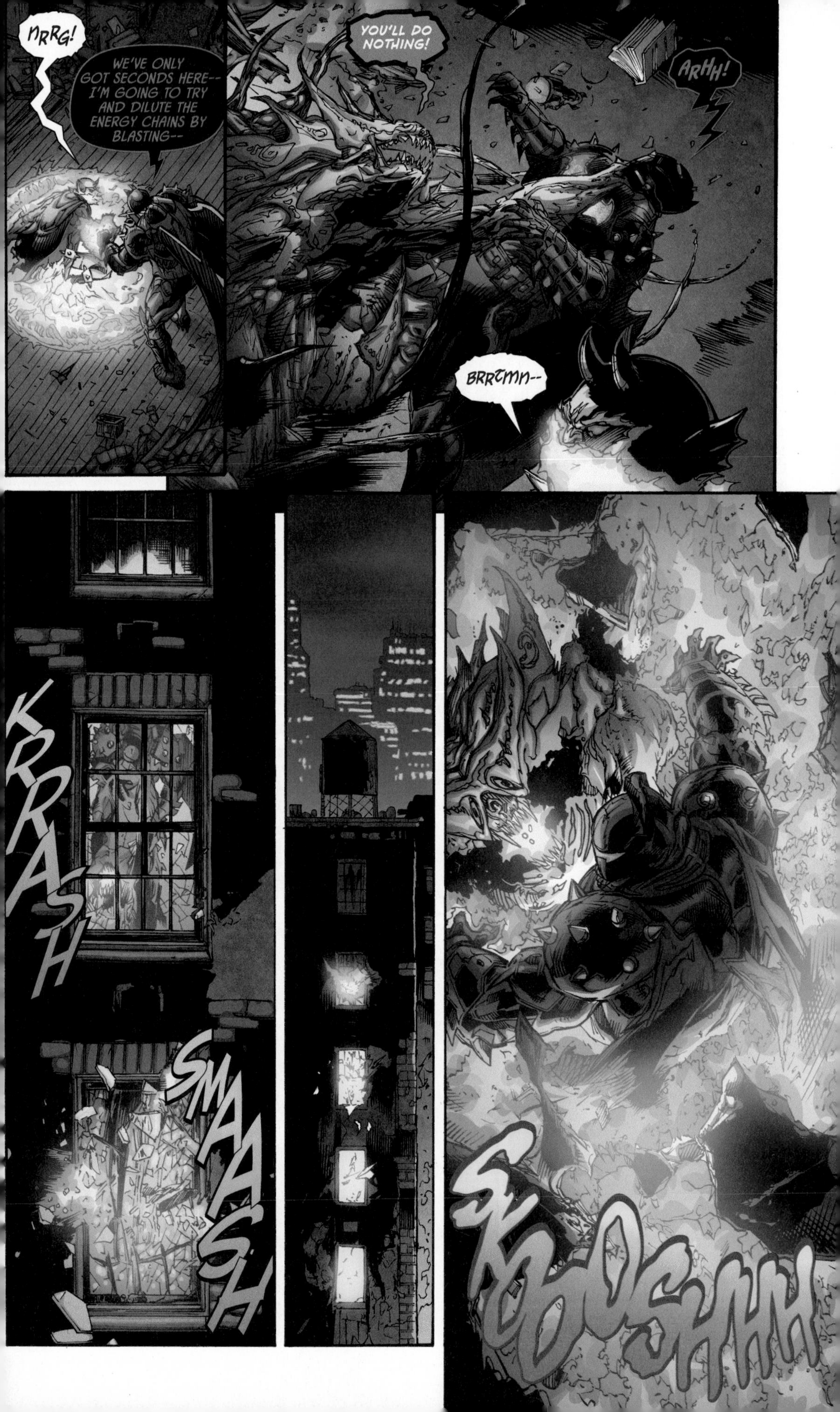
NRRG!
WE'VE ONLY GOT SECONDS HERE-- I'M GOING TO TRY AND DILUTE THE ENERGY CHAINS BY BLASTING--
YOU'LL DO NOTHING!
ARHH!
BRRTMN--
KRRASH
SMAAASH
SKOOSHHH

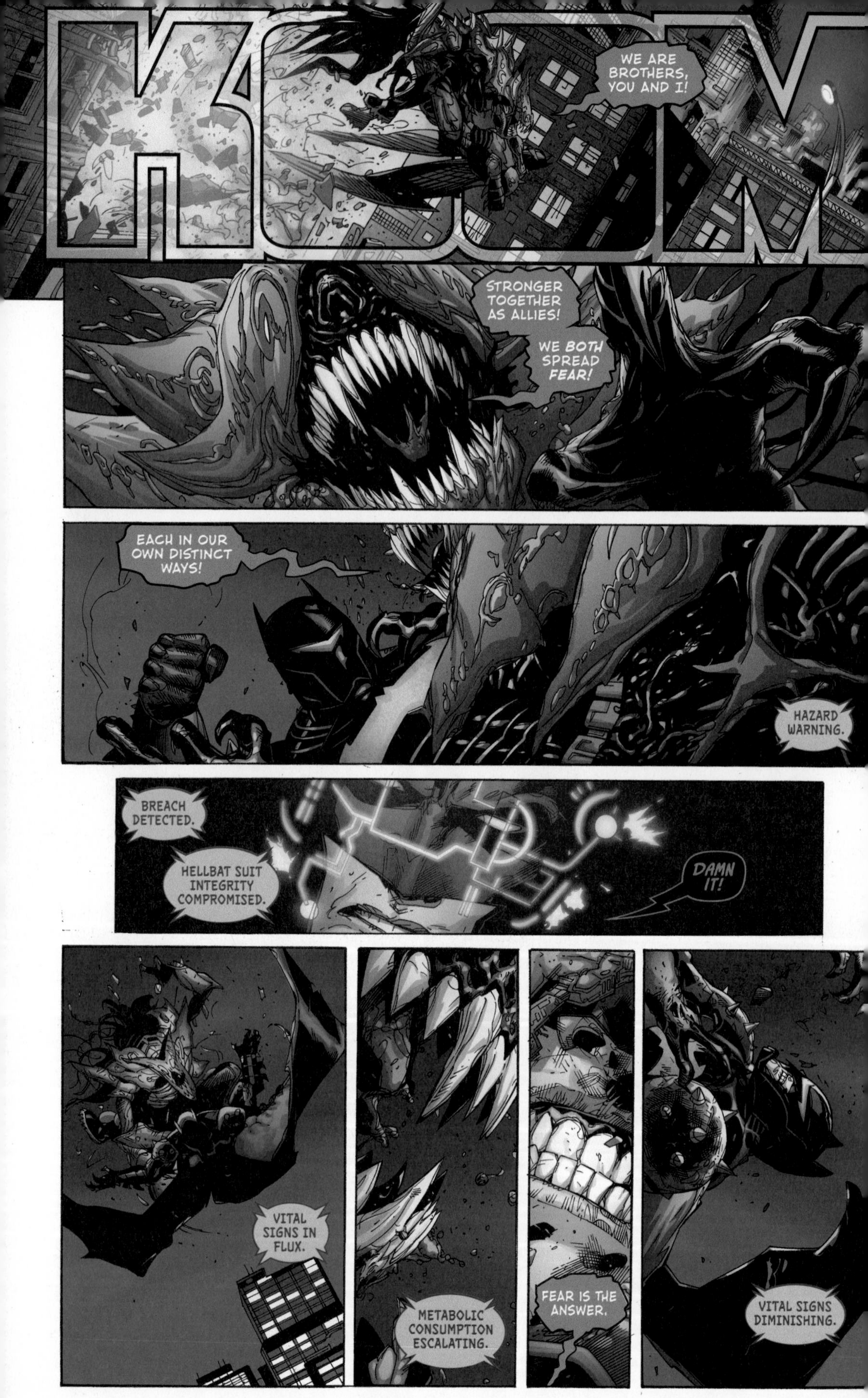
KOOOM
WE ARE BROTHERS, YOU AND I!
STRONGER TOGETHER AS ALLIES!
WE BOTH SPREAD FEAR!
EACH IN OUR OWN DISTINCT WAYS!
HAZARD WARNING.
BREACH DETECTED.
HELLBAT SUIT INTEGRITY COMPROMISED.
DAMN IT!
VITAL SIGNS IN FLUX.
METABOLIC CONSUMPTION ESCALATING.
FEAR IS THE ANSWER.
VITAL SIGNS DIMINISHING.

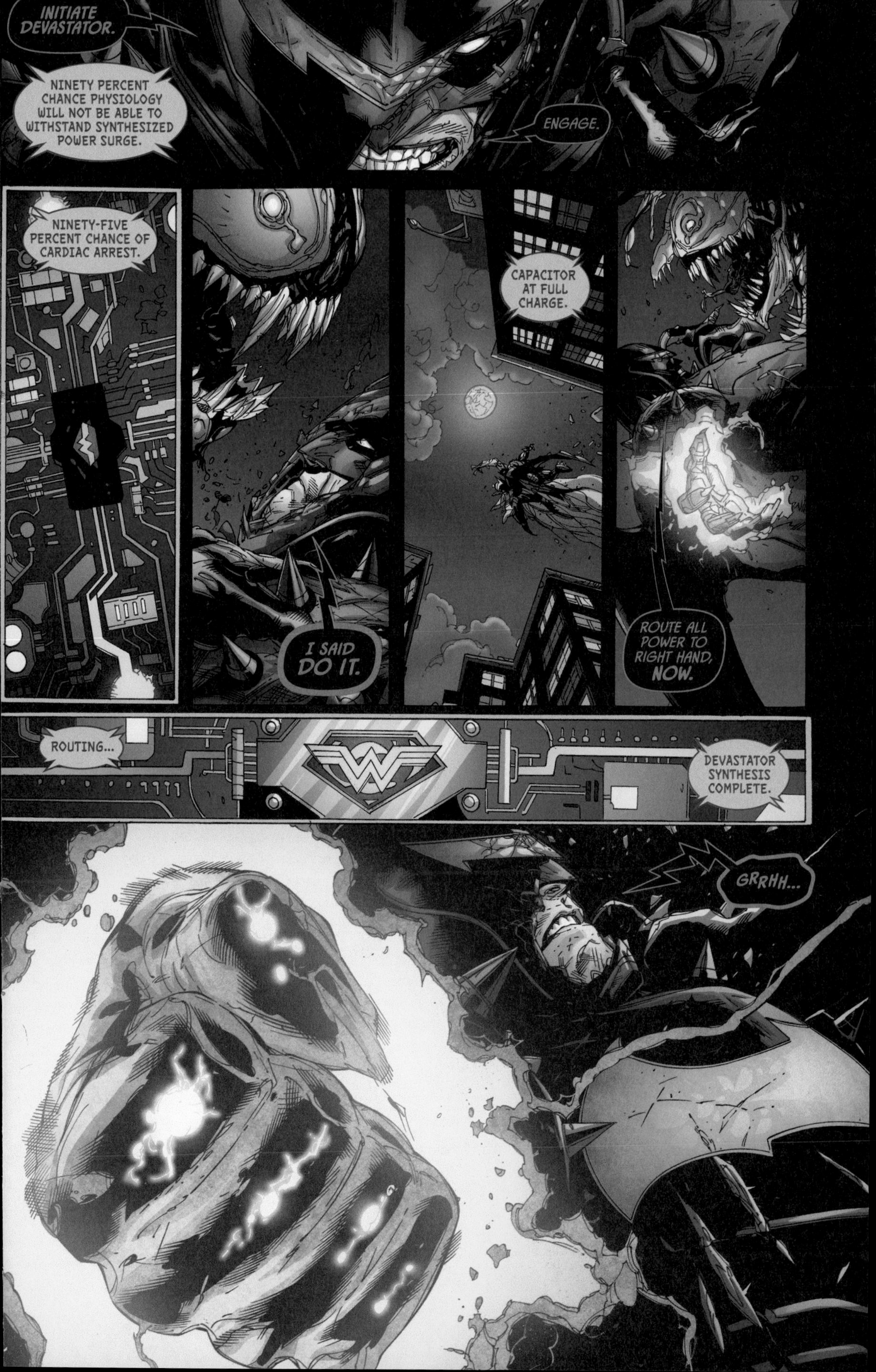
INITIATE DEVASTATOR.
NINETY PERCENT CHANCE PHYSIOLOGY WILL NOT BE ABLE TO WITHSTAND SYNTHESIZED POWER SURGE.
ENGAGE.
NINETY-FIVE PERCENT CHANCE OF CARDIAC ARREST.
I SAID DO IT.
CAPACITOR AT FULL CHARGE.
ROUTE ALL POWER TO RIGHT HAND, NOW.
ROUTING...
DEVASTATOR SYNTHESIS COMPLETE.
GRRHH...

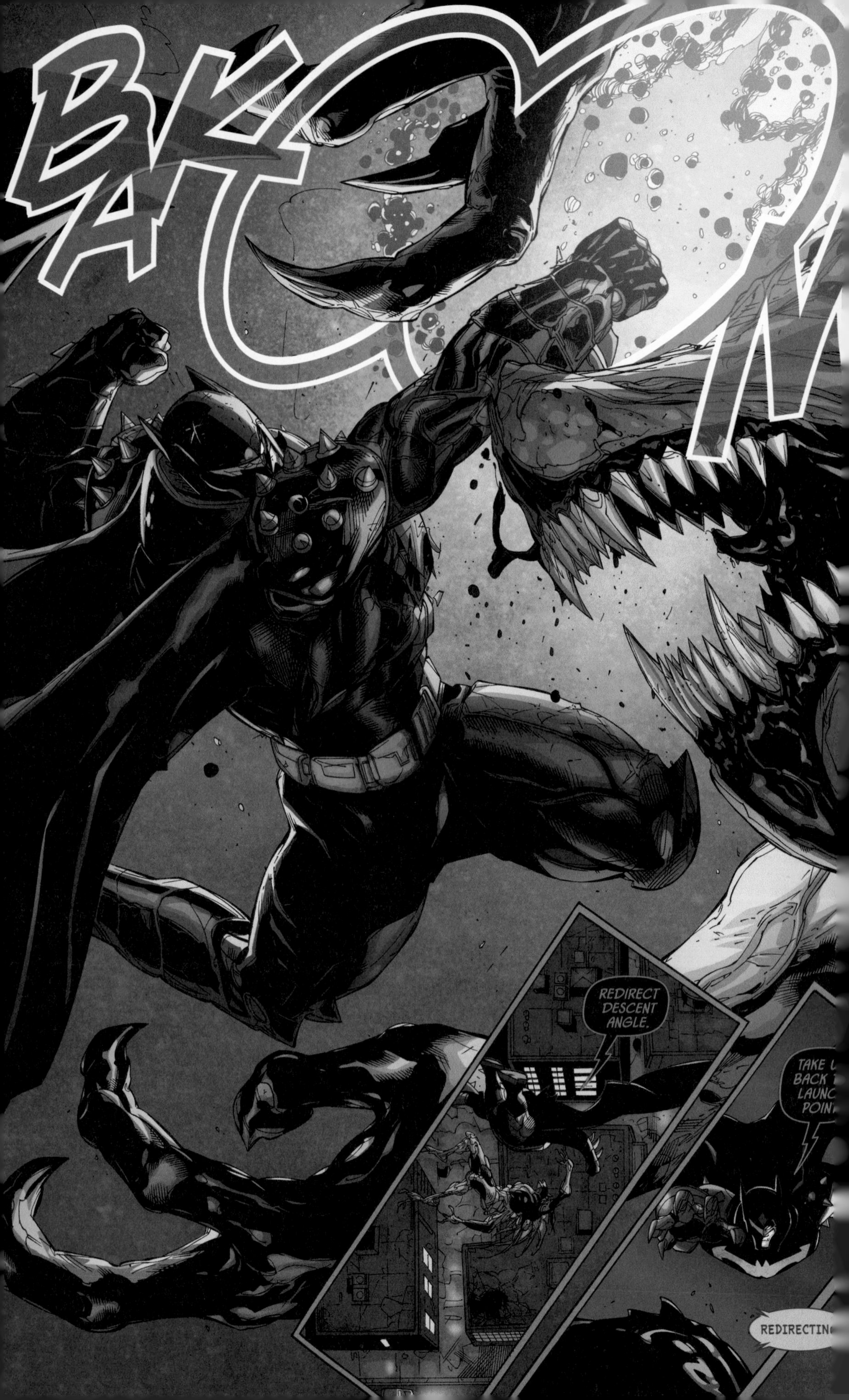
REDIRECT DESCENT ANGLE.

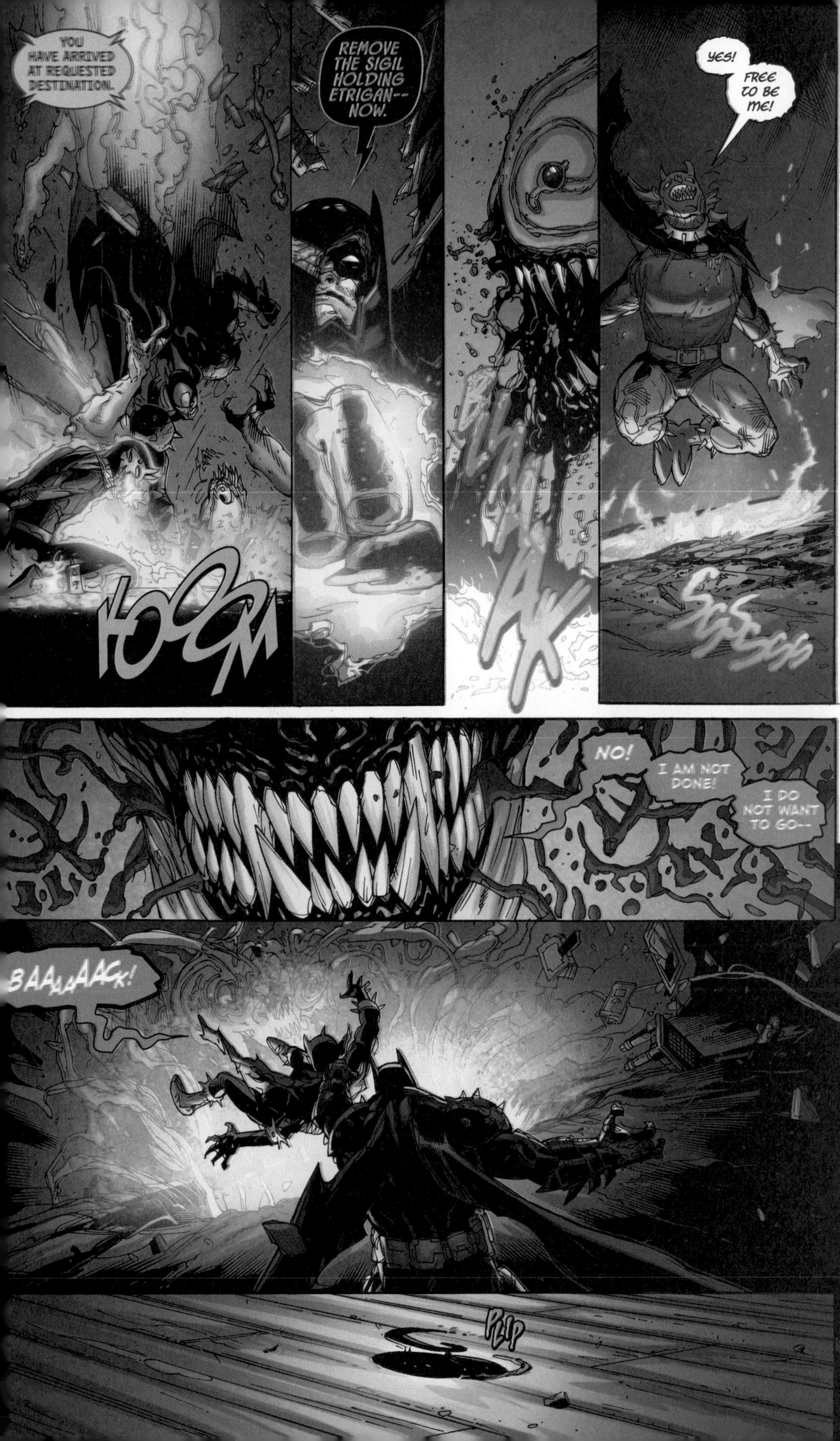
YOU HAVE ARRIVED AT REQUESTED DESTINATION.
KOOOM
REMOVE THE SIGIL HOLDING ETRIGAN-- NOW.
YES!
FREE TO BE ME!
SSSSSSS
NO!
I AM NOT DONE!
I DO NOT WANT TO GO--
BAAAAAACK!
PLIP

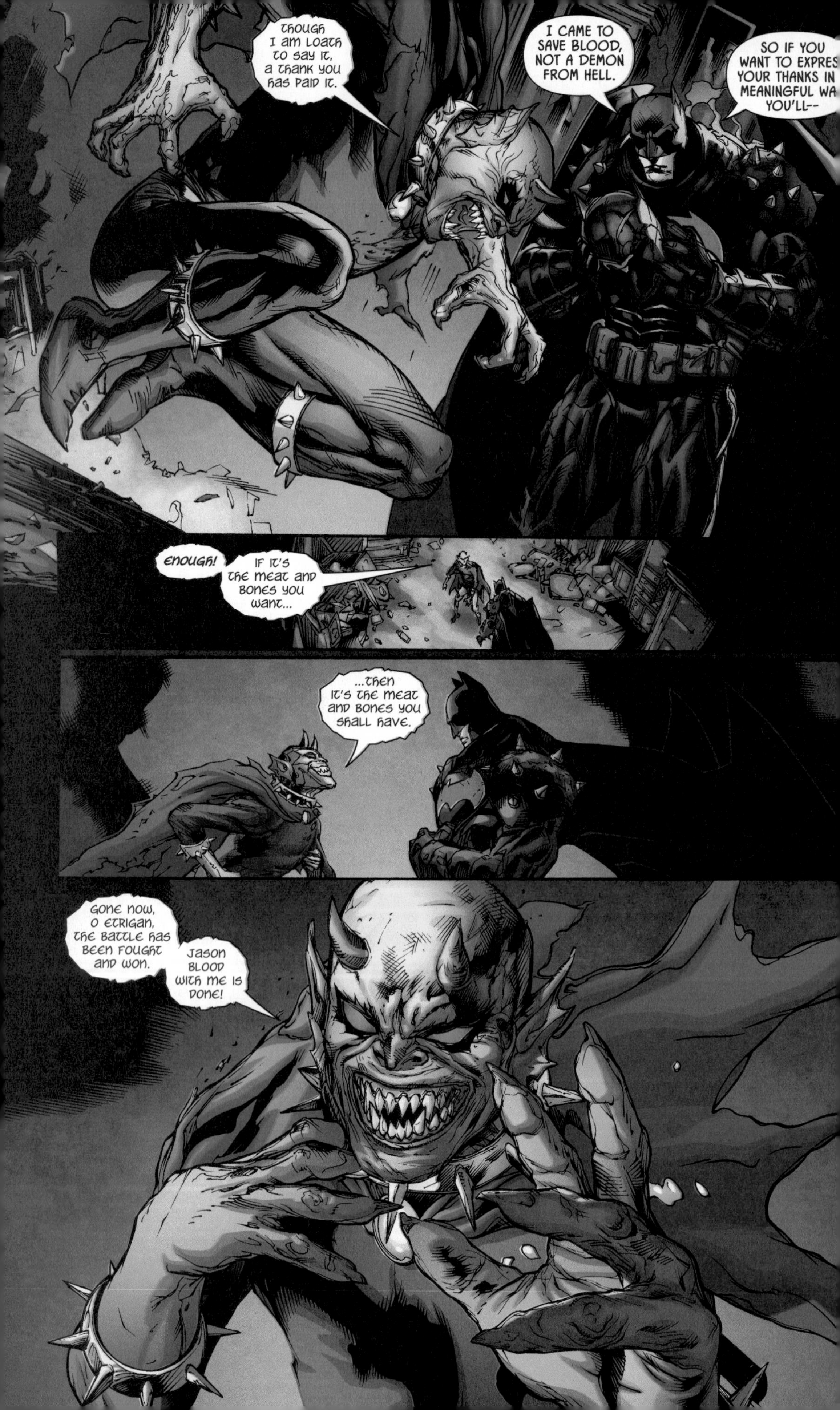
Though I am loath to say it, a thank you has paid it.
I CAME TO SAVE BLOOD, NOT A DEMON FROM HELL.
SO IF YOU WANT TO EXPRES YOUR THANKS IN MEANINGFUL WA YOU'LL--
ENOUGH!
IF IT'S THE MEAT AND BONES YOU WANT...
...THEN IT'S THE MEAT AND BONES YOU SHALL HAVE.
GONE NOW, O ETRIGAN, THE BATTLE HAS BEEN FOUGHT AND WON.
JASON BLOOD WITH ME IS DONE!

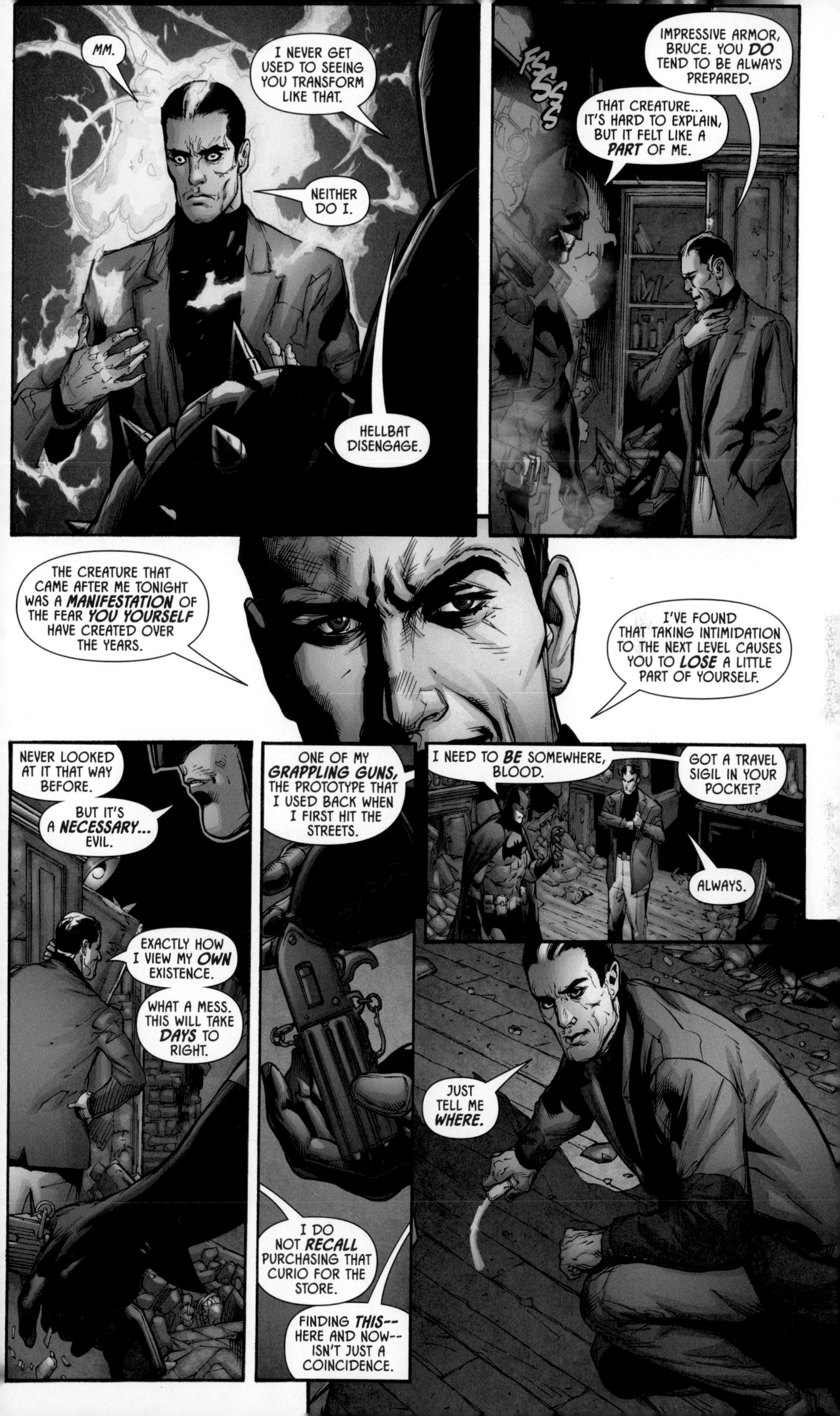
MM.
I NEVER GET USED TO SEEING YOU TRANSFORM LIKE THAT.
NEITHER DO I.
HELLBAT DISENGAGE.
FSSSS
IMPRESSIVE ARMOR, BRUCE. YOU DO TEND TO BE ALWAYS PREPARED.
THAT CREATURE... IT'S HARD TO EXPLAIN, BUT IT FELT LIKE A PART OF ME.
THE CREATURE THAT CAME AFTER ME TONIGHT WAS A MANIFESTATION OF THE FEAR YOU YOURSELF HAVE CREATED OVER THE YEARS.
I'VE FOUND THAT TAKING INTIMIDATION TO THE NEXT LEVEL CAUSES YOU TO LOSE A LITTLE PART OF YOURSELF.
NEVER LOOKED AT IT THAT WAY BEFORE.
BUT IT'S A NECESSARY... EVIL.
EXACTLY HOW I VIEW MY OWN EXISTENCE.
WHAT A MESS. THIS WILL TAKE DAYS TO RIGHT.
ONE OF MY GRAPPLING GUNS, THE PROTOTYPE THAT I USED BACK WHEN I FIRST HIT THE STREETS.
I DO NOT RECALL PURCHASING THAT CURIO FOR THE STORE.
FINDING THIS-- HERE AND NOW-- ISN'T JUST A COINCIDENCE.
I NEED TO BE SOMEWHERE, BLOOD.
GOT A TRAVEL SIGIL IN YOUR POCKET?
ALWAYS.
JUST TELL ME WHERE.

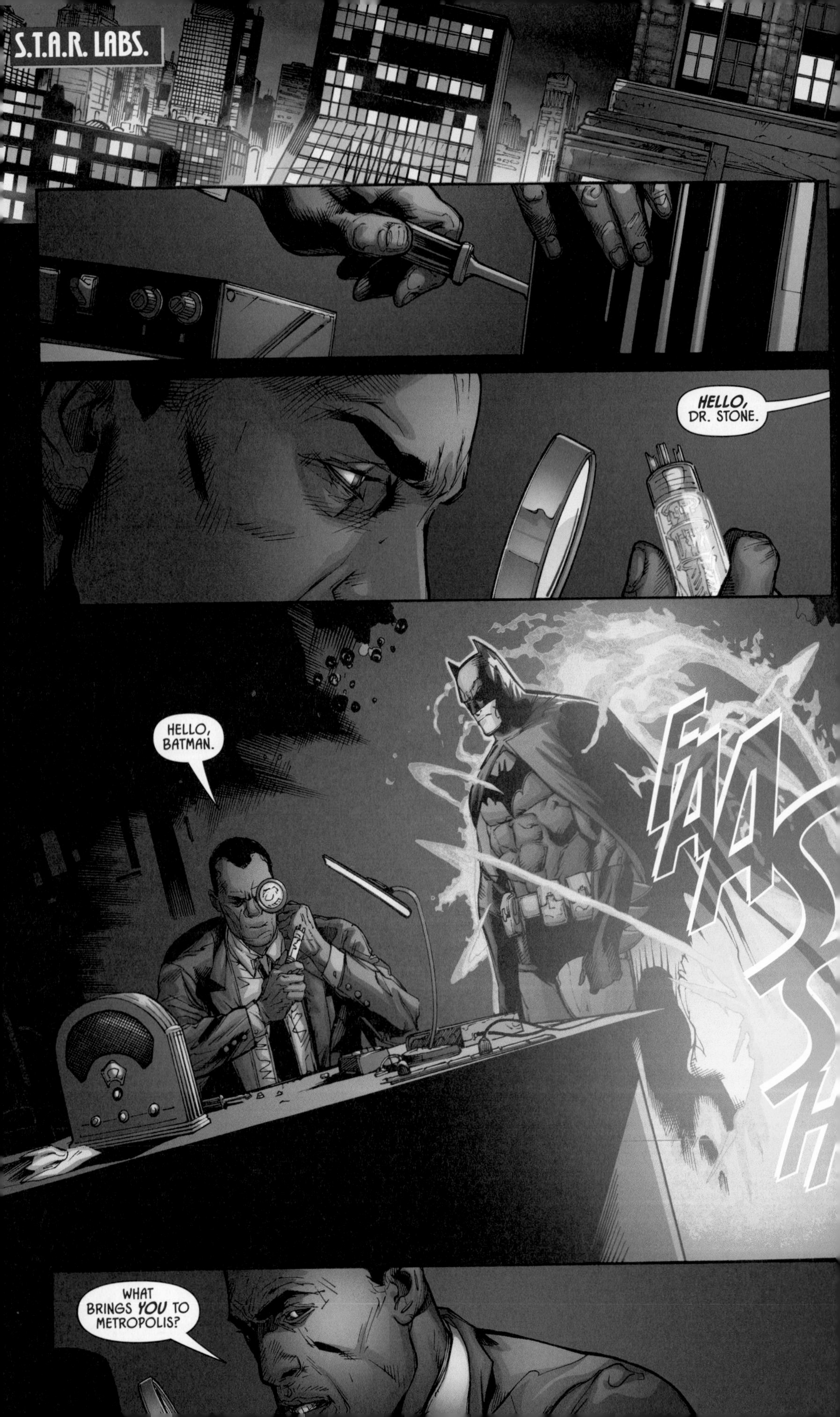
S.T.A.R. LABS.
HELLO, DR. STONE.
HELLO, BATMAN.
WHAT BRINGS *YOU* TO METROPOLIS?

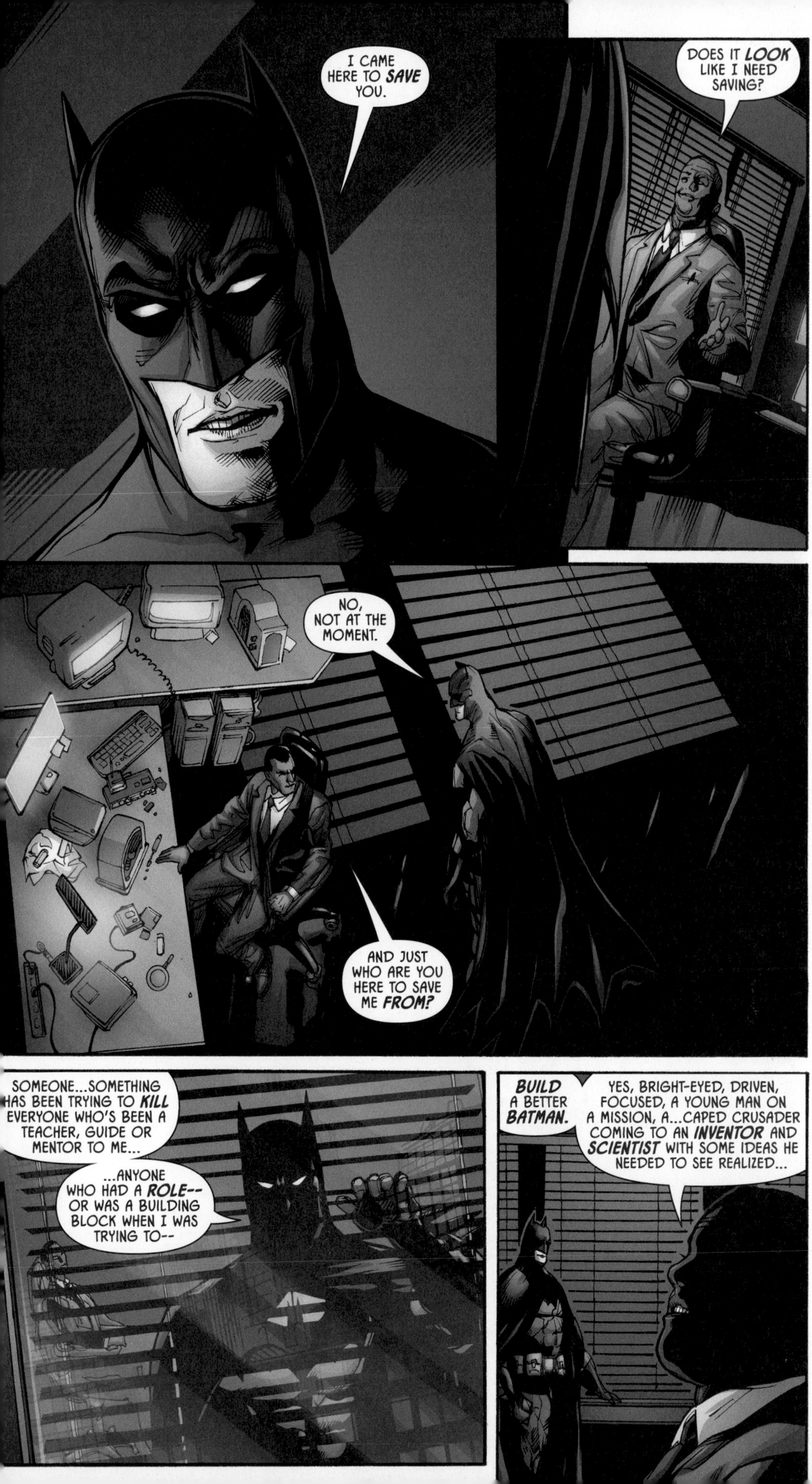
I CAME HERE TO SAVE YOU.
DOES IT LOOK LIKE I NEED SAVING?
NO, NOT AT THE MOMENT.
AND JUST WHO ARE YOU HERE TO SAVE ME FROM?
SOMEONE...SOMETHING HAS BEEN TRYING TO KILL EVERYONE WHO'S BEEN A TEACHER, GUIDE OR MENTOR TO ME...
...ANYONE WHO HAD A ROLE-- OR WAS A BUILDING BLOCK WHEN I WAS TRYING TO--
BUILD A BETTER BATMAN.
YES, BRIGHT-EYED, DRIVEN, FOCUSED, A YOUNG MAN ON A MISSION, A...CAPED CRUSADER COMING TO AN INVENTOR AND SCIENTIST WITH SOME IDEAS HE NEEDED TO SEE REALIZED...

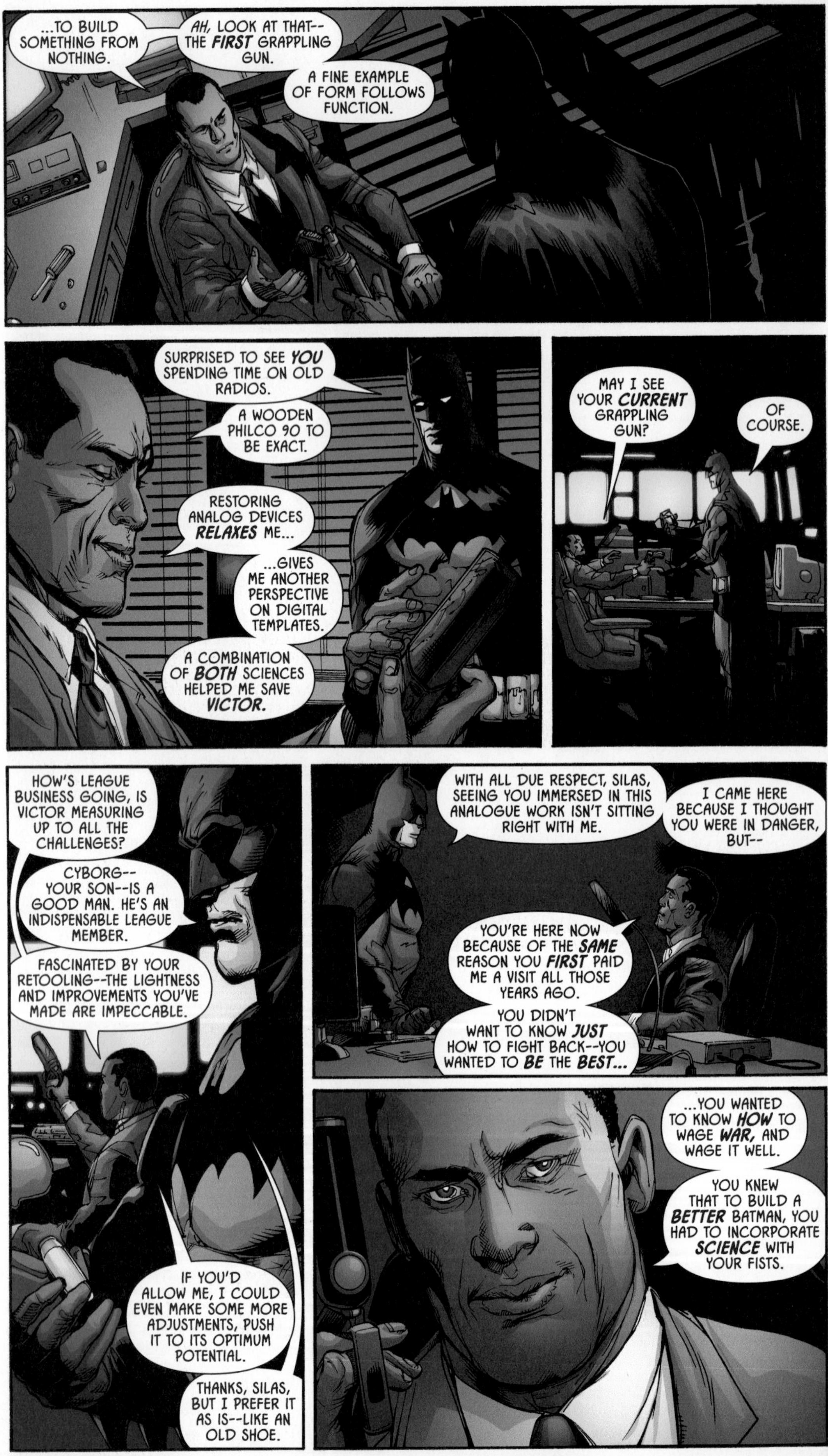
...TO BUILD SOMETHING FROM NOTHING.
AH, LOOK AT THAT-- THE FIRST GRAPPLING GUN.
A FINE EXAMPLE OF FORM FOLLOWS FUNCTION.
SURPRISED TO SEE YOU SPENDING TIME ON OLD RADIOS.
A WOODEN PHILCO 90 TO BE EXACT.
RESTORING ANALOG DEVICES RELAXES ME...
...GIVES ME ANOTHER PERSPECTIVE ON DIGITAL TEMPLATES.
A COMBINATION OF BOTH SCIENCES HELPED ME SAVE VICTOR.
MAY I SEE YOUR CURRENT GRAPPLING GUN?
OF COURSE.
HOW'S LEAGUE BUSINESS GOING, IS VICTOR MEASURING UP TO ALL THE CHALLENGES?
CYBORG-- YOUR SON--IS A GOOD MAN. HE'S AN INDISPENSABLE LEAGUE MEMBER.
FASCINATED BY YOUR RETOOLING--THE LIGHTNESS AND IMPROVEMENTS YOU'VE MADE ARE IMPECCABLE.
IF YOU'D ALLOW ME, I COULD EVEN MAKE SOME MORE ADJUSTMENTS, PUSH IT TO ITS OPTIMUM POTENTIAL.
THANKS, SILAS, BUT I PREFER IT AS IS--LIKE AN OLD SHOE.
WITH ALL DUE RESPECT, SILAS, SEEING YOU IMMERSED IN THIS ANALOGUE WORK ISN'T SITTING RIGHT WITH ME.
I CAME HERE BECAUSE I THOUGHT YOU WERE IN DANGER, BUT--
YOU'RE HERE NOW BECAUSE OF THE SAME REASON YOU FIRST PAID ME A VISIT ALL THOSE YEARS AGO.
YOU DIDN'T WANT TO KNOW JUST HOW TO FIGHT BACK--YOU WANTED TO BE THE BEST...
...YOU WANTED TO KNOW HOW TO WAGE WAR, AND WAGE IT WELL.
YOU KNEW THAT TO BUILD A BETTER BATMAN, YOU HAD TO INCORPORATE SCIENCE WITH YOUR FISTS.

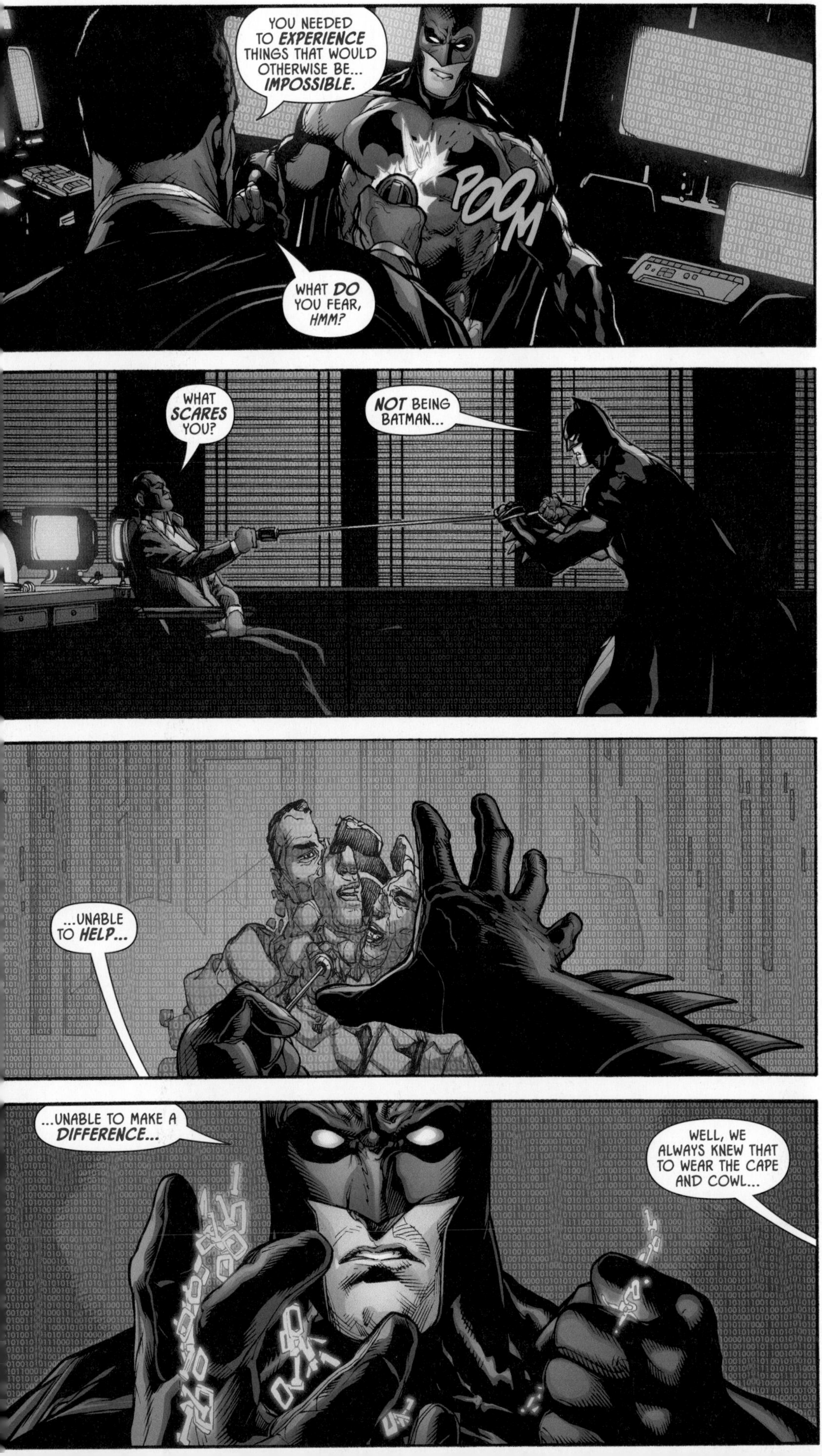
YOU NEEDED TO EXPERIENCE THINGS THAT WOULD OTHERWISE BE... IMPOSSIBLE.
POOM
WHAT DO YOU FEAR, HMM?
WHAT SCARES YOU?
NOT BEING BATMAN...
...UNABLE TO HELP...
...UNABLE TO MAKE A DIFFERENCE...
WELL, WE ALWAYS KNEW THAT TO WEAR THE CAPE AND COWL...

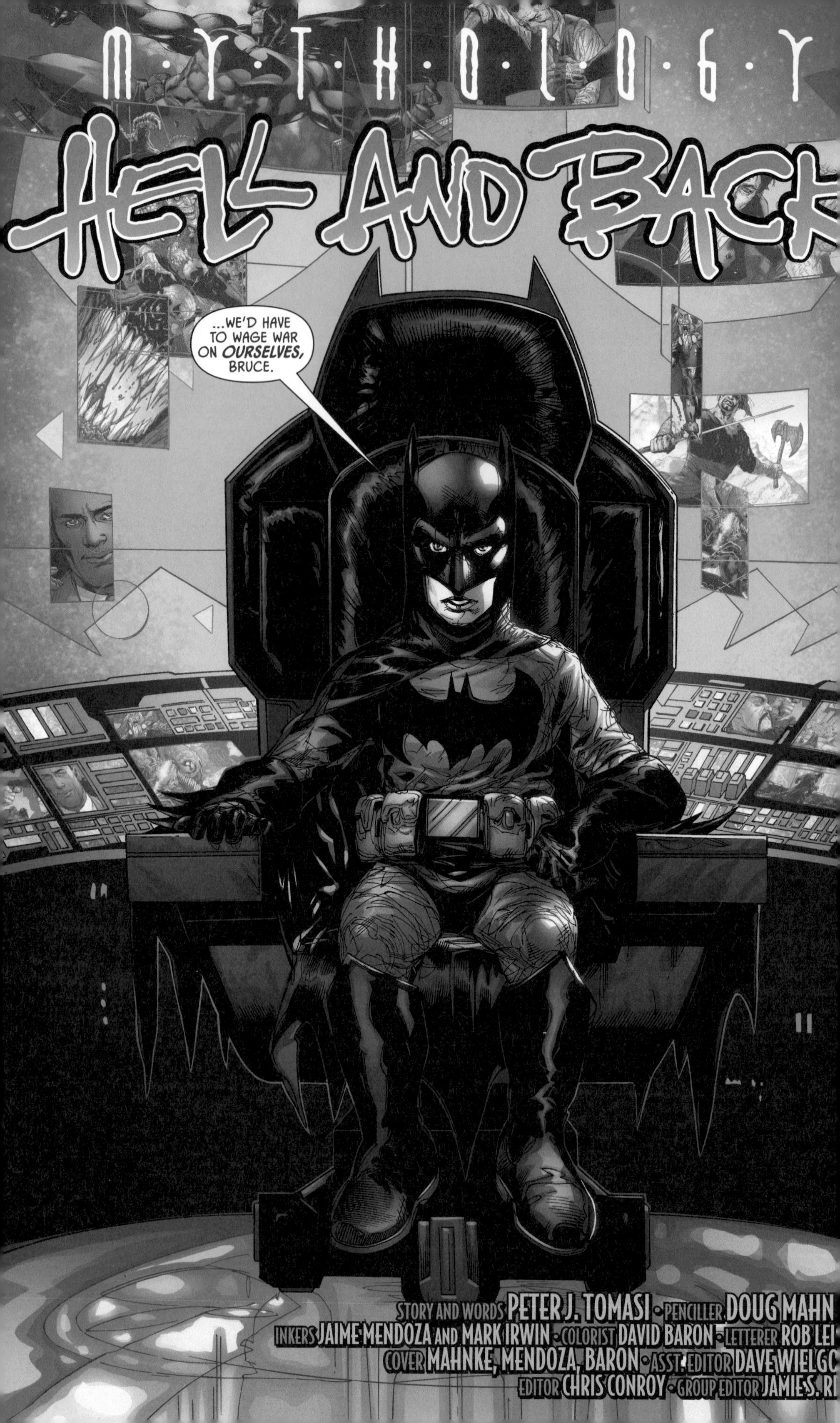
M·Y·T·H·O·L·O·G·Y
HELL AND BACK
...WE'D HAVE TO WAGE WAR ON *OURSELVES,* BRUCE.
STORY AND WORDS PETER J. TOMASI · PENCILLER DOUG MAHN
INKERS JAIME MENDOZA AND MARK IRWIN · COLORIST DAVID BARON · LETTERER ROB LEI
COVER MAHNKE, MENDOZA, BARON · ASST. EDITOR DAVE WIELGO
EDITOR CHRIS CONROY · GROUP EDITOR JAMIE S. RI

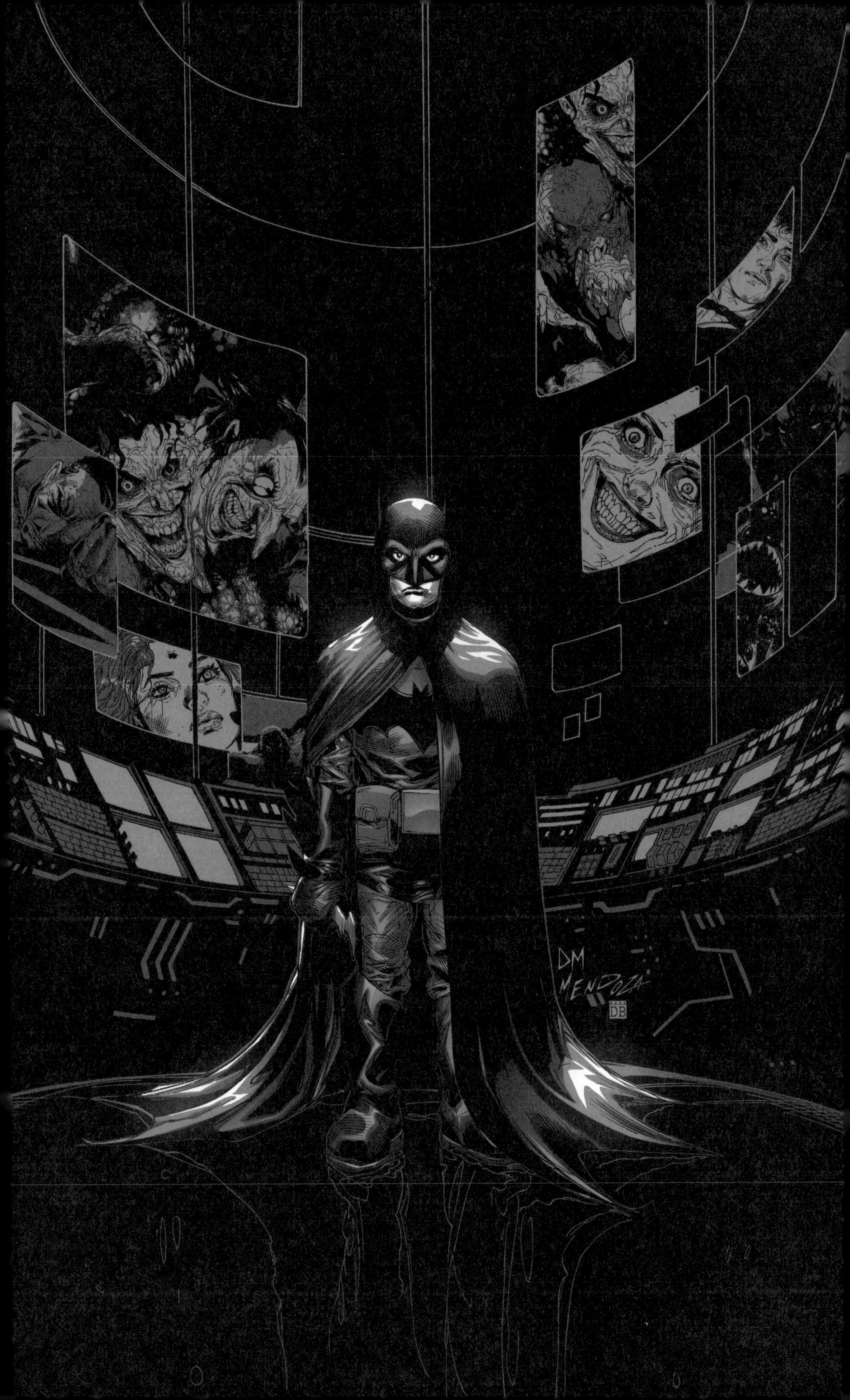
DM
MENDOZA
DB

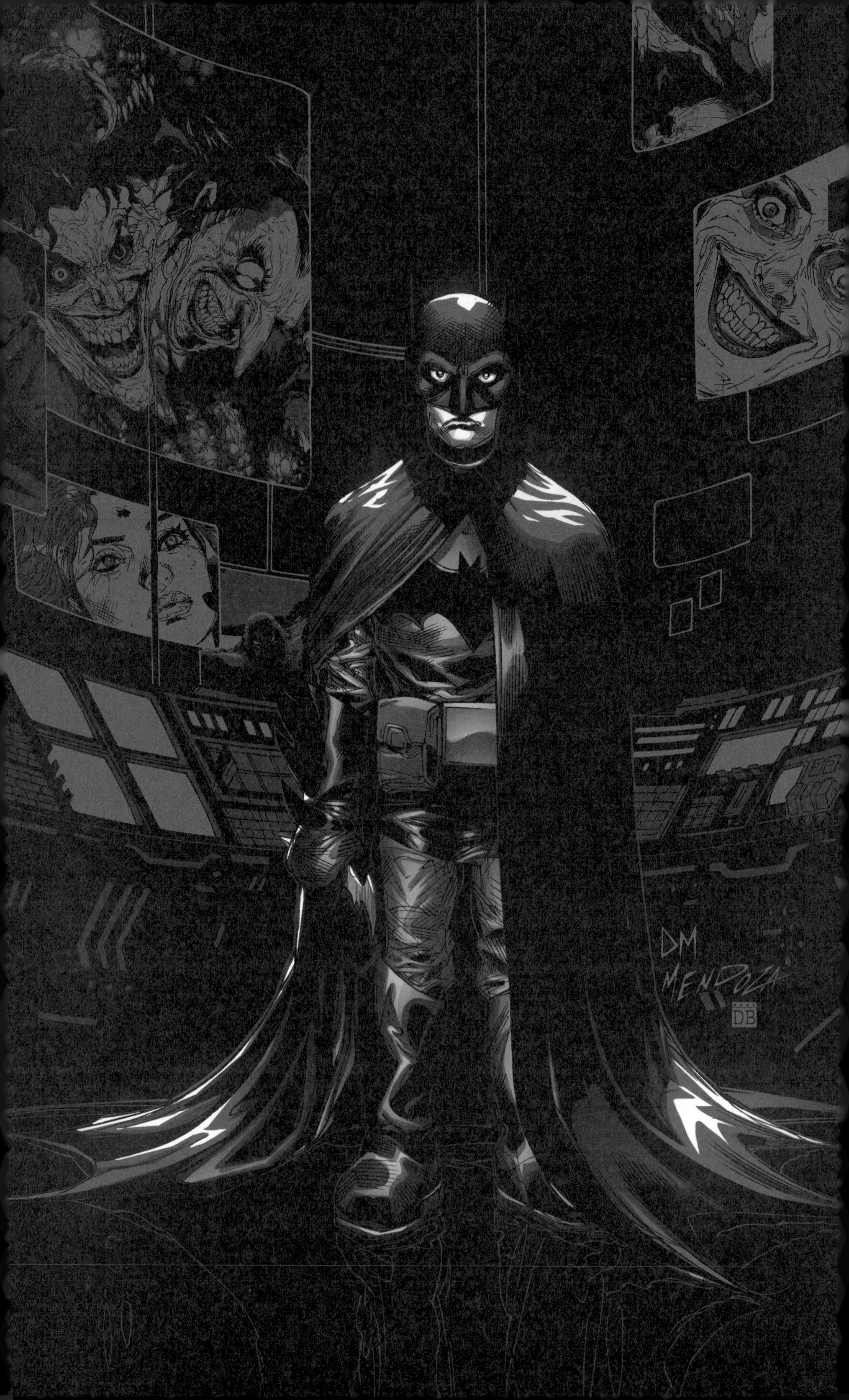
DM
MENDOZA
DB

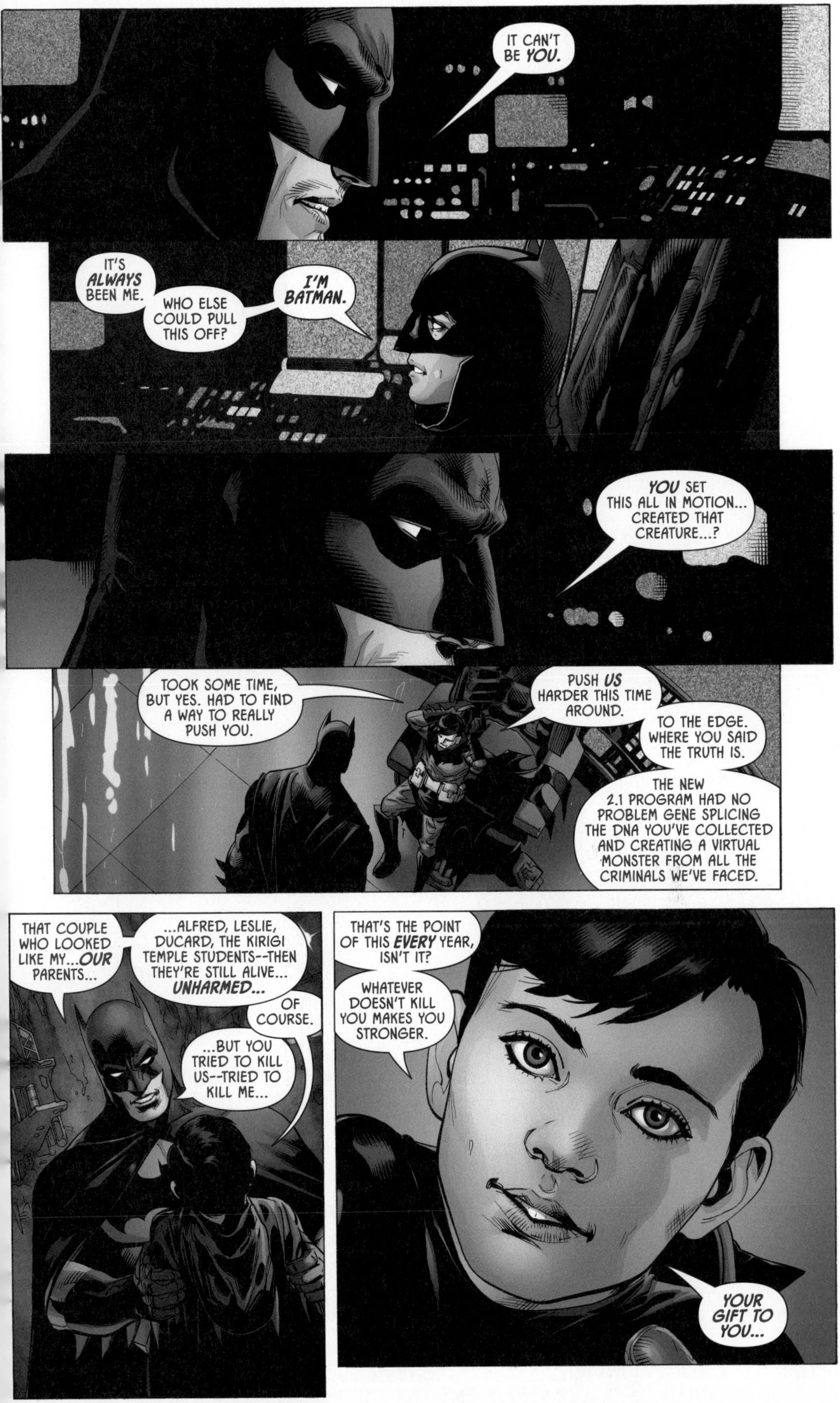
IT CAN'T BE *YOU.*
IT'S *ALWAYS* BEEN ME.
WHO ELSE COULD PULL THIS OFF?
I'M BATMAN.
YOU SET THIS ALL IN MOTION... CREATED THAT CREATURE...?
TOOK SOME TIME, BUT YES. HAD TO FIND A WAY TO REALLY PUSH YOU.
PUSH *US* HARDER THIS TIME AROUND.
TO THE EDGE. WHERE YOU SAID THE TRUTH IS.
THE NEW 2.1 PROGRAM HAD NO PROBLEM GENE SPLICING THE DNA YOU'VE COLLECTED AND CREATING A VIRTUAL MONSTER FROM ALL THE CRIMINALS WE'VE FACED.
THAT COUPLE WHO LOOKED LIKE MY...*OUR* PARENTS...
...ALFRED, LESLIE, DUCARD, THE KIRIGI TEMPLE STUDENTS--THEN THEY'RE STILL ALIVE... *UNHARMED...*
OF COURSE.
...BUT YOU TRIED TO KILL US--TRIED TO KILL ME...
THAT'S THE POINT OF THIS *EVERY* YEAR, ISN'T IT?
WHATEVER DOESN'T KILL YOU MAKES YOU STRONGER.
YOUR GIFT TO YOU...

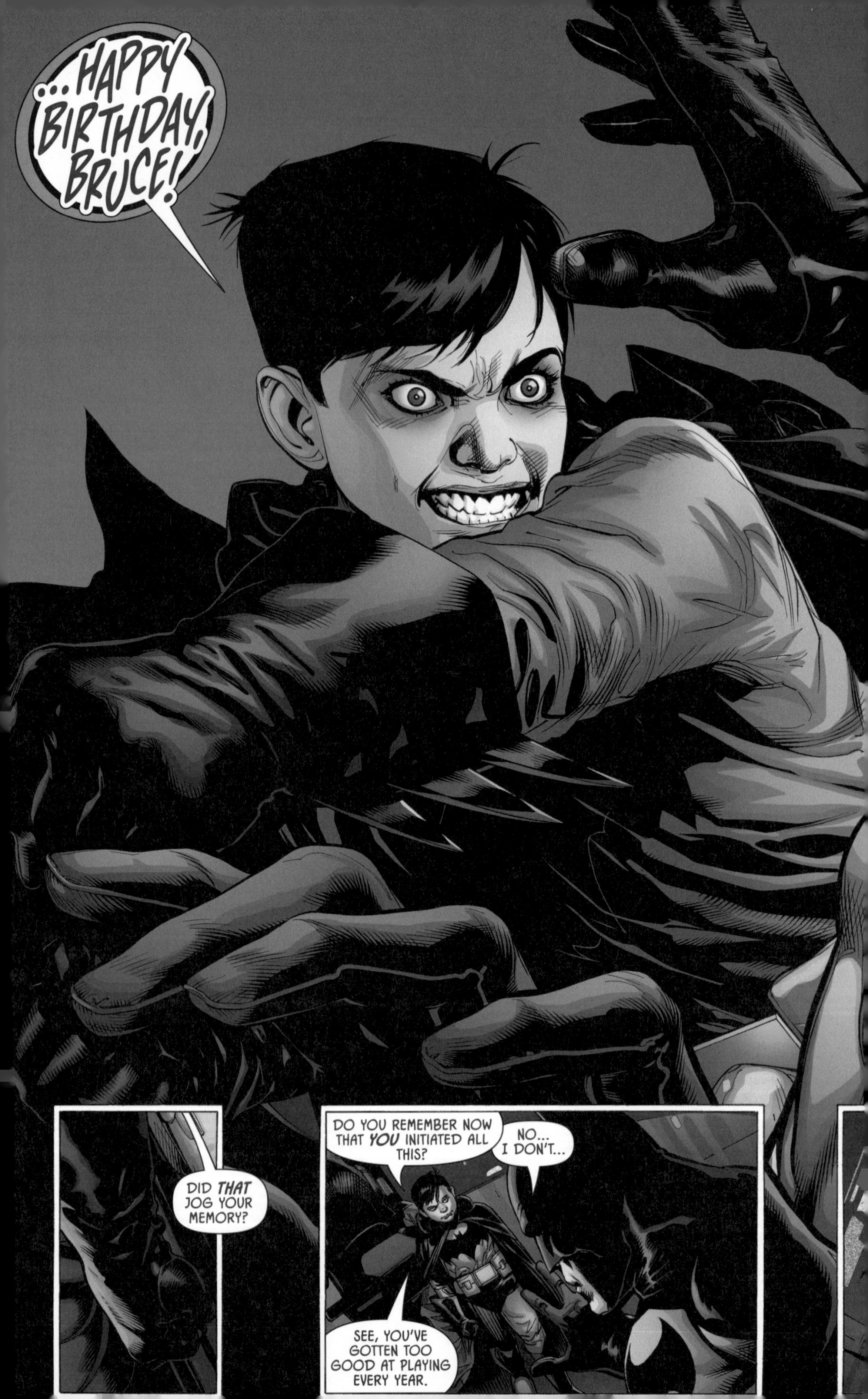
...HAPPY BIRTHDAY, BRUCE!
DID THAT JOG YOUR MEMORY?
DO YOU REMEMBER NOW THAT YOU INITIATED ALL THIS?
NO... I DON'T...
SEE, YOU'VE GOTTEN TOO GOOD AT PLAYING EVERY YEAR.

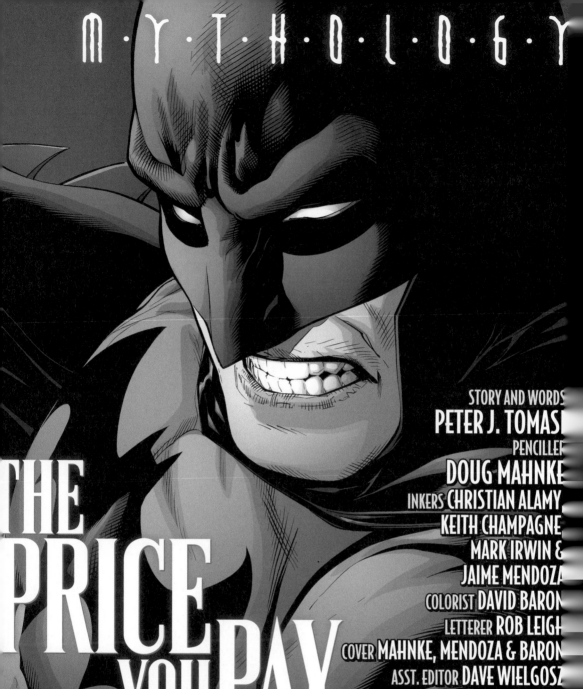

MYTHOLOGY

THE PRICE YOU PAY

STORY AND WORDS **PETER J. TOMASI**
PENCILLER **DOUG MAHNKE**
INKERS **CHRISTIAN ALAMY**
KEITH CHAMPAGNE
MARK IRWIN &
JAIME MENDOZA
COLORIST **DAVID BARON**
LETTERER **ROB LEIGH**
COVER **MAHNKE, MENDOZA & BARON**
ASST. EDITOR **DAVE WIELGOSZ**
EDITOR **CHRIS CONROY**
GROUP EDITOR **JAMIE S. RICH**

YOU DECIDED TO *DIVE DEEP* THIS TIME.

DEEPER THAN YOU'VE EVER GONE BEFORE.

KRAK

NO MATTER WHAT'S HAPPENING...*HERE*, I'M NOT GOING TO HIT A CHILD.

THAT'S ALL RIGHT, I'LL KEEP DOING THE HITTING.

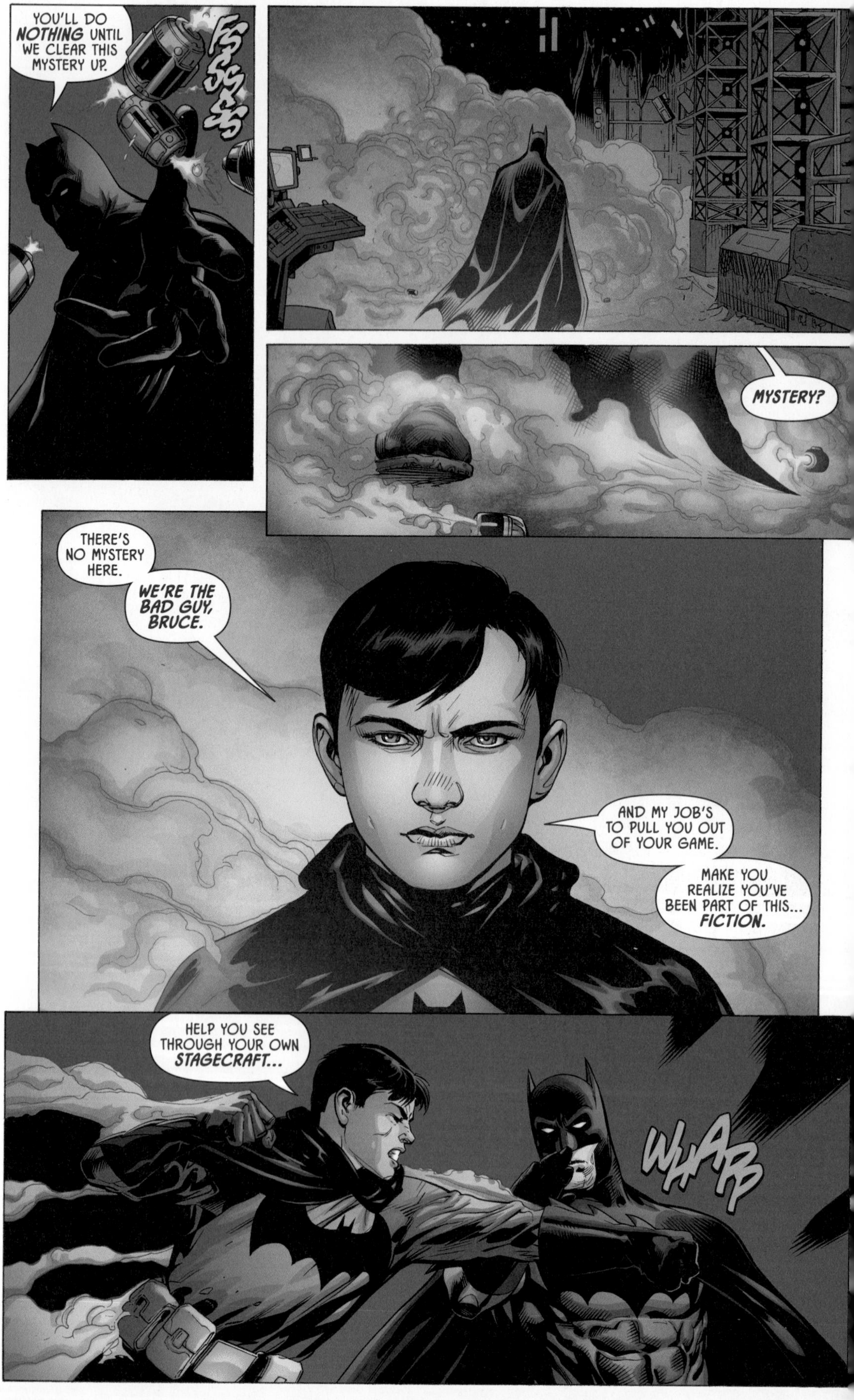

YOU'LL DO NOTHING UNTIL WE CLEAR THIS MYSTERY UP.
FSSSSS
MYSTERY?
THERE'S NO MYSTERY HERE.
WE'RE THE BAD GUY, BRUCE.
AND MY JOB'S TO PULL YOU OUT OF YOUR GAME.
MAKE YOU REALIZE YOU'VE BEEN PART OF THIS... FICTION.
HELP YOU SEE THROUGH YOUR OWN STAGECRAFT...
WHAP

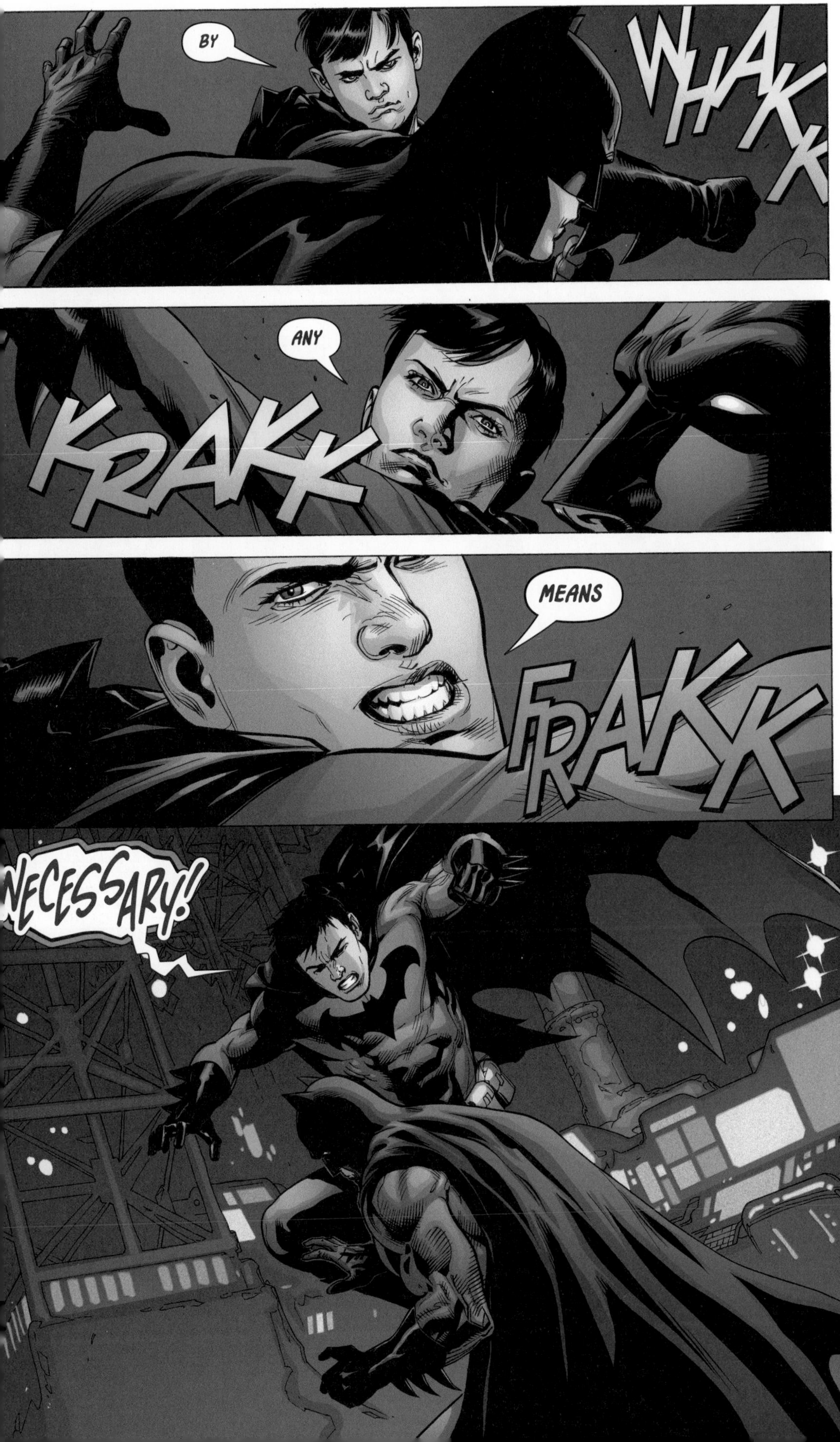
BY
WHAKK
ANY
KRAKK
MEANS
FRAKK
NECESSARY!

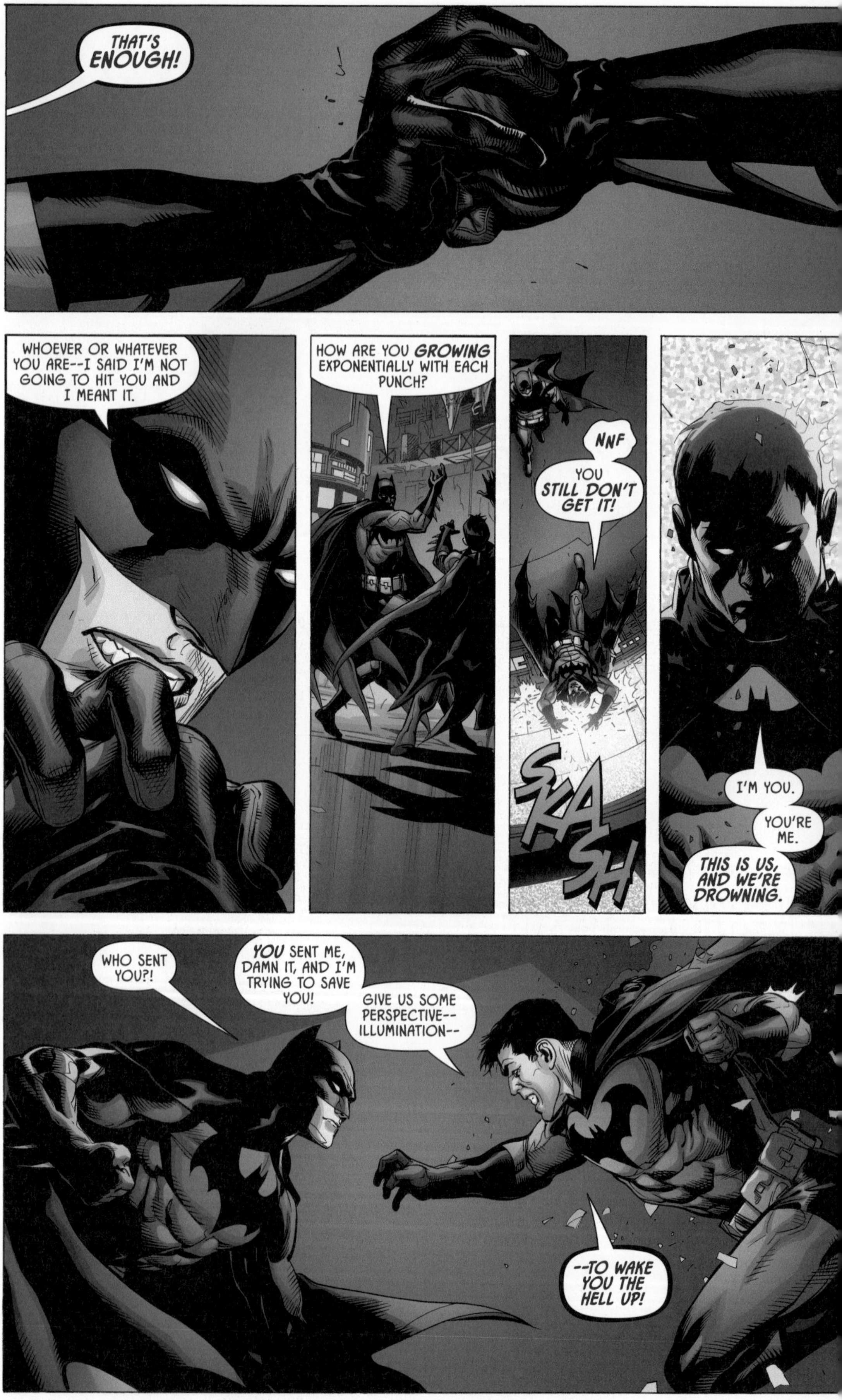
THAT'S ENOUGH!
WHOEVER OR WHATEVER YOU ARE--I SAID I'M NOT GOING TO HIT YOU AND I MEANT IT.
HOW ARE YOU GROWING EXPONENTIALLY WITH EACH PUNCH?
NNF
YOU STILL DON'T GET IT!
SKASH
I'M YOU.
YOU'RE ME.
THIS IS US, AND WE'RE DROWNING.
WHO SENT YOU?!
YOU SENT ME, DAMN IT, AND I'M TRYING TO SAVE YOU!
GIVE US SOME PERSPECTIVE-- ILLUMINATION--
--TO WAKE YOU THE HELL UP!

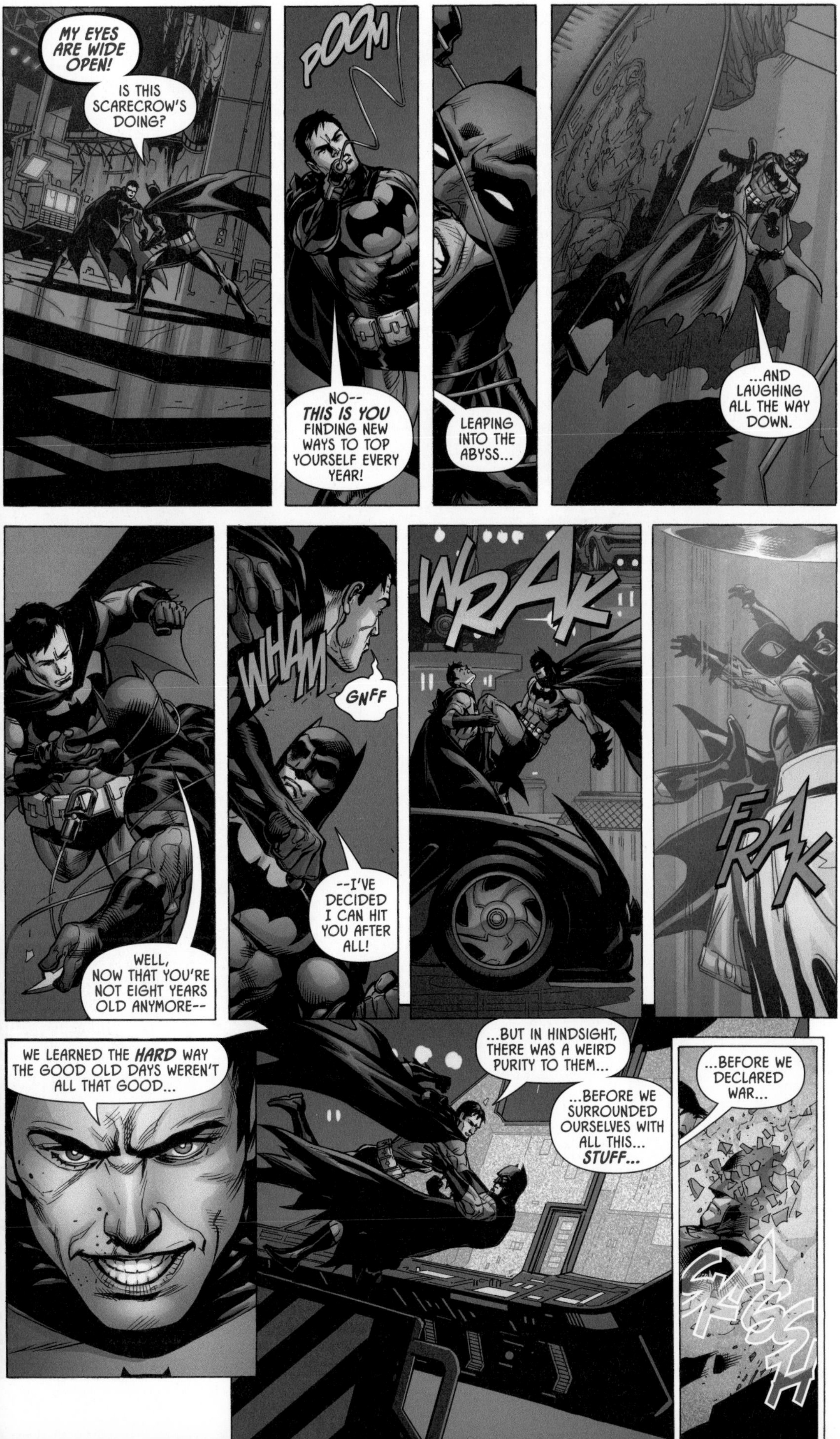
MY EYES ARE WIDE OPEN!
IS THIS SCARECROW'S DOING?
POOM
NO-- THIS IS YOU FINDING NEW WAYS TO TOP YOURSELF EVERY YEAR!
LEAPING INTO THE ABYSS...
...AND LAUGHING ALL THE WAY DOWN.
WELL, NOW THAT YOU'RE NOT EIGHT YEARS OLD ANYMORE--
WHAM
GNFF
--I'VE DECIDED I CAN HIT YOU AFTER ALL!
WRAK
FRAK
WE LEARNED THE HARD WAY THE GOOD OLD DAYS WEREN'T ALL THAT GOOD...
...BUT IN HINDSIGHT, THERE WAS A WEIRD PURITY TO THEM...
...BEFORE WE SURROUNDED OURSELVES WITH ALL THIS... STUFF...
...BEFORE WE DECLARED WAR...

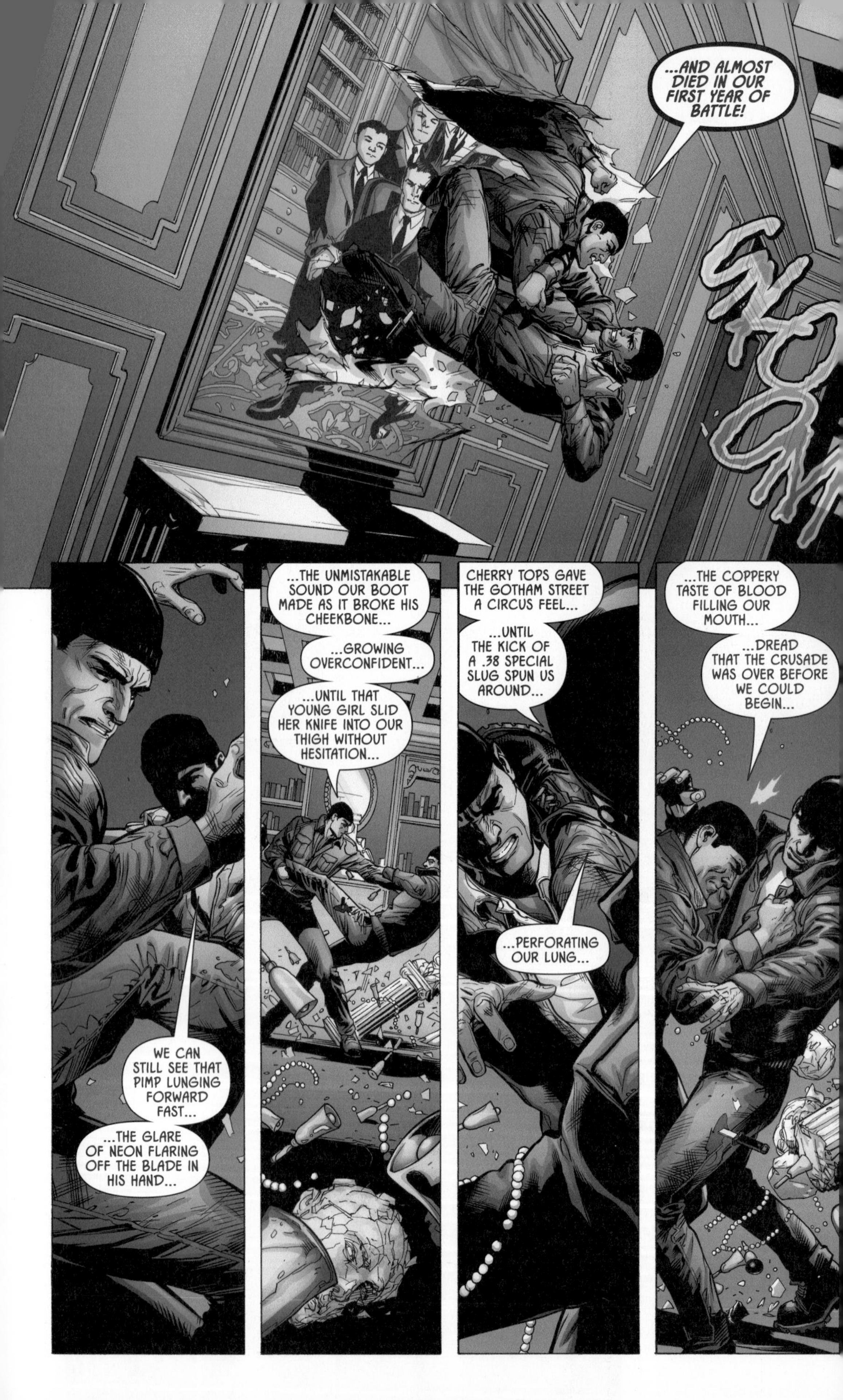
...AND ALMOST DIED IN OUR FIRST YEAR OF BATTLE!
WE CAN STILL SEE THAT PIMP LUNGING FORWARD FAST...
...THE GLARE OF NEON FLARING OFF THE BLADE IN HIS HAND...
...THE UNMISTAKABLE SOUND OUR BOOT MADE AS IT BROKE HIS CHEEKBONE...
...GROWING OVERCONFIDENT...
...UNTIL THAT YOUNG GIRL SLID HER KNIFE INTO OUR THIGH WITHOUT HESITATION...
CHERRY TOPS GAVE THE GOTHAM STREET A CIRCUS FEEL...
...UNTIL THE KICK OF A .38 SPECIAL SLUG SPUN US AROUND...
...PERFORATING OUR LUNG...
...THE COPPERY TASTE OF BLOOD FILLING OUR MOUTH...
...DREAD THAT THE CRUSADE WAS OVER BEFORE WE COULD BEGIN...

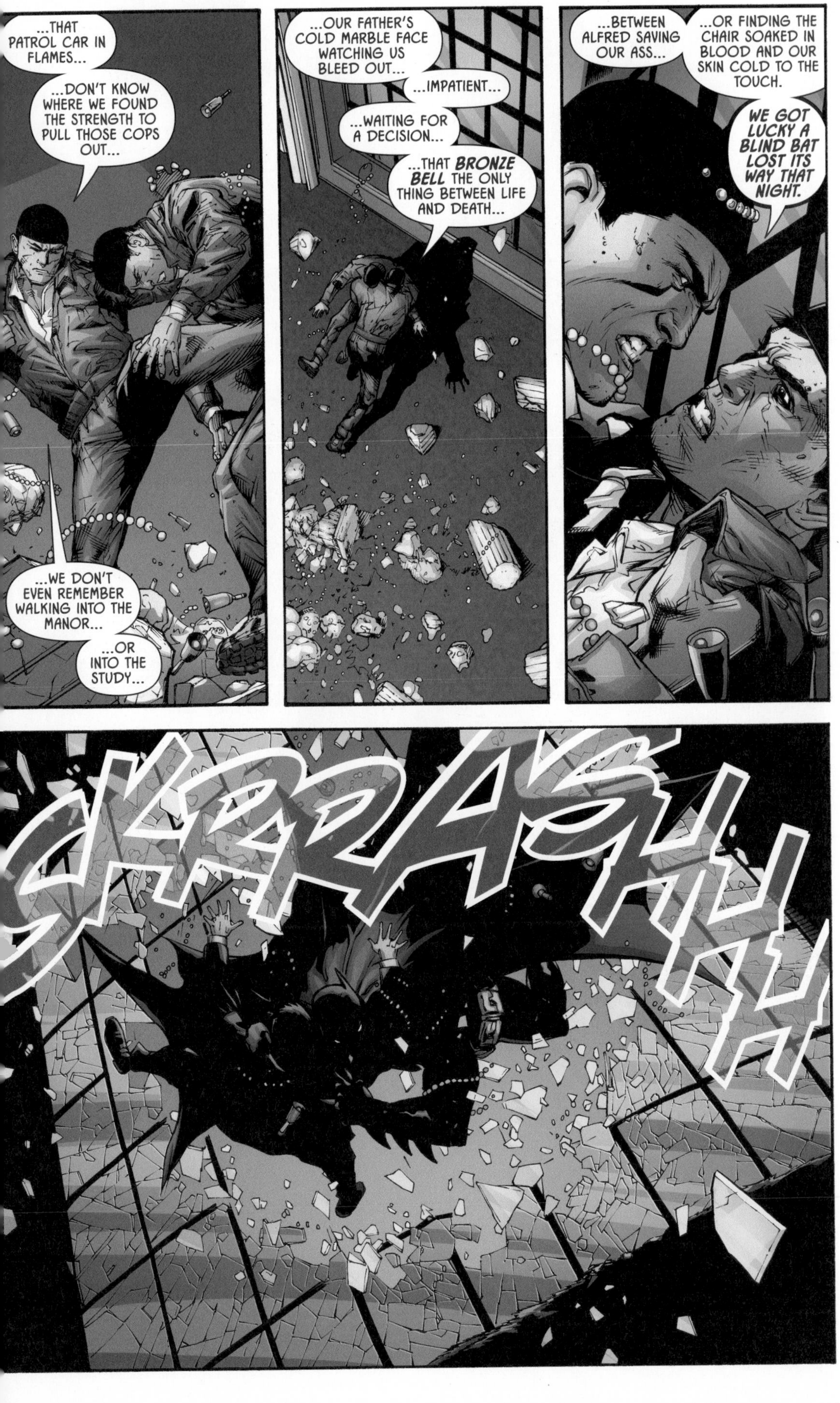
...THAT PATROL CAR IN FLAMES...
...DON'T KNOW WHERE WE FOUND THE STRENGTH TO PULL THOSE COPS OUT...
...WE DON'T EVEN REMEMBER WALKING INTO THE MANOR...
...OR INTO THE STUDY...
...OUR FATHER'S COLD MARBLE FACE WATCHING US BLEED OUT...
...IMPATIENT...
...WAITING FOR A DECISION...
...THAT BRONZE BELL THE ONLY THING BETWEEN LIFE AND DEATH...
...BETWEEN ALFRED SAVING OUR ASS...
...OR FINDING THE CHAIR SOAKED IN BLOOD AND OUR SKIN COLD TO THE TOUCH.
WE GOT LUCKY A BLIND BAT LOST ITS WAY THAT NIGHT.
CKRASHHH

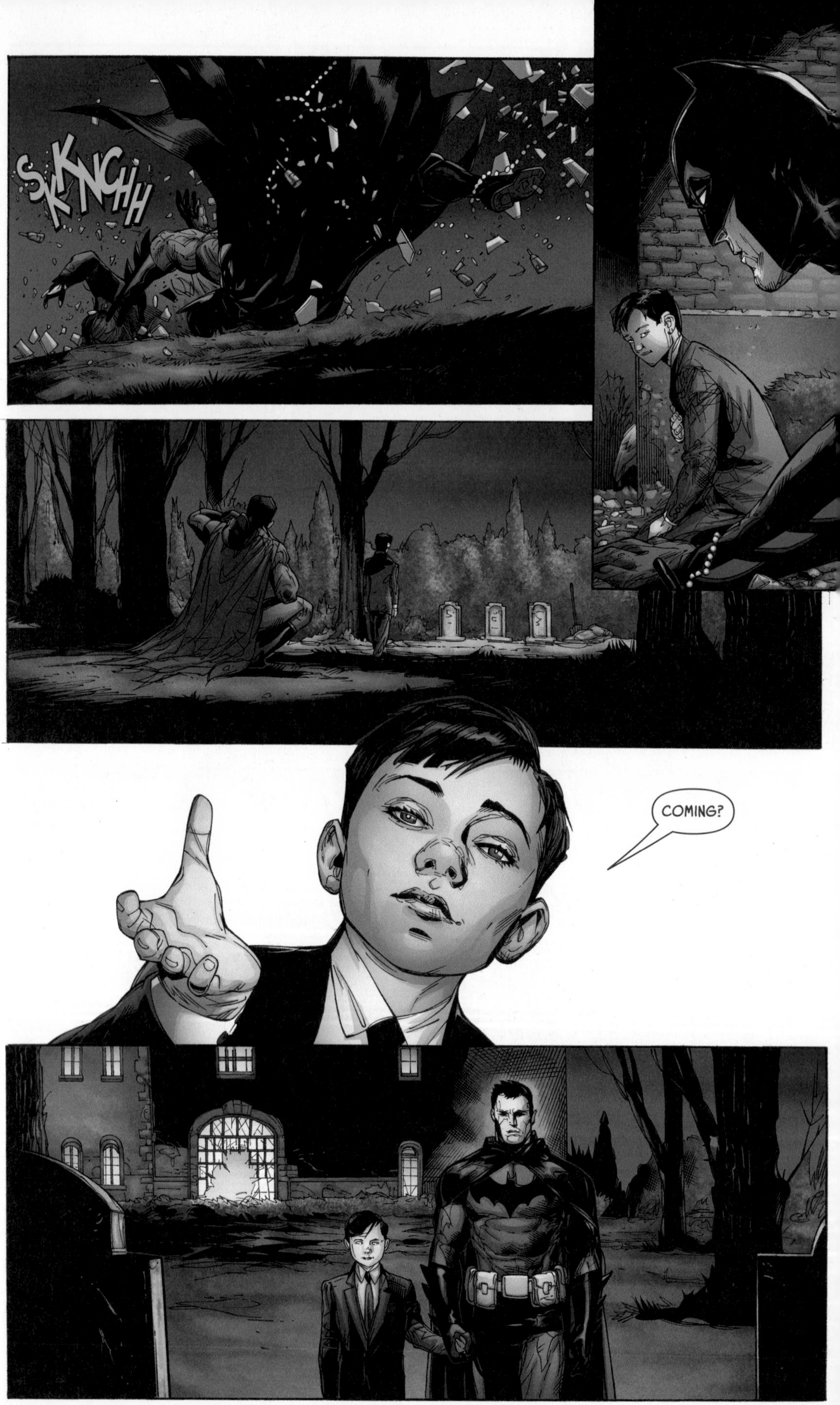
SKKNCHH
COMING?

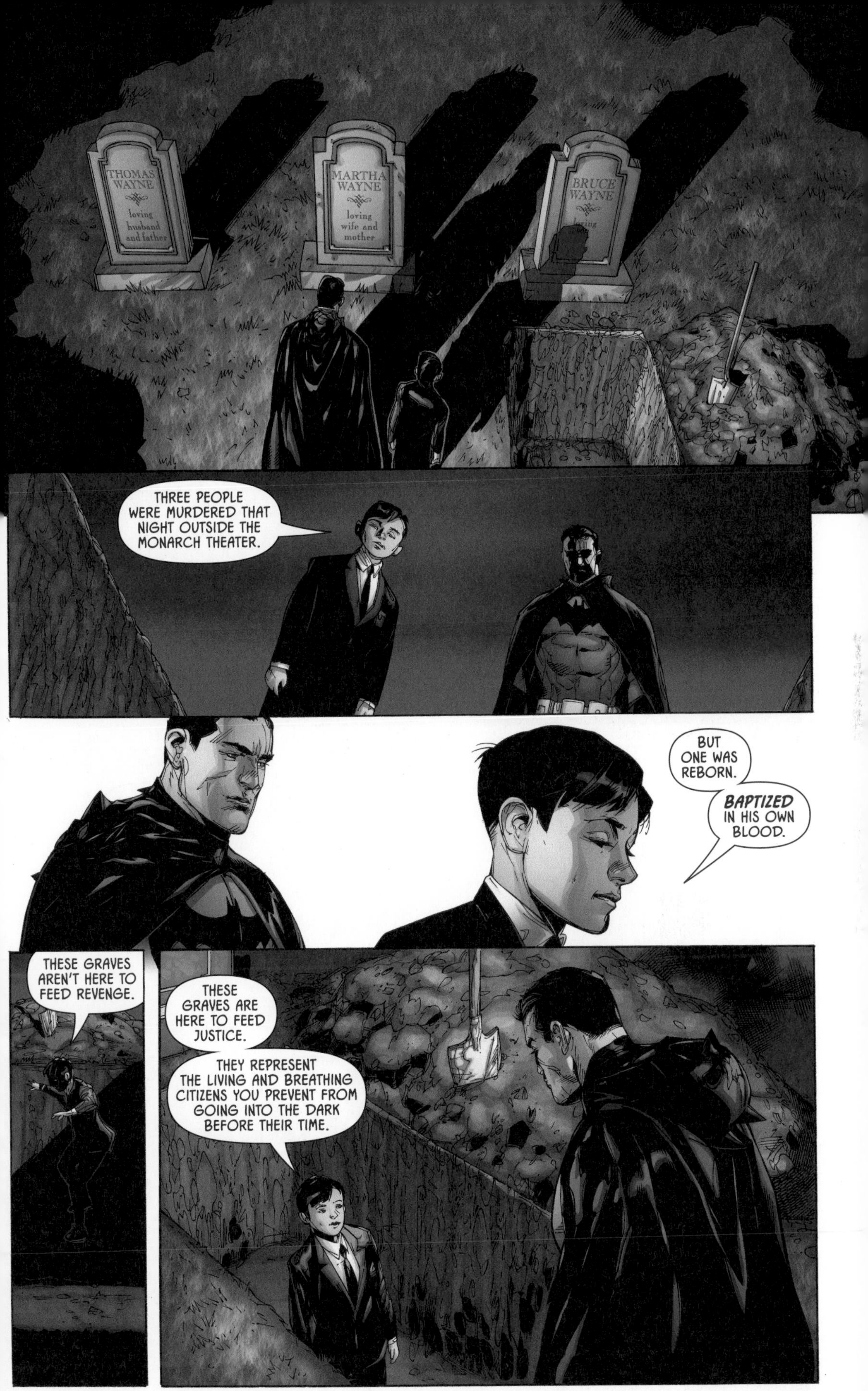
THOMAS WAYNE loving husband and father
MARTHA WAYNE loving wife and mother
BRUCE WAYNE
THREE PEOPLE WERE MURDERED THAT NIGHT OUTSIDE THE MONARCH THEATER.
BUT ONE WAS REBORN.
BAPTIZED IN HIS OWN BLOOD.
THESE GRAVES AREN'T HERE TO FEED REVENGE.
THESE GRAVES ARE HERE TO FEED JUSTICE.
THEY REPRESENT THE LIVING AND BREATHING CITIZENS YOU PREVENT FROM GOING INTO THE DARK BEFORE THEIR TIME.

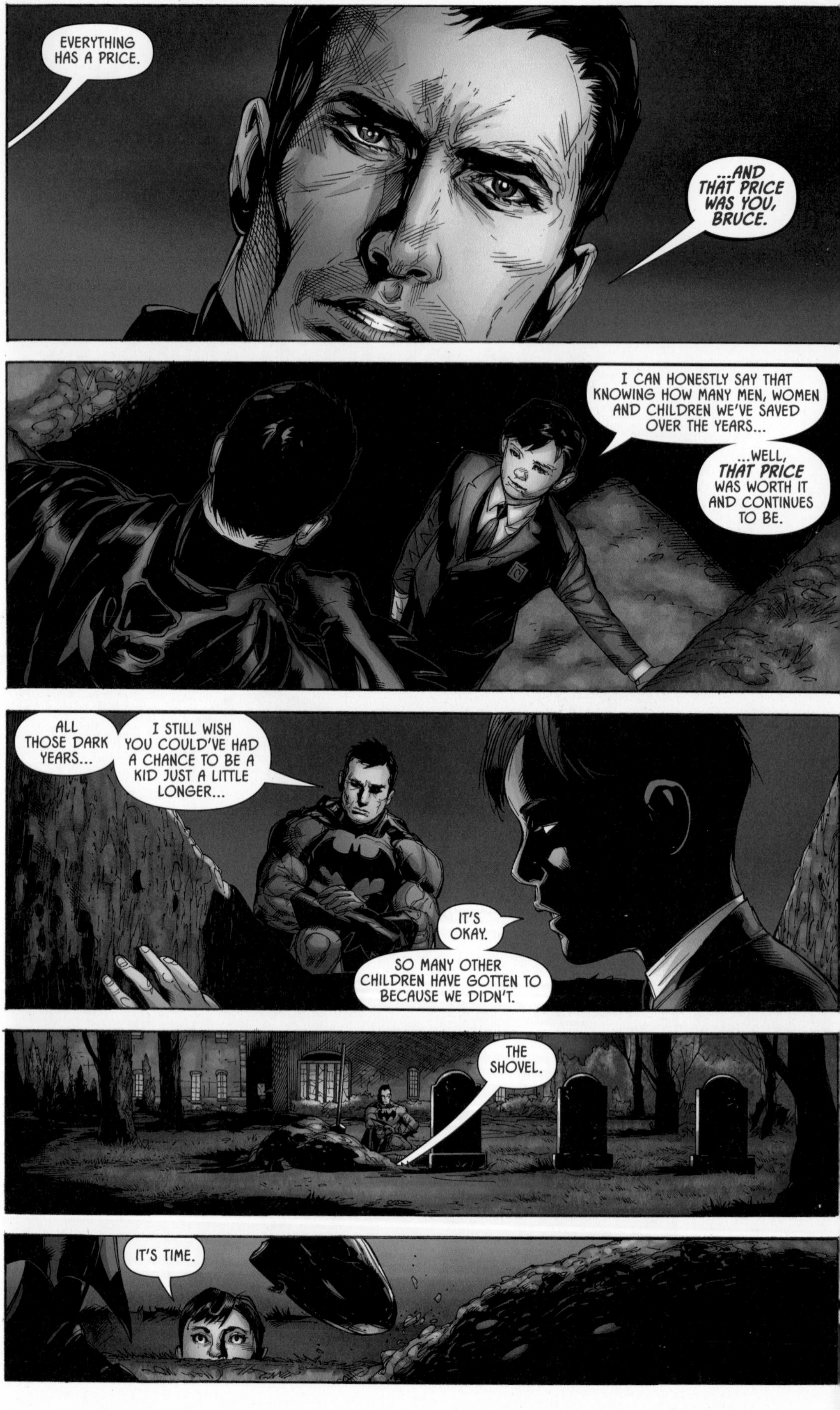
EVERYTHING HAS A PRICE.
...AND THAT PRICE WAS YOU, BRUCE.
I CAN HONESTLY SAY THAT KNOWING HOW MANY MEN, WOMEN AND CHILDREN WE'VE SAVED OVER THE YEARS...
...WELL, THAT PRICE WAS WORTH IT AND CONTINUES TO BE.
ALL THOSE DARK YEARS...
I STILL WISH YOU COULD'VE HAD A CHANCE TO BE A KID JUST A LITTLE LONGER...
IT'S OKAY.
SO MANY OTHER CHILDREN HAVE GOTTEN TO BECAUSE WE DIDN'T.
THE SHOVEL.
IT'S TIME.

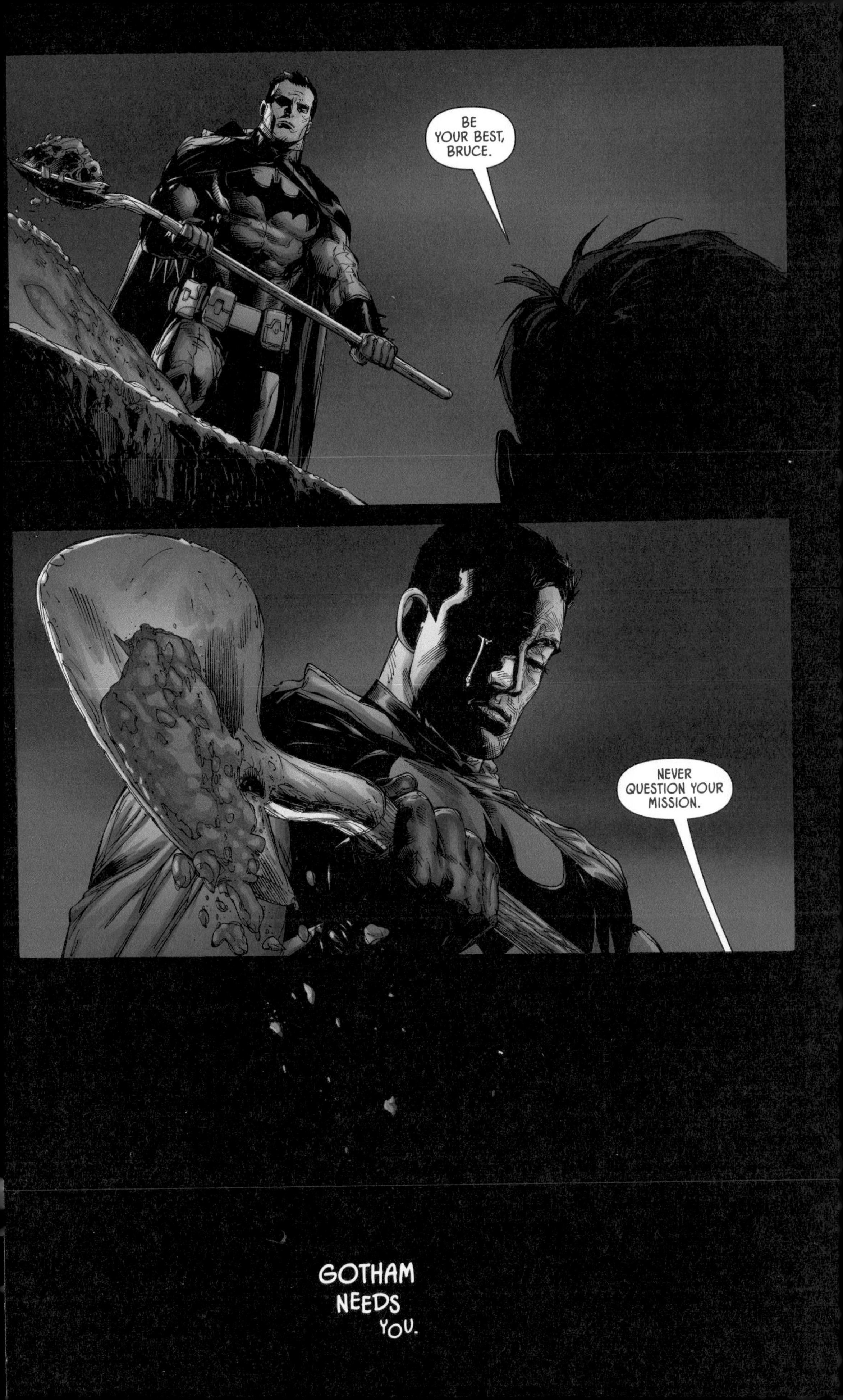
BE YOUR BEST, BRUCE.
NEVER QUESTION YOUR MISSION.
GOTHAM NEEDS YOU.

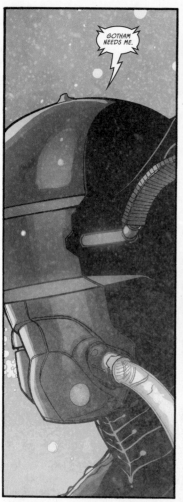

GOTHAM NEEDS ME.

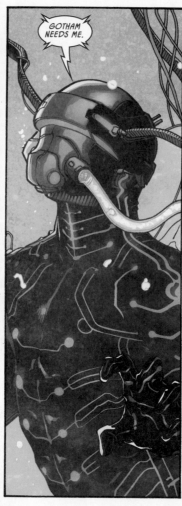

GOTHAM NEEDS ME.

GOTHAM NEEDS ME!

CALM DOWN, BRUCE...

...THE WATER IS DRAINING.

I'VE HACKED IN-- THE PROGRAM'S ALREADY CYCLING DOWN--IT'S COME TO AN END.

GOTHAM NEEDS ME!

SK KRK

HOW LONG'S HE BEEN IN THAT THING, ALFRED?

SK KRK

GOTHAM NEEDS ME!

I DON'T KNOW, DAMIAN...

...SEEMS HE INITIATED THIS...STEALTH SEQUENCE HIMSELF.

GOTHAM NEEDS ME!

STEALTH. →TT← YOU MEAN SECRET, DON'T YOU?

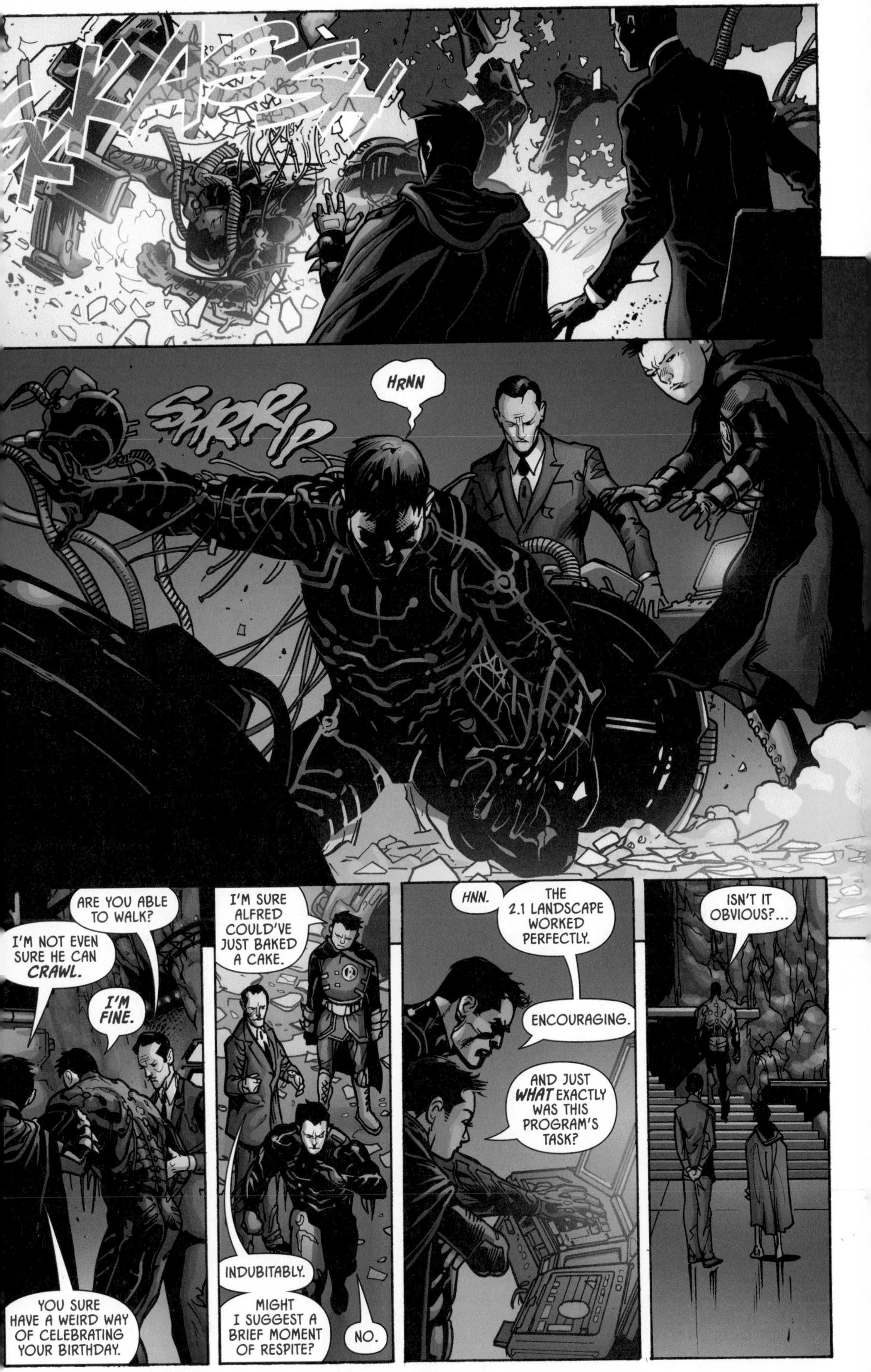
KRASSH
HRNN
SHRIP
ARE YOU ABLE TO WALK?
I'M NOT EVEN SURE HE CAN CRAWL.
I'M FINE.
YOU SURE HAVE A WEIRD WAY OF CELEBRATING YOUR BIRTHDAY.
I'M SURE ALFRED COULD'VE JUST BAKED A CAKE.
INDUBITABLY.
MIGHT I SUGGEST A BRIEF MOMENT OF RESPITE?
NO.
HNN.
THE 2.1 LANDSCAPE WORKED PERFECTLY.
ENCOURAGING.
AND JUST WHAT EXACTLY WAS THIS PROGRAM'S TASK?
ISN'T IT OBVIOUS?...

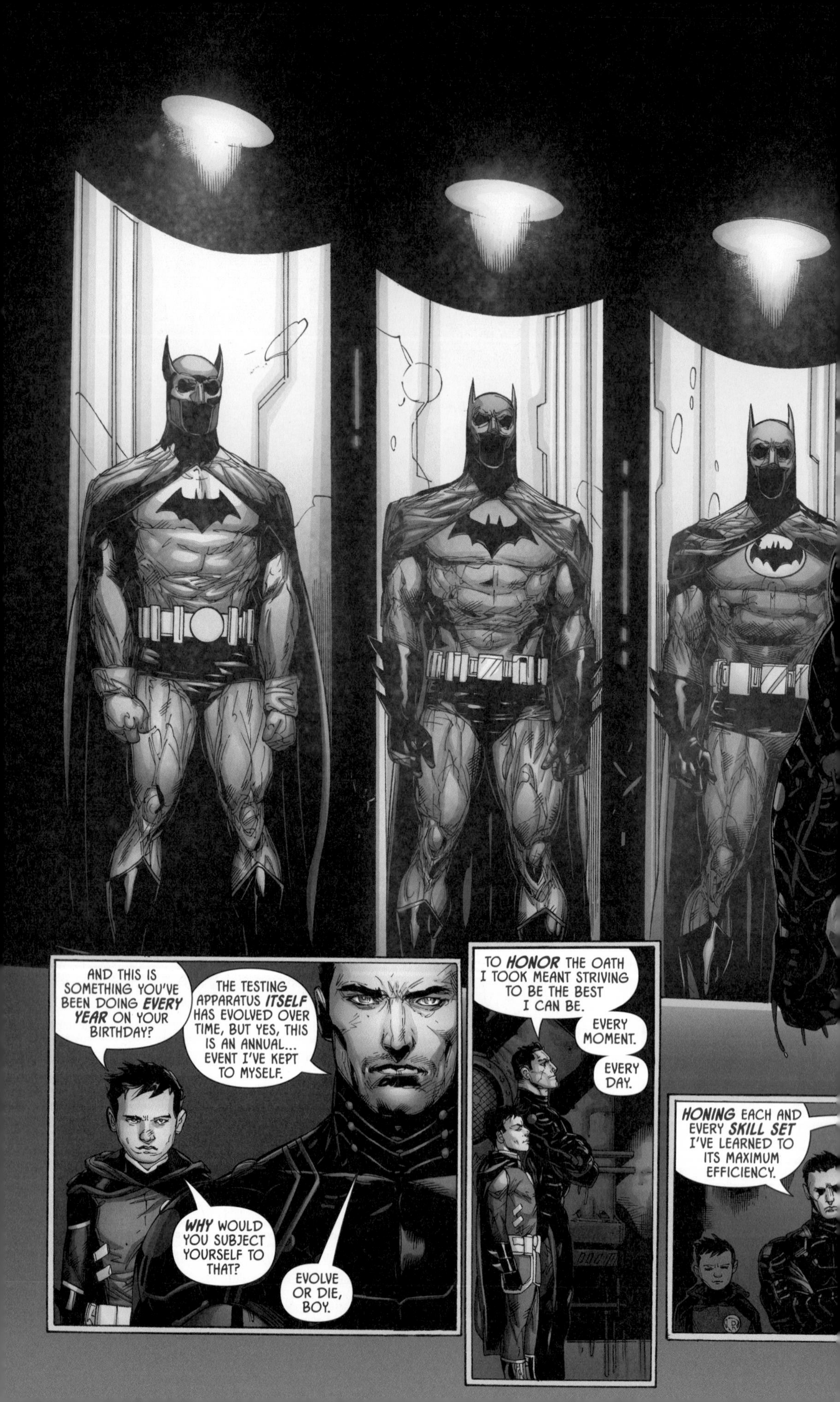
AND THIS IS SOMETHING YOU'VE BEEN DOING EVERY YEAR ON YOUR BIRTHDAY?
THE TESTING APPARATUS ITSELF HAS EVOLVED OVER TIME, BUT YES, THIS IS AN ANNUAL... EVENT I'VE KEPT TO MYSELF.
WHY WOULD YOU SUBJECT YOURSELF TO THAT?
EVOLVE OR DIE, BOY.
TO HONOR THE OATH I TOOK MEANT STRIVING TO BE THE BEST I CAN BE.
EVERY MOMENT.
EVERY DAY.
HONING EACH AND EVERY SKILL SET I'VE LEARNED TO ITS MAXIMUM EFFICIENCY.

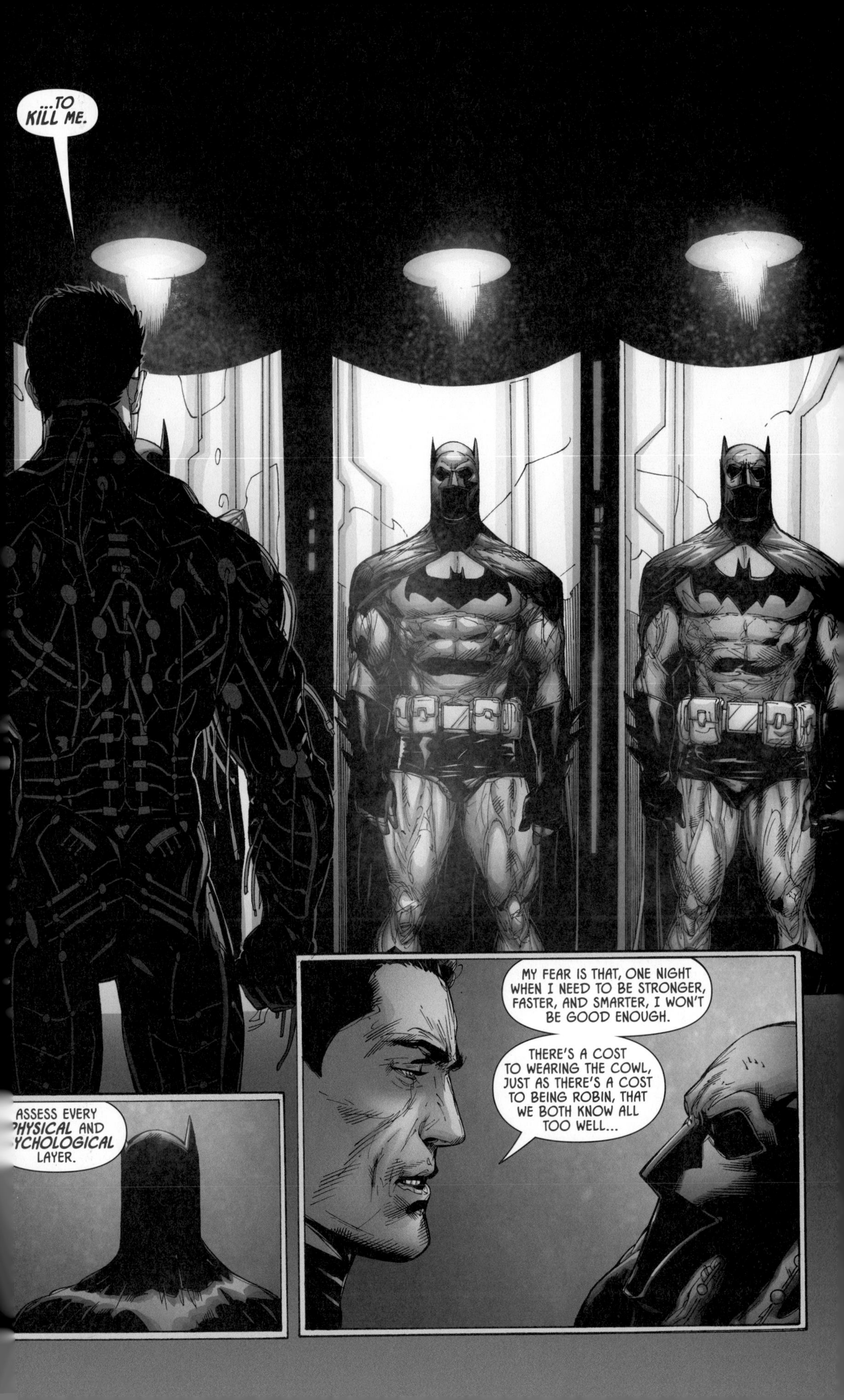
...TO KILL ME.
ASSESS EVERY PHYSICAL AND YCHOLOGICAL LAYER.
MY FEAR IS THAT, ONE NIGHT WHEN I NEED TO BE STRONGER, FASTER, AND SMARTER, I WON'T BE GOOD ENOUGH.
THERE'S A COST TO WEARING THE COWL, JUST AS THERE'S A COST TO BEING ROBIN, THAT WE BOTH KNOW ALL TOO WELL...

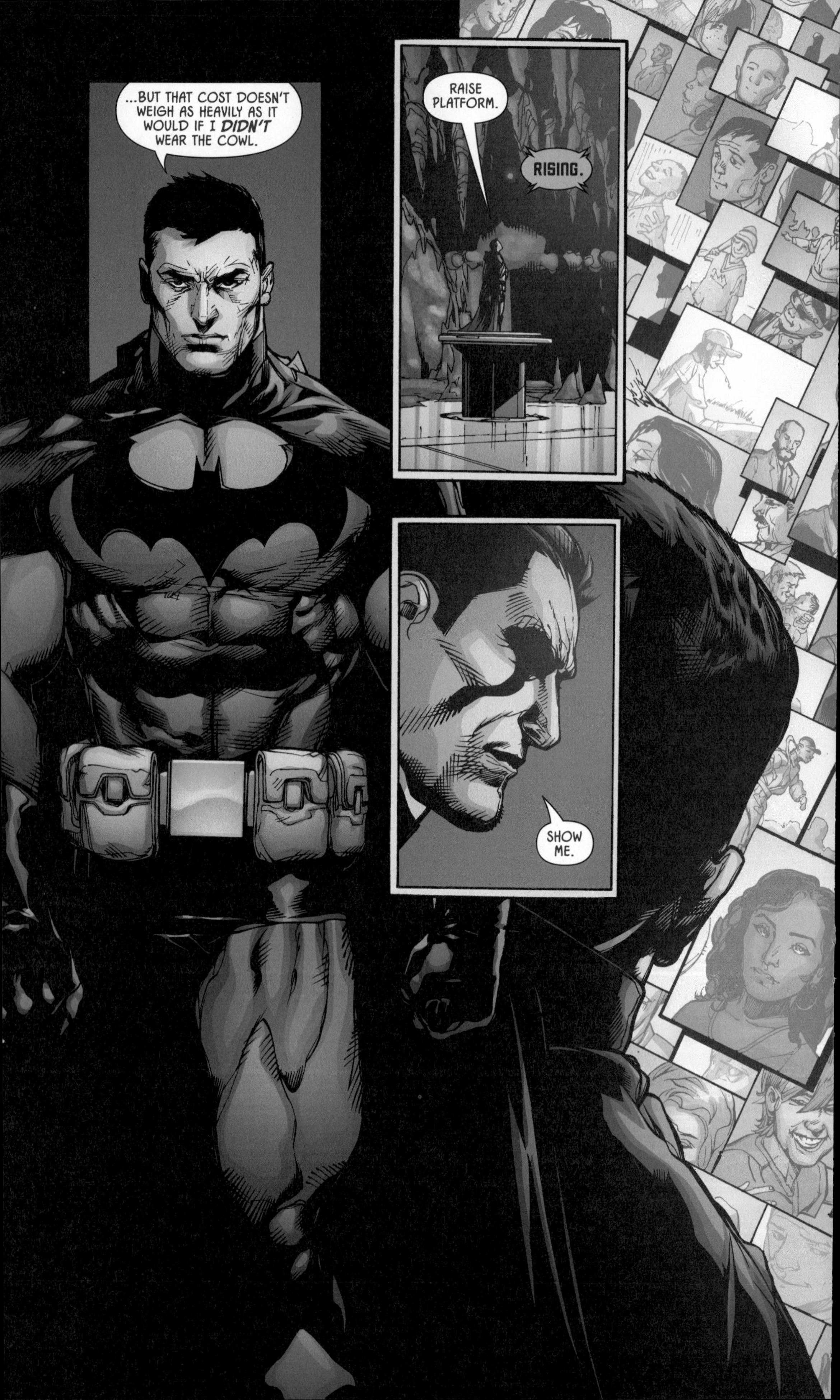

...BUT THAT COST DOESN'T WEIGH AS HEAVILY AS IT WOULD IF I *DIDN'T* WEAR THE COWL.
RAISE PLATFORM.
RISING.
SHOW ME.

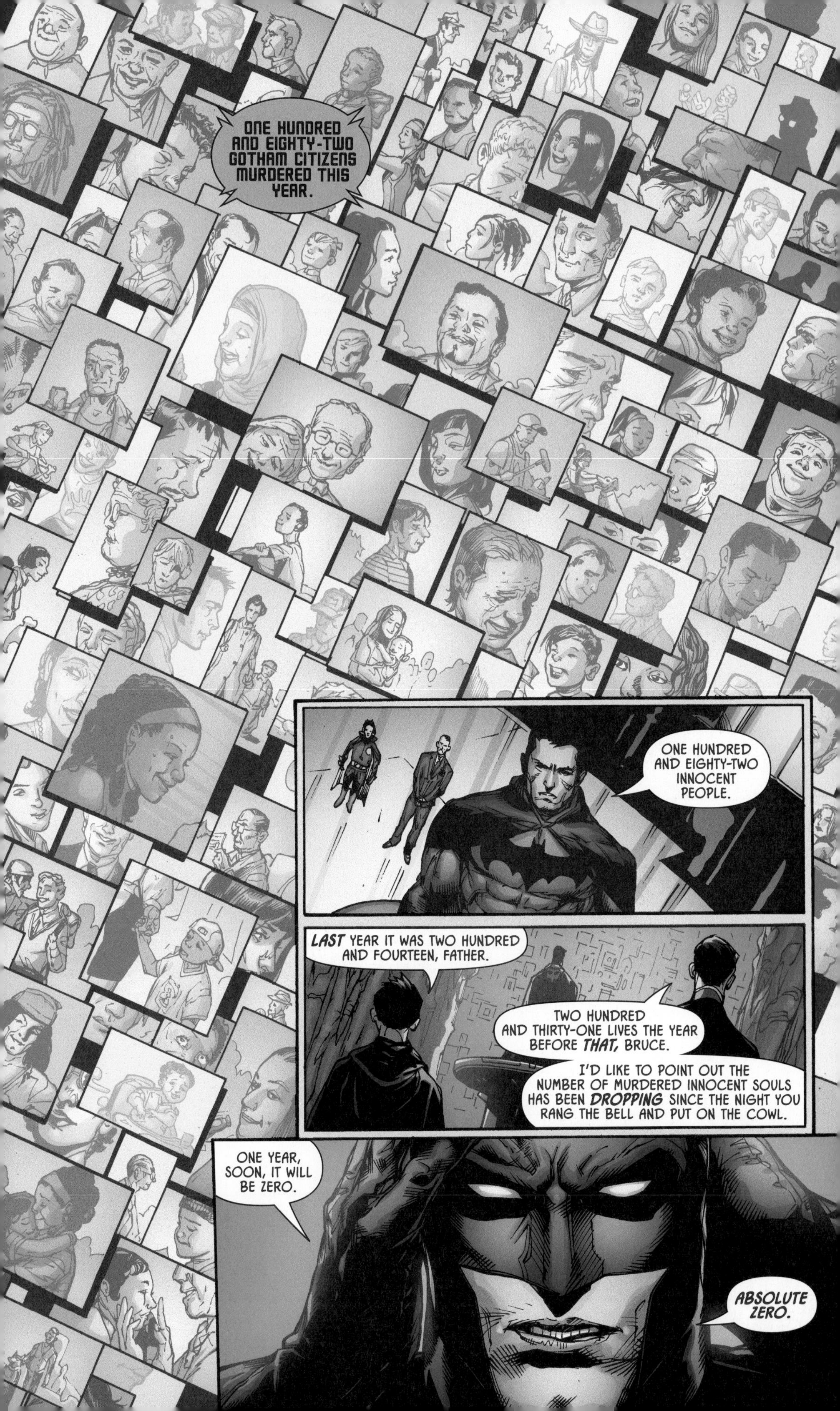
ONE HUNDRED AND EIGHTY-TWO GOTHAM CITIZENS MURDERED THIS YEAR.
ONE HUNDRED AND EIGHTY-TWO INNOCENT PEOPLE.
LAST YEAR IT WAS TWO HUNDRED AND FOURTEEN, FATHER.
TWO HUNDRED AND THIRTY-ONE LIVES THE YEAR BEFORE THAT, BRUCE.
I'D LIKE TO POINT OUT THE NUMBER OF MURDERED INNOCENT SOULS HAS BEEN DROPPING SINCE THE NIGHT YOU RANG THE BELL AND PUT ON THE COWL.
ONE YEAR, SOON, IT WILL BE ZERO.
ABSOLUTE ZERO.

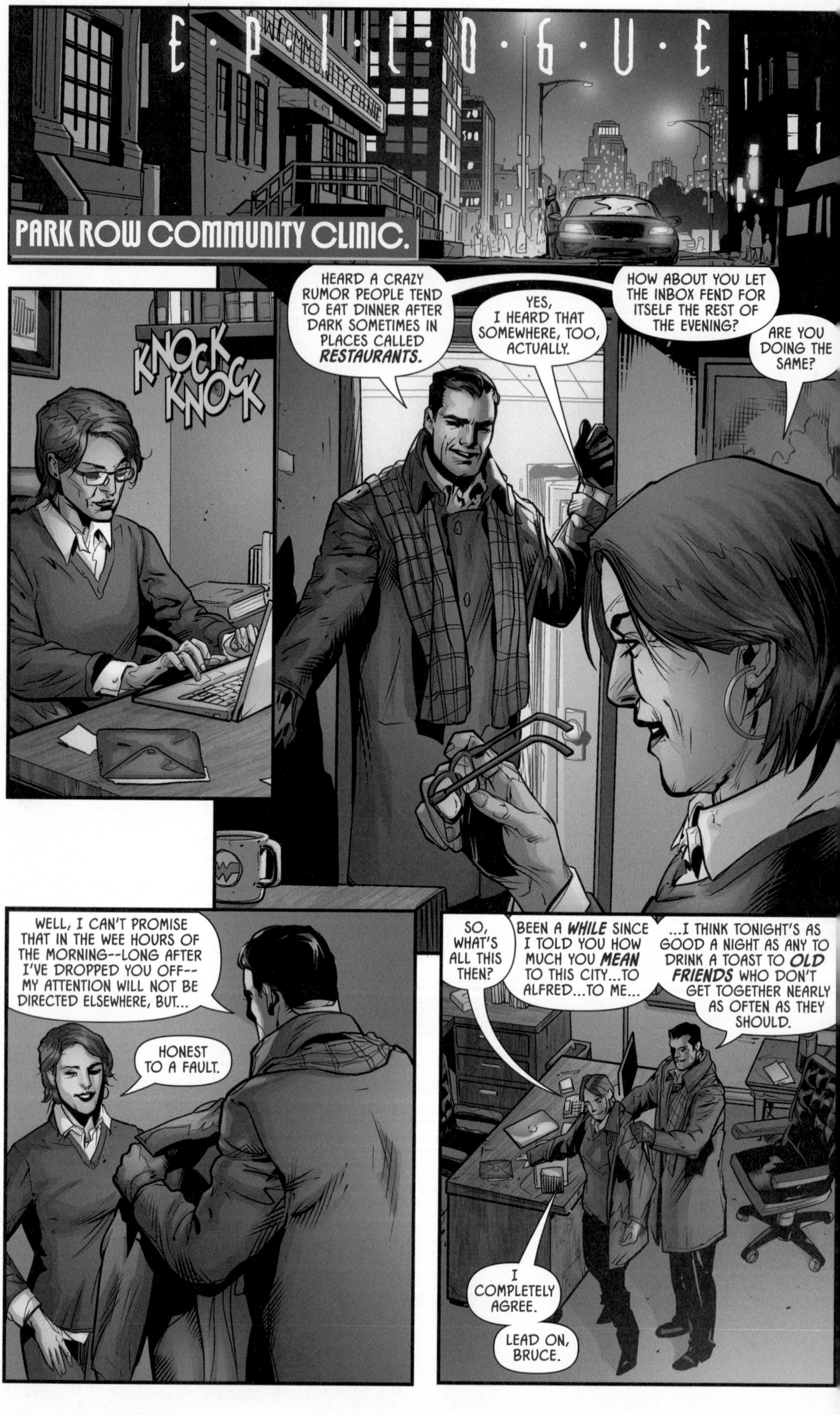
E·P·I·L·O·G·U·E!
PARK ROW COMMUNITY CLINIC.
KNOCK KNOCK
HEARD A CRAZY RUMOR PEOPLE TEND TO EAT DINNER AFTER DARK SOMETIMES IN PLACES CALLED RESTAURANTS.
YES, I HEARD THAT SOMEWHERE, TOO, ACTUALLY.
HOW ABOUT YOU LET THE INBOX FEND FOR ITSELF THE REST OF THE EVENING?
ARE YOU DOING THE SAME?
WELL, I CAN'T PROMISE THAT IN THE WEE HOURS OF THE MORNING--LONG AFTER I'VE DROPPED YOU OFF--MY ATTENTION WILL NOT BE DIRECTED ELSEWHERE, BUT...
HONEST TO A FAULT.
SO, WHAT'S ALL THIS THEN?
BEEN A WHILE SINCE I TOLD YOU HOW MUCH YOU MEAN TO THIS CITY...TO ALFRED...TO ME...
...I THINK TONIGHT'S AS GOOD A NIGHT AS ANY TO DRINK A TOAST TO OLD FRIENDS WHO DON'T GET TOGETHER NEARLY AS OFTEN AS THEY SHOULD.
I COMPLETELY AGREE.
LEAD ON, BRUCE.

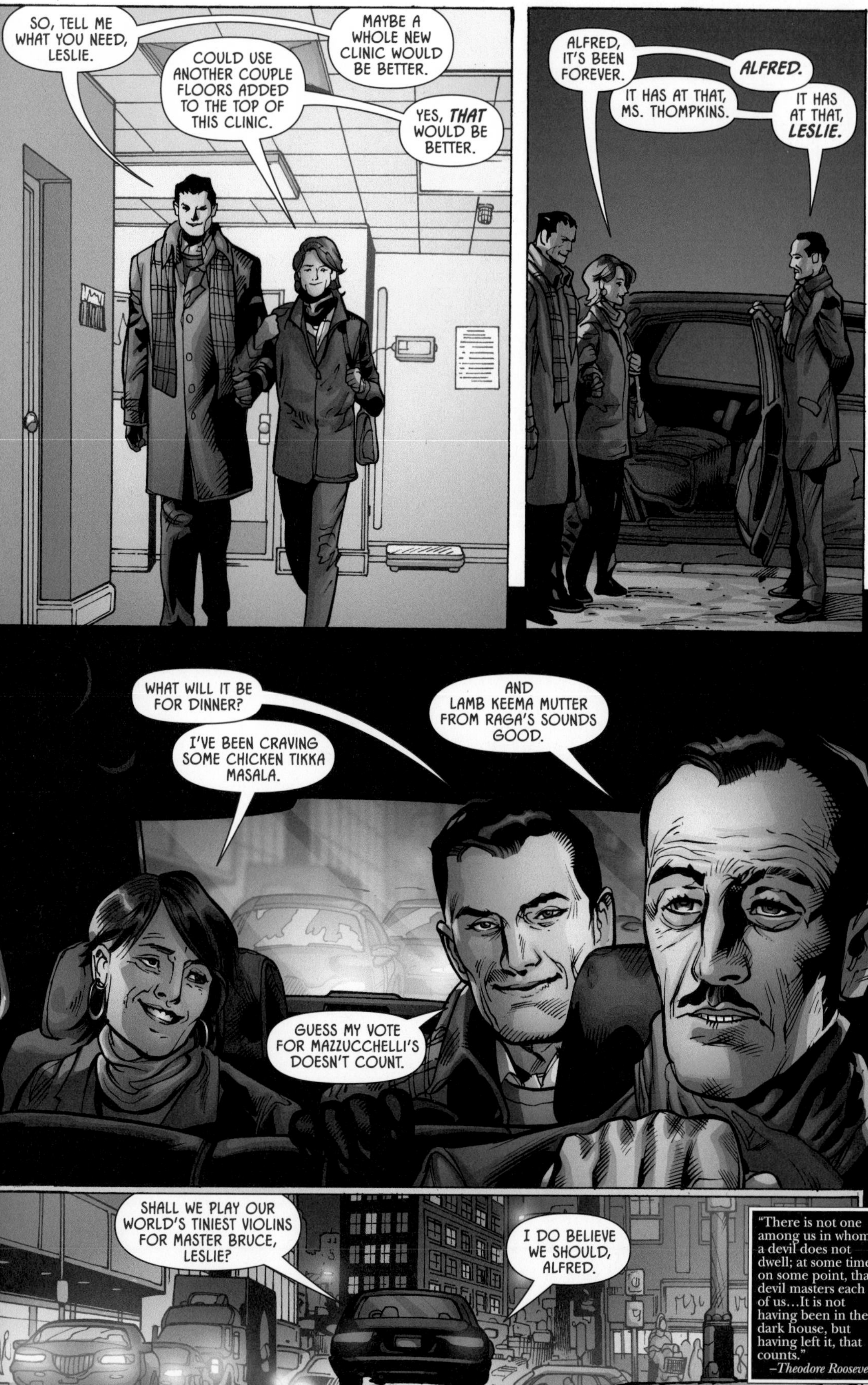
SO, TELL ME WHAT YOU NEED, LESLIE.
COULD USE ANOTHER COUPLE FLOORS ADDED TO THE TOP OF THIS CLINIC.
MAYBE A WHOLE NEW CLINIC WOULD BE BETTER.
YES, ***THAT*** WOULD BE BETTER.
ALFRED, IT'S BEEN FOREVER.
IT HAS AT THAT, MS. THOMPKINS.
ALFRED.
IT HAS AT THAT, ***LESLIE.***
WHAT WILL IT BE FOR DINNER?
I'VE BEEN CRAVING SOME CHICKEN TIKKA MASALA.
AND LAMB KEEMA MUTTER FROM RAGA'S SOUNDS GOOD.
GUESS MY VOTE FOR MAZZUCCHELLI'S DOESN'T COUNT.
SHALL WE PLAY OUR WORLD'S TINIEST VIOLINS FOR MASTER BRUCE, LESLIE?
I DO BELIEVE WE SHOULD, ALFRED.
"There is not one among us in whom a devil does not dwell; at some time, on some point, that devil masters each of us...It is not having been in the dark house, but having left it, that counts."
–*Theodore Roosevelt*

VARIANT COVER GALLERY

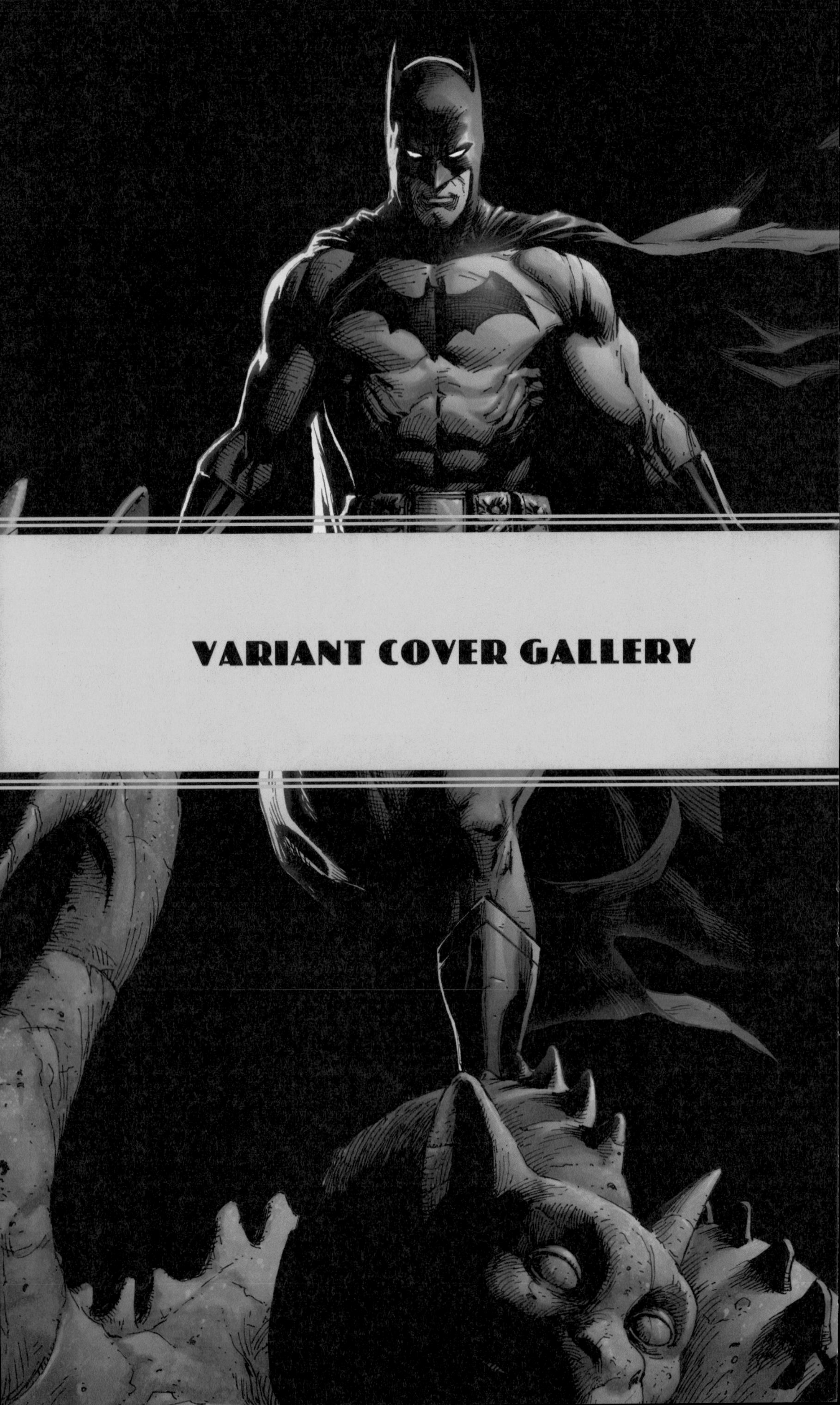

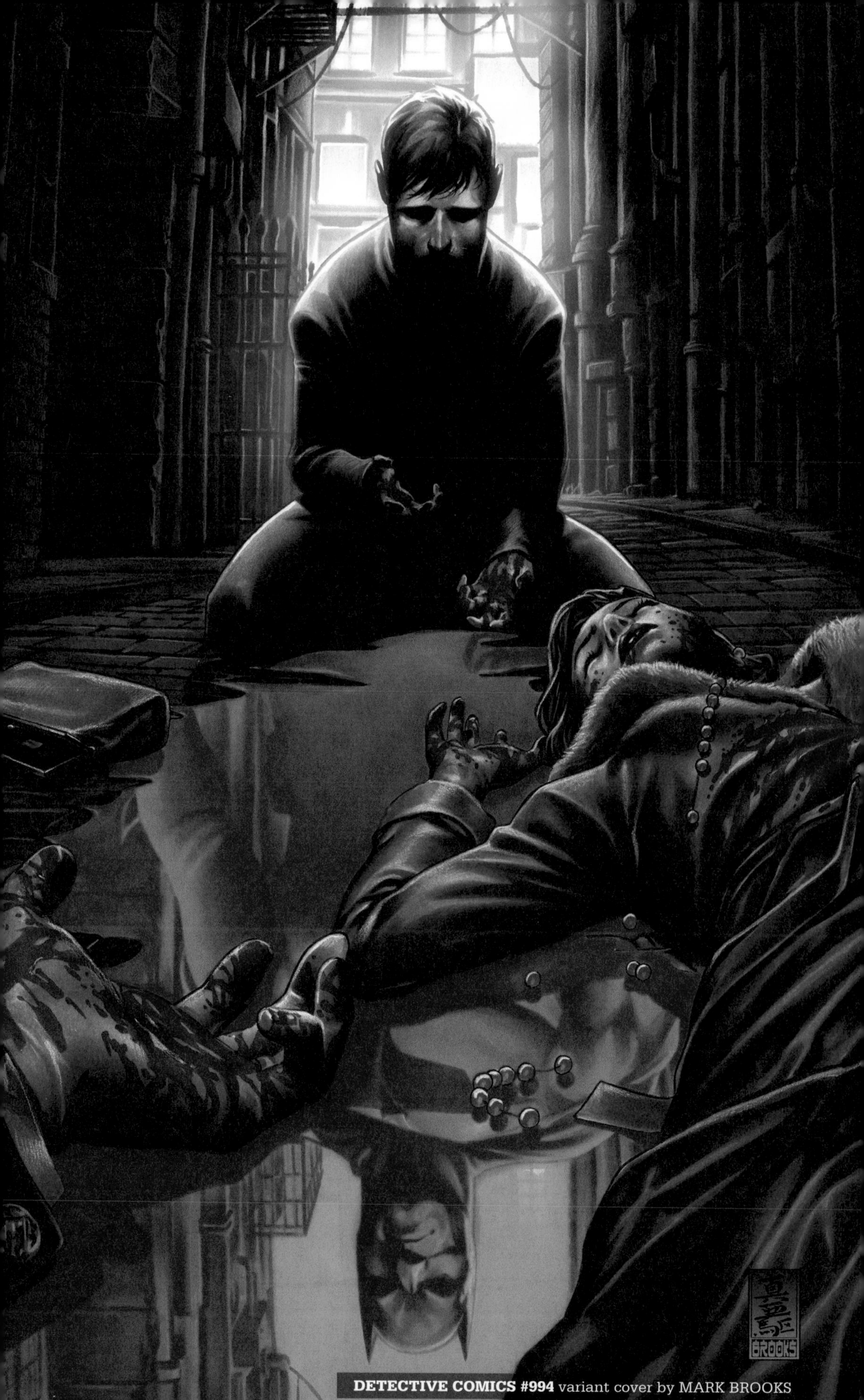
BROOKS

DETECTIVE COMICS #994 variant cover by MARK BROOKS

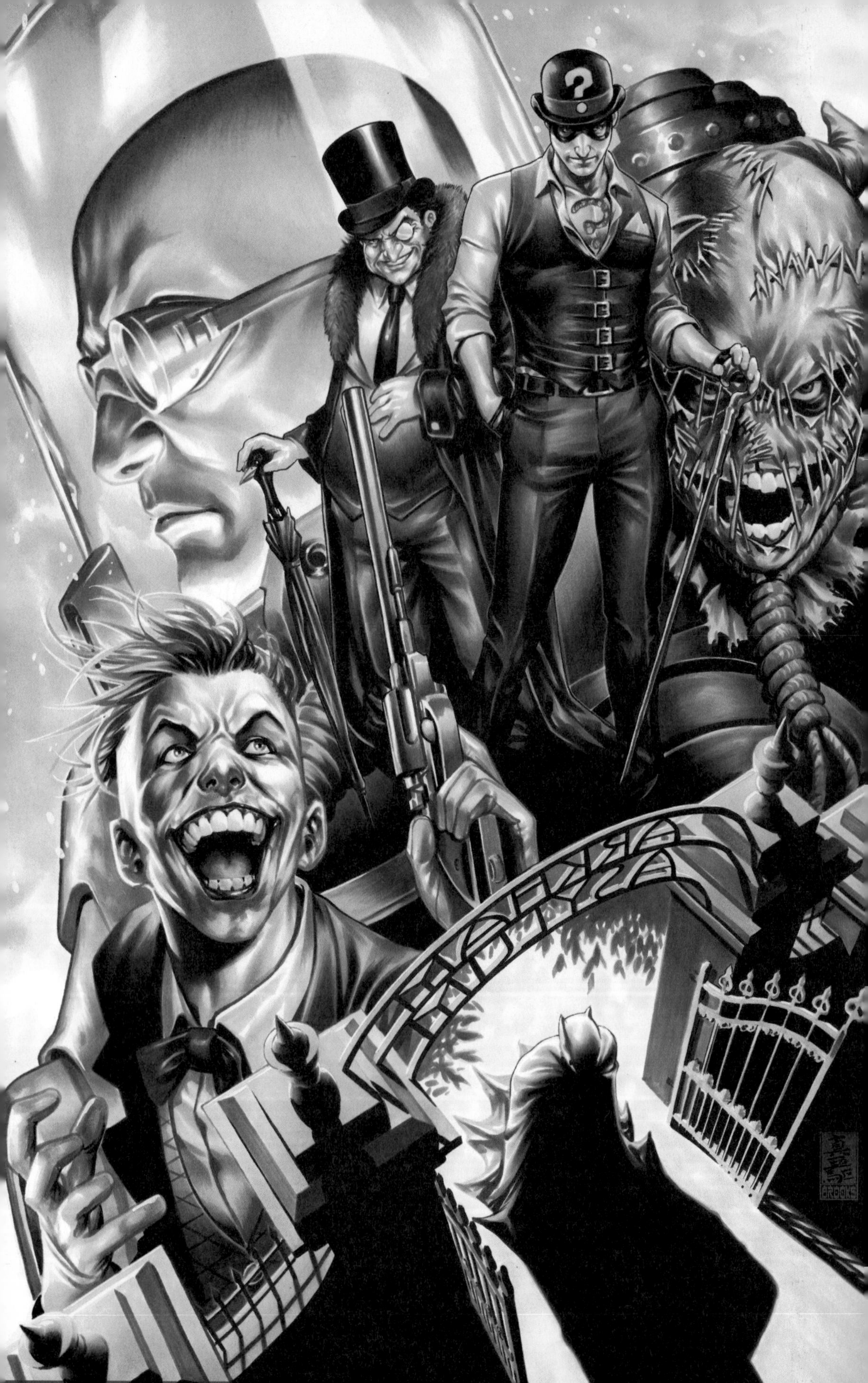

DETECTIVE COMICS #995 variant cover by MARK BROOKS

DETECTIVE COMICS #996 variant cover by BRIAN STELFREEZE

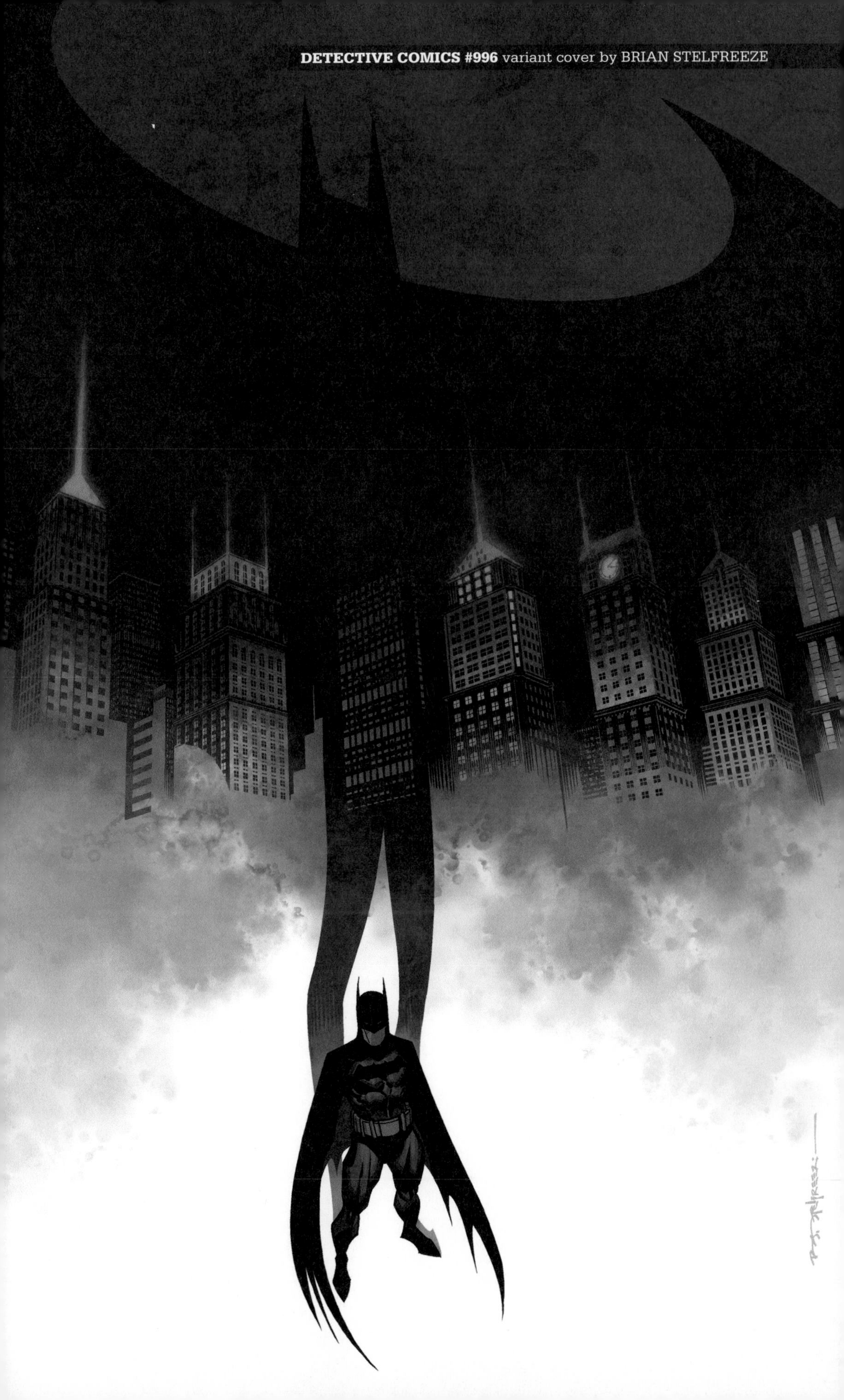

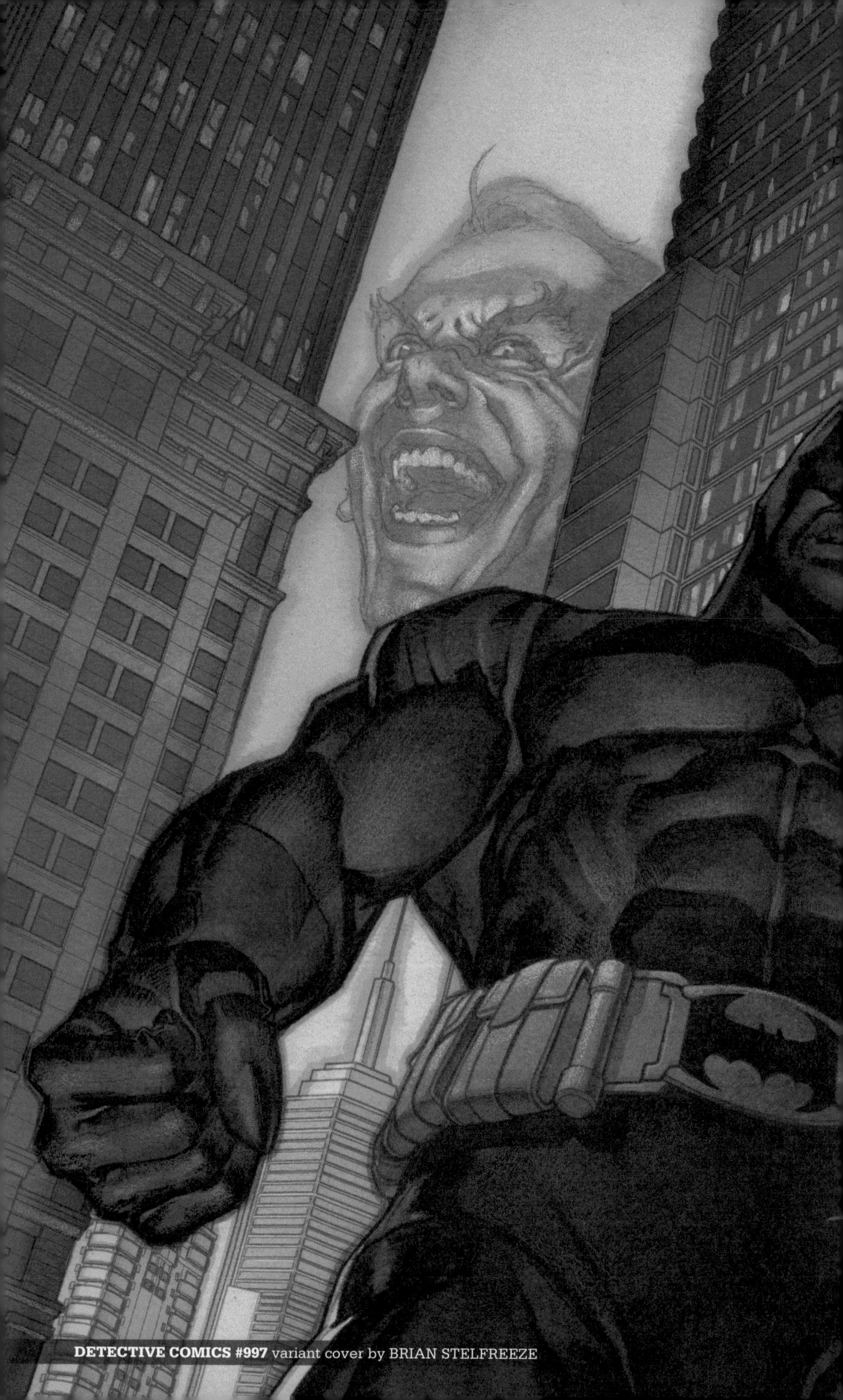

DETECTIVE COMICS #997 variant cover by BRIAN STELFREEZE

DETECTIVE COMICS #998 variant cover by GARY **FRANK** and BRAD ANDERSON

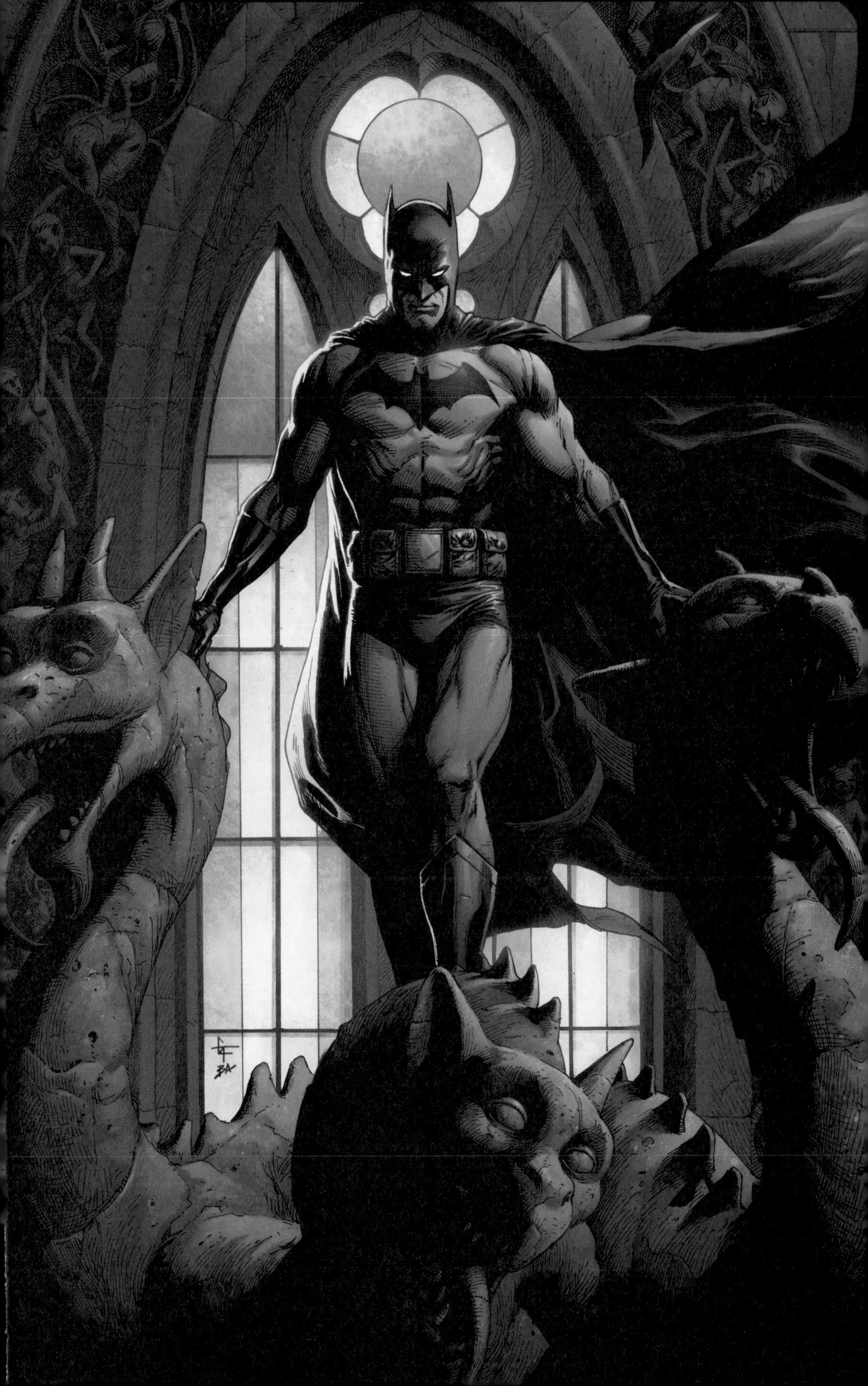
GF
BA

DETECTIVE COMICS #999 variant cover by JOHN BYRNE and TRISH MULVIHILL

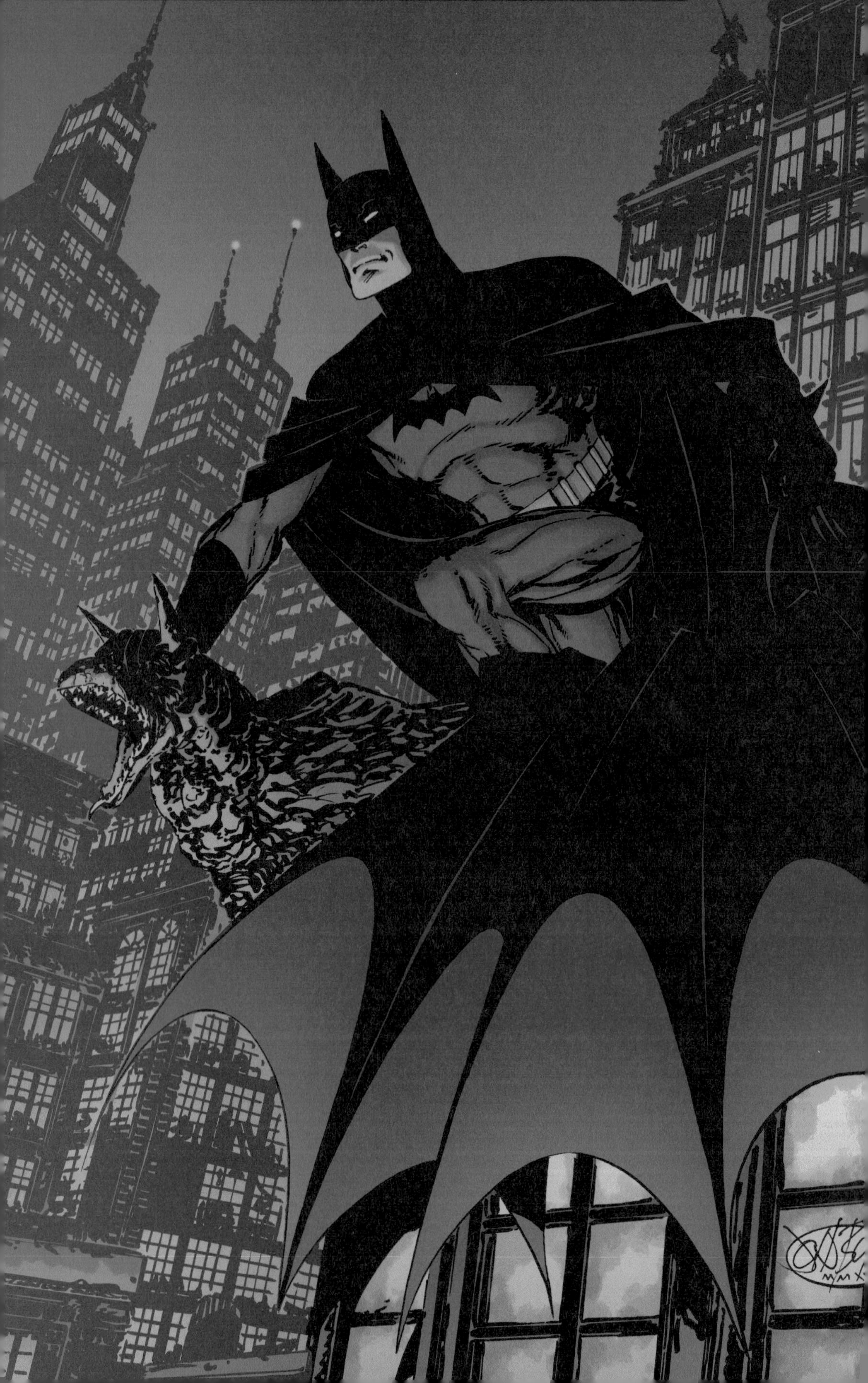